A Spiritual Economy

SYNKRISIS

Comparative Approaches to Early Christianity in Greco-Roman Culture

SERIES EDITORS

Dale B. Martin (Yale University) and L. L. Welborn (Fordham University)

Synkrisis is a project that invites scholars of early Christianity and the Greco-Roman world to collaborate toward the goal of rigorous comparison. Each volume in the series provides immersion in an aspect of Greco-Roman culture, so as to make possible a comparison of the controlling logics that emerge from the discourses of Greco-Roman and early Christian writers. In contrast to older "history of religions" approaches, which looked for similarities between religions in order to posit relations of influence and dependency, Synkrisis embraces a fuller conception of the complexities of culture, viewing Greco-Roman religions and early Christianity as members of a comparative class. The differential comparisons promoted by Synkrisis may serve to refine and correct the theoretical and historical models employed by scholars who seek to understand and interpret the Greco-Roman world. With its allusion to the rhetorical exercises of the Greco-Roman world, the series title recognizes that the comparative enterprise is a construction of the scholar's mind and serves the scholar's theoretical interests.

EDITORIAL BOARD

Loveday Alexander (Sheffield University)
John Bodell (Brown University)
Kimberly Bowes (University of Pennsylvania)
Daniel Boyarin (University of California, Berkeley)
Fritz Graf (Ohio State University)
Ronald F. Hock (University of Southern California)
Hans-Josef Klauck (University of Chicago)
Stanley K. Stowers (Brown University)
Angela Standhartinger (Marburg University)

A Spiritual Economy

Gift Exchange in the Letters of Paul of Tarsus

Thomas R. Blanton, IV

Yale
UNIVERSITY PRESS
New Haven & London

Published with assistance from the foundation established in memory of
Philip Hamilton McMillan of the Class of 1894, Yale College.

Copyright © 2017 by Yale University.
All rights reserved.
This book may not be reproduced, in whole or in part, including illustrations, in any form (beyond that copying permitted by Sections 107 and 108 of the U.S. Copyright Law and except by reviewers for the public press), without written permission from the publishers.

Yale University Press books may be purchased in quantity for educational, business, or promotional use. For information, please e-mail sales.press@yale.edu (U.S. office) or sales@yaleup.co.uk (U.K. office).

Set in Bulmer type by Westchester Publishing Services.
Printed in the United States of America.

Library of Congress Control Number: 2016936128
ISBN 978-0-300-22040-7 (hardcover : alk. paper)

A catalogue record for this book is available from the British Library.

This paper meets the requirements of ANSI/NISO Z39.48-1992 (Permanence of Paper).

10 9 8 7 6 5 4 3 2 1

Contents

Acknowledgments vii

ONE
Introduction 1

TWO
Symbolic Goods as Media of Exchange in Paul's Gift Economy 15

THREE
The Benefactor's Account Book: The Rhetoric of Gift Reciprocation According to Seneca and Paul 27

FOUR
Gift or Commodity? On the Classification of Paul's Unremunerated Labor 41

FIVE
Classification and Social Relations: The Dark Side of the Gift 61

SIX
The Gift of Status 76

SEVEN
Spiritual Gifts and Status Inversion 104

EIGHT
Summary and Conclusions 134

*Appendix: Letters and Events Significantly Shaping Paul's Relations
with the Corinthian Assembly: A Relative Chronology*   143
List of Abbreviations   145
Notes   147
Bibliography   191
Index of Subjects   213
Index of Modern Authors   215
Index of Biblical and Early Jewish Sources   219
Index of Greek and Roman Sources   225

Acknowledgments

During the course of my work on *A Spiritual Economy,* I have incurred gift-debts too numerous to count, which I do not pretend to be able to discharge. I offer this book in the hope that it may, however inadequately, serve to "pay forward" some of the gifts that I have received during the course of my research and writing.

It was my reading of Troels Engberg-Pedersen's *Harvard Theological Review* article on reciprocity in Paul and Seneca in 2010 that piqued my interest in gift exchange; it was then that I began to read the material that forms the basis of many of the arguments I put forth in this book: Marcel Mauss's *The Gift* and Seneca's *On Benefits.* Initial forays into the logic of Paul's system of divine-human exchanges based on the *charis* of reciprocal exchange resulted in the essay that appears herein as chapter 2, which I first presented at the Early Christianity and the Ancient Economy program unit at the International Society of Biblical Literature (SBL) Meeting in Tartu, Estonia, in August 2010. I am grateful to Alanna Nobbs and Don Barker for inviting me to present a version of the paper at the "Corinth: Paul, People, and Politics" conference hosted by the Society for the Study of Early Christianity at Macquarie University in May 2011.

Gratitude is due to those who have read or commented on various chapters of the book. Larry Welborn has been a constant support since the inception of the project and has read and provided helpful feedback on virtually every chapter. It was he who, as an editor of the Synkrisis series, invited me to submit a book proposal. John Fitzgerald and David Hollander have read portions of the manuscript and offered feedback during sessions of the Early Christianity and the Ancient Economy SBL program unit, domestically in San Francisco, Chicago, and Baltimore and internationally in Vienna and St. Andrews. Gratitude is also due to participants who offered valuable comments during those sessions. I thank John Barclay for offering valuable feedback on chapter 3, originally published as (and slightly adapted from) "The Benefactor's Account-book: The Rhetoric of Gift

Reciprocation in Seneca and Paul," in *New Testament Studies* 59.3 (July 2013): 396–414, copyright © Cambridge University Press 2013 and reprinted with permission by Cambridge University Press.

I recall fondly the students in my "Gift Exchange in Religion and Society" class at Luther College during spring semester 2013; it was there that the insights now contained in chapters 4 and 5 began to take shape. Students in my "Life and Letters of Paul" courses at the Lutheran School of Theology at Chicago (LSTC) in 2014 and 2015 provided a source of renewed stimulation and spurred me to refine and nuance my understanding of Paul's complex relationship with gifting discourses and practices. I thank Ray Pickett and my academic dean, Esther Menn, for their continued support and collegial friendship at LSTC.

No academic book can be written without the support of research libraries; I thank Kathy Buzza, the Interlibrary Loan Coordinator at Preus Library, for her assiduity in fulfilling numerous requests for materials from 2010 to 2013. Barry Hopkins, Associate Librarian for Public Services, and Elaine Bonner, Access Services Manager, at the JKM Library in Hyde Park (Chicago) have facilitated my research since I was a graduate student at the University of Chicago Divinity School; it is a pleasure to be able to work with them both at LSTC. I also express my appreciation to Bill Beermann, Catalog Librarian at JKM, for speedily fulfilling a last-minute request.

I thank Jennifer Banks and Heather Gold of Yale University Press for their support and advice and the Synkrisis series editors, Larry Welborn and Dale Martin, for backing *A Spiritual Economy* throughout the various stages of its review. Jessie Dolch reviewed the entire manuscript with keen editorial eyes.

Finally, I thank my wife, May May Latt, whose support enabled me to complete the manuscript of this book during the spring of 2015, and my sister-in-law, Kyi Kyi Latt, and Cho Cho Win for graciously making available their house in Wisconsin.

For all of these unrepayable debts, I issue my wholly inadequate but nonetheless heartfelt "thank you."

A Spiritual Economy

ONE

Introduction

Prolegomenon: In What Sense Is the Gift "Free"?

The gift, argues Jacques Derrida, is an impossibility. It is impossible, in Derrida's view, because "for there to be a gift, there must be no reciprocity, return, exchange, countergift, or debt."[1] The gift is "aneconomic" in that it must always remain outside the "circle" of reciprocal exchange that characterizes the marketplace, a context in which, when a good or service is transmitted, another good or service—or, better, currency—must be transmitted in return: "If the other *gives* me back or *owes* me or has to give me back what I gave him or her, there will not have been a gift."[2] The gift is impossible because, as soon as it is recognized as "gift," its recognition as such calls into play a network of symbolic associations: gratitude, reciprocity, gift-debt, and countergift. These associations, in Derrida's view, disqualify that which is transmitted from being categorized as "gift."

Central to Derrida's argument is his construal of that which is "economic," a term that he restricts in its application to mercantile exchange, conceptualized using the metaphor of the circle: the "law of the economy" demands a "return to the point of departure, to the origin, also to the home."[3] The "economy" entails circulation: reciprocity and return. The gift remains "aneconomic" in the sense that "it must not circulate, it must not be exchanged, it must not in any case be exhausted, as a gift, by the process of exchange, by the movement of circulation of the circle in the form of return to the point of departure."[4]

Derrida's definition, however, fails in several respects. First, as Pierre Bourdieu has shown, the "economy" can only with difficulty be limited to transactions that occur within the context of mercantile exchange.⁵ Goods and services are frequently transmitted in extramercantile contexts: in the home, among friends, or, in the classic anthropological literature on gift exchange, between clans. The Greek term *oikonomia,* from which "economy" derives, originally referred to the ordering of relations within the household—the location par excellence in which mercantile exchanges are suppressed in favor of gifts.⁶

Second—more damaging to the thesis—is the fact that, as André Petitat has shown, Derrida's definition of the gift results not from an examination of the actual processes involved in the transmission of what we might label "gifts," but rather from a denial or inversion of characteristics associated with market exchange: circulation and return, calculation, self-interest, and obligation.⁷ As such, Derrida's notion of a "pure," unilateral gift inhabits an imaginary symbolic space—a utopia of exchange, or an "inverted dream" in which all of the purportedly negative characteristics of mercantile exchanges are absent. Rather than resulting from a robust analysis of the actual processes involved in gift exchange, Derrida's understanding rests on the postulate that "gift" may be defined simply on the basis of the denial that it possesses characteristics of the market economy: it represents that which is "aneconomic." The "gift" constitutes that imaginary space which "must *keep* a relation of foreignness to the circle" of reciprocity. However, as Derrida himself seems to have recognized, the appearance of a gift under the conditions that he describes is "impossible": the "simple *recognition* of gift *as* gift" is sufficient "to annul the gift as gift."⁸ As Petitat makes clear, Derrida's definition entirely removes his discussion of the gift from the actual world of human exchange, locating it instead in an impossible, utopian space.

Although Derrida was right to point to distinctions between gift and market economies, any definition of the gift that operates solely according to the logic of negation is clearly inadequate. Gift exchanges in the "real world" of socioeconomic interaction exhibit an array of characteristics, only some of which are opposed to mercantile exchanges (a point to which we will return). Although, as Petitat points out, the range of what we might call gift exchange covers a host of diverse interactions that cannot be reduced to a single typology or set of principles,⁹ nevertheless some regularities may be observed. Jacques Godbout and Alain Caillé point out that the gift may be viewed as a "catalyst and an outward sign of elective affinities," or as "the embodiment of the system of interpersonal social relations."¹⁰ In the opinion of the first-century CE Roman senator Seneca the Younger, gift exchange constitutes the "chief bond of human society."¹¹ Derrida omits the socially formative aspects of gift exchange entirely from his account. The distinction between gift and mercantile exchange lies not, as Derrida assumed, in the supposedly irreciprocal character of the gift, but in the type of obligation implied in the reciprocal donation: unlike the obligation to render payment in market transactions, the obligation of reciprocity in gift exchange is not enforceable in a court of law; its sanctions reside in social disapproval and the weakening or dissolution of social bonds. As the gift is "the embodiment of the system of interpersonal social relations," its refusal or reticence to reciprocate it—whether with a countergift, a display of gratitude, or, what is perhaps the most valuable gift, the gift of oneself: one's time and one's presence—constitutes a denial of social relations.

In attempting to distance the gift from mercantile transactions, Derrida's definition of the gift inadvertently ceded too much to the marketplace. Assuming that circularity, reciprocation, and return were characteristics only of the market, he was compelled to deny that the unilateral, irreciprocal gift was possible. It became instead "*the* impossible": it is that which, once recognized as gift, ceases to exist as such. The interpreter must be careful, however, not to concede too much ground to the marketplace by assuming, with Derrida, that "return" nullifies the gift. The "circle" of exchange is not solely the province of the market; it is territory over which the gift also shares a claim.

Derrida's "impossible" gift bears some similarity to the "free gift" sometimes posited by Christian theology.¹² Robert Duvall's film *The Apostle* features an itinerant, outlaw preacher who, like Paul of Tarsus, styles himself an "apostle." In a climactic scene, the "Apostle E.F."—whose self-ascribed title overshadows his name, indicated only by initials¹³—preaches a farewell sermon to the congregation that he had painstakingly assembled in a one-room church in fictive Bayou Boutte, Louisiana.¹⁴ In an impassioned discourse on the death of Jesus, understood as a "gift" to humanity, an act of sacrifice by which sins might be forgiven, providing "salvation" for the sinner, the "Apostle" opines: "He died for us so that we could be saved. It's free, but it ain't cheap."[15] The "free gift" of salvation did not come cheaply in Christian theology: it was "purchased" at the price of Jesus' death. It is "free" in the sense that the recipient need not, in the manner of most market transactions, offer repayment in the form of a specified amount of currency, exchanged at a time and place negotiated before the transaction: "salvation" cannot be bought.

The characterization of the gift as "free," however, ought not be taken to imply that no reciprocal action is expected within the Christian "economy of salvation": affective bonds are forged between "believers" and their God, who sacrificed his only son, and Jesus, who willingly gave himself so that others might live. Tears in the eyes of the "Apostle's" parishioners testify to the depth of affect that may be activated by an impassioned account of self-sacrifice for the benefit of others. Nor is the gift unilateral: those who have been "saved" willingly offer their tithes, their time, their thanksgiving, and their praise to the authors of such great gifts, the heavenly Father and Jesus, his son. The gift, along with the affect and gratitude that it inspires, establishes a circle that, in the view of those who participate in it, unites the human and the divine, the terrestrial and the heavenly, in a system of social relations: worshipers give of themselves because their savior first gave of himself. The "free gift" does not fail to generate reciprocity, nor does it for that reason cease to function as "gift." On the contrary, the constitution and reconstitution of social bonds, both actual and imagined, are among its most salient characteristics.

The "free gift" can be neither bought nor sold under the conditions of the marketplace, but like market transactions, it "returns" to its giver countergifts, gratitude, thanksgiving, or services: both the market and the gift may aptly be described by the metaphor of the circle. But there is a crucial difference: with market exchange, once the circle is completed by the rendering of payment, it ceases to exist as such—no reciprocal obligation remains to lend it permanence. It is otherwise with the gift: when the countergift is offered, the circle persists, as donors becomes donees, themselves

INTRODUCTION   5

obliged to make a return. The "circle" of the gift progresses through the dimension of time, in spirals.

The Aims of This Book

The aim of the present work is neither to clarify theological issues concerning relations between humans and their culturally postulated god or gods, nor to reiterate insights into the nature of gift exchange already registered by the anthropologists and sociologists whose work has been central to the explication of "the gift" in its myriad cultural forms. Rather, the aim is twofold: (1) to delineate the characteristics of the "economy" of gift exchange evident in the letters of the first-century Jewish evangelist Paul of Tarsus; and (2) to make use of Paul's letters as a heuristic device through which to clarify and elaborate issues not yet raised in previous studies of gift exchange. The task is necessarily multidisciplinary, involving the detailed study of Paul's letters (an exercise familiar to New Testament scholars) within the economic context of the Roman empire (involving classics and economic history), prompted by questions of gift exchange more frequently pursued in departments of sociology or anthropology. Readers are invited to exercise clemency in their judgments regarding the book's success in this endeavor: these fields are broad—each one too broad to be fully mastered by a single individual, and collectively far too large for such mastery even to be conceived. My aims are therefore circumscribed: I hope to make use of studies of gift exchange to illuminate Paul, and to make use of Paul to refine and elaborate the study of gift exchange.

In a series of books and essays that have spanned his career, Jonathan Z. Smith has developed the notion that the academic study of religion ought to entail—in addition to an examination of the social context and history of interpretation of a given text—three crucial elements: "comparison," "redescription" and "rectification."[16] Predicated on the view that knowledge is constituted on the basis of systems of classification and discrimination, comparison is the prerequisite to a nuanced understanding of primary data—in Smith's case, those of "religion."[17] He writes: "With at least two exempla in view, one is prepared to undertake their comparison both in terms of aspects and relations held to be significant, expressed in the tropes of similarities and differences, and with respect to some category, question, theory, or model of interest to the study of religion."[18] The goal of comparison, in Smith's view, is "the redescription of the exempla (each in light of the other) and a rectification of the academic categories in relation to which they have been imagined."[19] The present work involves a number of comparisons between primary sources from the Roman imperial period, as for example, comparisons between Paul and Seneca on aspects of gift exchange (chapters 2 and 3) and between Paul and Pliny on "gifts" of status (chapter 6). In other chapters, comparisons are made between Paul's letters and the formulations of recent theorists of gift exchange (chapters 4–6) and sociopolitical status (chapters 6 and 7). In each case, the "aim" of comparison entails, as Smith suggests, a redescription of the primary source material and a "rectification" of the academic categories in relation to which gift exchange has been imagined. It is my hope that this procedure will result not only in an interesting and informative redescription of Paul's discourses and practices, but—more importantly—an elaboration and refinement of theories of gift exchange that will be of utility within a number of academic disciplines, including sociology, anthropology, classics, and religious studies.

The Necessity of a Multidisciplinary Approach

The discussion of gift exchange necessarily involves interdisciplinarity. The patriarch of academic discussions of the subject, Marcel Mauss, the nephew of and collaborator with Émile Durkheim and a founding editor of *L'Année sociologique* (1898), received a chair in the religions of "primitive" peoples at the École Pratique des Hautes Études in 1902.[20] His work traversed three academic disciplines: sociology, anthropology, and religion. Each of these disciplines has subsequently interpreted, critiqued, and elaborated the seminal insights outlined in his *Essai sur le don* (*The Gift*), first published in 1925.

Alvin Gouldner's 1960 article in the *American Sociological Review* posited that reciprocity was a "universal" norm, although "its concrete formulations may vary with time and place."[21] Even if, faced with data that are necessarily incomplete, one may hesitate to label any practice or norm "universal," it is certain that reciprocity is widespread: it is evident in a number of cultures globally throughout recorded history.[22] Gift exchange, one of the most prominent types of reciprocal interaction, is likewise alive and well, even in the present situation of globalized corporate capitalism: the gift has not been eradicated by the market.[23]

Recent studies in primatology have demonstrated just how "widespread" reciprocity really is: not only humans, but also primates exhibit patterns of reciprocal exchange. Frans de Waal has demonstrated that chimpanzees (Pan troglodytes) groomed by companions are more likely later to share food with their groomers than with other members of their group.[24] In an analysis of studies on the subject, Gabriele Schino and Filippo Aureli have shown that reciprocity plays a larger role than kinship in grooming among primates.[25] In a separate meta-analysis, Schino and Aureli demonstrated that "female primates groom preferentially those group mates that groom them most";[26] this is a "general pattern that seems to be widespread across the primate order."[27] These and other data suggest that "primates are indeed able to exchange grooming both for itself and for different rank-related benefits."[28] As a phenomenon that is exhibited not only by humans across disparate geographic and historical locations, but also by our closest nonhuman relatives, the reciprocal exchange of goods and services, which we might otherwise label "gift exchange," is too broad a topic to be adequately addressed from within the confines of any given academic discipline. Gift exchange is a topic that invites—indeed demands—a multidisciplinary approach.

There is, however, an aspect of gift exchange exhibited in the letters of Paul that has not yet been demonstrated in our primate relatives. The goods and services exchanged among orangutans, chimpanzees, and capuchin monkeys involve grooming, food sharing, sexual access, and protection—evident material benefits. In contrast, the "goods" to which Paul claimed to have access were symbolic in nature; they existed not in the form of material objects or services, but in the form of assurances of salvation from an apocalyptic judgment that he deemed imminent and the promise of eternal life in a heavenly existence. The gifts that Paul claimed to mediate differ from those of the capuchin monkey in that the former entail the analytical category "religion"—a category that, as Jonathan Z. Smith and others have cogently argued, "is not a native term; it is a term created by scholars for their intellectual purposes and therefore is theirs to define. It is a second-order, generic concept that plays the same role in establishing a disciplinary horizon that a concept such as 'language' plays in linguistics or 'culture' plays in anthropology."[29] The concept is not, on that account, any less useful in the service of academic analysis. As a second-order, academic construct, the category of "religion" serves useful heuristic functions, providing a rubric under which particular exempla might be juxtaposed, their similarities and differences identified, and the significance of those comparisons for the critique or elaboration of various theoretical constructs explicated.[30]

Understanding the "Gift"

Like "religion," "gift"—the term central to the analyses offered in this book—is an unstable signifier, with the potential to be defined in multiple, often contradictory ways. For Derrida, as we have seen, "gift" implied an "aneconomic" system, devoid of reciprocation or return of any kind. For Mauss, it was quite otherwise: "the gift" constitutes part of a "system of total services" that performs economic functions inasmuch as it involves "the exchange of goods, wealth, and products" on a collective scale.[31] Using the developmental model that prevailed in nineteenth-century Europe and the United States (a model that, incidentally, has been implicated as part of the ideological apparatus of colonialism),[32] Mauss posited that "primitive" societies operated on the basis of a "system of exchange that is different" from "our" modern market economy: "it functioned before the discovery of forms of contract and sale that may be said to be modern (Semitic, Hellenic, and Roman), and also before money, minted and inscribed."[33] The instruments of enforcement of this "system of total services" were not legal, but moral, religious, and spiritual.[34]

INTRODUCTION   9

The moral basis of Mauss's "system of total services" rested on three obligations: to give, to receive, and to reciprocate. The failure to meet any of these obligations carried penalties: the loss of honor, prestige, and authority and, in extreme cases, even warfare between tribes or clans.[35] Gifts are in theory voluntary, but "in reality they are given and reciprocated obligatorily."[36] They are "apparently free and disinterested, but nevertheless constrained and self-interested," resting on "a polite fiction, formalism, and social deceit . . . when really there is obligation and economic self-interest."[37]

As Mauss makes clear, two of the characteristics often predicated of gift-giving, voluntarism and disinterest, do not constitute definitive characteristics of gift exchange; these attributes constitute nothing more than "a polite fiction, formalism, and social deceit." Mauss's logic of binary opposition, however, oversimplifies the complex character of transactions that we might label "gift exchange." It is this oppositional logic, by which freedom and constraint, voluntarism and obligation, self-interest and disinterest are viewed as stark alternatives, that prompts Mauss's unflattering characterization of gift exchange as "fiction" and "social deceit." According to this logic, the gift may be characterized by only one term within each of these sets of paired descriptors, but never both, in varying degrees. It is likewise the logic of binary opposition that prompts Derrida to argue that the gift is impossible: the gift is defined as that which is "aneconomic" rather than "economic," nonreciprocal rather than reciprocated, gratuitous rather than calculated.

The binary logic that both Mauss and Derrida use, however, fails to capture the nuance of gift exchange. It leads to the inevitable conclusions: either the gift is a "fiction" and "social" deceit, or it is an impossibility, existing only in a utopia of exchange. Most gift exchanges, however, exist somewhere between the binary extremes: given neither wholly freely nor entirely under constraint, neither wholly voluntarily nor entirely out of obligation, neither from unadulterated self-interest nor due wholly to concern for the other, neither calculating costs and benefits with precision nor entirely lacking such calculation. Existing in the spaces between imagined binary extremes, "the gift" resists easy definition or systematization.

Given its myriad cultural variations, gift exchange is characterized by an "irreducible heterogeneity," despite all attempts to specify its rules, norms, or definitive qualities.[38] Nevertheless, the notion of the gift is not without utility. We may identify several characteristics associated with gift exchange that, although failing to amount to a formal definition, nonetheless serve as useful heuristic devices for distinguishing gifts from other types of exchange:

1. The gift is that which is described by the parties involved in an exchange as a "gift," "donation," "present," "offering," or a synonymous term;
2. actors describe the transmission in question using forms of the verb "to give," "to donate," "to present," or synonymous terms. The "gift" is that which is construed as "given";[39]
3. the "gift" is often, but not always, followed by a reciprocal gift ("countergift") offered in return;
4. the presentation of the countergift is often, but not always, deferred for a period deemed appropriate on the basis of local practices;
5. distinguishing it from both "barter" and "sale," neither the value of the potential countergift nor the time and place at which it might be presented is negotiated in advance of the initial exchange;
6. generally, the failure of a recipient to offer a countergift incurs no legal sanction; it may, however, precipitate social sanctions (loss of honor, prestige, authority; the termination of friendly relations; or the initiation of hostile relations);
7. the reception of a gift is often acknowledged by a display of gratitude and thanksgiving.

Although the fulfillment of one or more of the conditions set forth in items three through seven above offers good indications that a given transaction might be categorized as "gift," the attributions of the actors involved are paramount to the classification of the transaction, as indicated by items one and two. Gift exchange entails cognitive and symbolic elements, consisting in its classification and description as "gift" by those party to the exchange, and behavioral elements, consisting of a display of gratitude, the offering of a countergift, and so on. Since they are not observable criteria, and since they likely exist in varying degrees in multiple types of exchanges, schemes based on dyads such as freedom/constraint, self-interest/concern for the other, and calculation/gratuitousness are not useful criteria for distinguishing "gifts" from other types of exchange.

A Preview of the Questions Addressed in This Book

Paul's letters present an opportunity for the elaboration of two domains of discourse and practice: "religion" and "gift." Although the category of "religion" may well have been foreign to Paul[40]—there is no exact equivalent in the Koine Greek in which he wrote and spoke—nevertheless it is of utility to the contemporary observer, as the classification invites comparisons and contrasts with other individuals and groups whose discourses and practices make significant reference to culturally postulated divine beings.[41] The "gift" was, in contrast, a native category for Paul; his Greek includes a rich vocabulary of gifting terminology: *dōron* ("gift"), *anathema* ("offering"), *didōmi* ("to give"), *charis* ("gift," "favor," "thanks"), *charizomai* ("to give graciously"). It has long been recognized that gift exchange was a foundational element in Greco-Roman religions (a genus of which Paul's religion was a species), as sacrifices offered at temples and shrines were construed as gifts to the gods that invited reciprocation according to the principle *do ut des,* "I give in order that you might give."[42] Paul, too, claimed to function as a mediator of gifts between humans and the god of Israel. Gifts of Israel's god were rendered accessible, in his view, through his preaching of the "good news" about Jesus' crucifixion, resurrection, and future authority over beings both heavenly and terrestrial. Conversely, gifts offered to Paul could be construed as gifts to Israel's god: his person served as a substitute temple, a mobile mediator between humans and the divine.

As Mauss recognized, gift exchange forms a "system of total services" by which material goods and services of various types are circulated. Paul, however, offers an opportunity to delineate the consequences of a different, albeit parallel, set of interactions in which symbolic gifts—those posited as proceeding to or from a deity or deities—enter into a system of exchange with material goods and services. The concern of each of the chapters that follow is to delineate the material consequences of the symbolic exchanges that Paul posits, as "religion" meets "gift" within the sociopolitical contexts of various early Christian assemblies in the mid-first century CE.

Following this introduction, the second chapter, "Symbolic Goods as Media of Exchange in Paul's Gift Economy," enlists Pierre Bourdieu's notion of the "economy of symbolic goods," in conjunction with Seneca the Younger's extended meditation on benefaction, as points of comparison illuminating Paul's notions of gift exchange between humans and the god of Israel. Axioms of reciprocal gift exchange between humans, Israel's god, and Jesus, interpreted as a divine being, are examined in Paul's letter to the Romans, 2 Corinthians, and the letter to Philemon, indicating a "system of total services" in which both material and postulated "spiritual" goods play significant roles. The delineation of the logic by which goods and services were transmitted in early Christian assemblies associated with Paul lays the foundation for the discussions in subsequent chapters.

Chapter 3, "The Benefactor's Account Book: The Rhetoric of Gift Reciprocation According to Seneca and Paul," extends the comparison between Paul and Seneca. Whereas Seneca advises against issuing reminders of a gift given, in his letter to Philemon, Paul obliquely calls attention to the "gift of salvation" the he claimed to mediate. This difference in rhetoric and praxis is examined in relation to the diametrically opposed economic situations of the two agents, and its implications, both for the circulation of goods and services and for the allocation of honor and prestige, are discussed. The chapter indicates the extent to which cultural discourses and practices associated with gift exchange may be strategically modified and adapted by sociopolitical agents in their attempts to access valued resources.

Chapter 4, "Gift or Commodity? On the Classification of Paul's Unremunerated Labor," elaborates on the distinction between gift and commodity developed by James Carrier and problematized by Gretchen Herrmann and William Miller. The chapter examines the ways in which the categorization of a good or service exchanged does not rest simply on the basis of the "objective" characteristics of the transaction, but results instead from a "politics of classification" in which agents negotiate, classify, and reclassify exchanges in order to exploit or activate the possibilities, associations, and sociopolitical consequences inherent in various classificatory categories.

Chapter 5, "Classification and Social Relations: The Dark Side of the Gift," analyzes the process of contestation and negotiation involved in the classification of Paul's unremunerated labor as an itinerant evangelist periodically active in the city of Corinth. The characterization of the social relations (whether friendly or hostile) of traveling evangelists temporarily resident in the city was both contingent on and a constitutive factor in the classification of "apostolic" labor and the various forms of support that it entailed as "gift," "theft," "sale," or "parasitic" exploitation. The chapter constitutes a case study in the politics of classification that is a constitutive element of the exchange process.

Chapter 6, "The Gift of Status," distinguishes two types of status: positional status, entailing roles or positions, each with its own obligations, duties, privileges, and responsibilities; and accorded status, or honor and prestige. On the basis of examples in the letters of Pliny the Younger, the chapter demonstrates that positional status was often granted as a gift or donation by highly placed patrons—a role fulfilled in Pliny's letters by the emperor Trajan. Like Pliny, Paul viewed positional status as a gift from those in authority; however, he believed it was primarily the god of Israel who was able to grant positional status. The chapter examines the role of postulated "gifts of status" in orchestrating a hierarchical sociopolitical organization within the early Christian assemblies. The discussion advances the study of gift exchange in that, although sociological and anthropological studies have long noted the close correlation between gift-giving and status, the fact that positional status may itself be granted as a gift has not to my knowledge previously been recognized.

Chapter 7, "Spiritual Gifts and Status Inversion," enlists Carole Crumley's notion of "heterarchy" as a means both to critique and to elaborate Wayne Meeks's fundamental insights regarding "status inconsistency" within early Christian assemblies. Within the heterarchical situation of the assemblies, various schemes for according honor and prestige were readily available. In opposition to schemes in which honor and prestige were strongly correlated with wealth, Paul proposed an alternative paradigm in which prestige was associated with the "gifts of the spirit" of Israel's god. Chapter 8 briefly summarizes the findings of the preceding chapters and considers their implications, both for religious studies and for studies of "the gift."

TWO

Symbolic Goods as Media of Exchange in Paul's Gift Economy

Economies of Symbolic Goods

In the wake of Paul Veyne's *Le Pain et le cirque* (1976),[1] historians of Mediterranean antiquity have recognized that systems characterized by reciprocity served to reproduce forms of social and political order.[2] This system operated according to the logic of exchange; gifts and favors, whether personal or political, obliged the recipient to respond with a gift or favor in return. Both gift and countergift could take various forms, including money, material goods, public honor and recognition, and access to social networks.[3] Inasmuch as these gifts and countergifts consisted of exchanges in material goods and services involving human labor, their regular transmission functioned as an economic system. Gift exchange, however, was not conducted on a mercantile basis, according to fixed rates of exchange and dates of repayment. Neither the exact value of the reciprocal gift nor the date on which it would be presented was predetermined. The reciprocity system served an economic function, albeit in accordance with nonmercantile principles.

This chapter argues that there also existed another type of exchangeable product within the reciprocity systems of Mediterranean antiquity. This type, the "religious symbolic good," consists of benefits ostensibly mediated by the power of a divine being.[4] Since this type involves nonmaterial, linguistically mediated productions, it falls into the broader category of "symbolic goods" identified by sociologist Pierre Bourdieu. In his discussion of the economy of the Catholic Church, Bourdieu treats the "goods of salvation" (i.e., the bestowal of a beatific afterlife) as an exchangeable product, access to which is controlled by the monopoly of a clerical elite.[5] Reciprocal systems in which symbolic productions play a constitutive role are designated "economies of symbolic goods."

The argument developed in this chapter proceeds in two steps. First, on the basis of a treatise of Seneca the Younger, the chapter outlines the main tenets of the system of reciprocity as it was practiced in Greco-Roman antiquity. A system of reciprocity is salutary for the operation of economies of symbolic goods, as it provides the conditions under which religious discourse may function as a product exchangeable with other products. Second, the chapter considers one writer of this period, Paul of Tarsus, as a test case to determine whether religious economies of symbolic goods were operative in early Christian communities. Paul, I argue, describes situations in which religious discourse, material goods, and services involving human labor are held to be exchangeable within the context of an ethic of reciprocity. Paul, in other words, operates within the framework of a religious economy of symbolic goods. Although other Pauline letters are pertinent, a brief survey of Romans, 2 Corinthians, and Philemon suffices to convey the key concepts.

Seneca on Systems of Reciprocity

During the latter half of the first century CE, the Roman rhetorician and statesman Seneca wrote a sustained reflection on the theory and practice of gift-giving, *De Beneficiis* ("On Benefits"). Seneca describes a system of reciprocity similar to those that have been attested in a variety of cultural contexts.[6] He outlines a simple principle: a gift given elicits a return from the recipient. This principle is demonstrated in artistic depictions of the Graces, who were often portrayed as three youthful sisters dressed in loose, transparent veils and dancing hand in hand. Seneca interprets the picture allegorically:

> Why do the sisters hand in hand dance in a ring which returns upon itself? For the reason that a benefit [*beneficium*] passing in its course from hand to hand returns nevertheless to the giver

[*ad dantem revertitur*]; the beauty of the whole is destroyed if the course is anywhere broken, and it has most beauty if it is continuous and maintains an uninterrupted succession.[7]

Gifts, ideally, pass "from hand to hand," eventually returning to their giver. For the system to operate successfully, it must "maintain an uninterrupted succession" (i.e., gifts given must be reciprocated). Ingratitude, for Seneca, is the ultimate vice (*Ben.* 1.1.2; 1.10.4; 3.1.1; 3.6.1–2), because it interrupts the pattern in which gift is followed by countergift. When there is no gratitude, no return is made; the ring of the Graces is broken.

Although Seneca defines a benefit (*beneficium*) as a gift concerning which the giver takes no thought of return (*Ben.* 2.31.2; 1.1.9; 1.2.4), it is clear that, in his view, the receiver ought to have the thought of return uppermost in his or her mind: "The man who intends to be grateful, immediately, while he is receiving, should turn his thought to repaying" (2.25.3). There is a stark contrast between the (ideal) attitudes of giver and receiver: "the one should be taught to make no record of the amount, the other to feel indebted for more than the amount" (1.4.2–4). Ingratitude, or the refusal to perceive oneself as indebted to a gift-giver, is the paradigmatic vice (1.1.2; 1.10.4; 3.1.1; 3.6.1–2). The giver is entitled to a return, above all in the form of gratitude (*gratia*) from the recipient, but also—as Seneca is at pains to point out—in the form of a material countergift (2.35.1). Although it is bad form for the giver to acknowledge an expectation of a return (1.2.3; 2.6.2; 2.10.4), nonetheless the reciprocity system demands that one be made. Giving a benefit is analogous to farming, writes Seneca: one must cultivate it—while avoiding the appearance of doing so—from the time of planting until harvest. Eventually, a well-cultivated benefit yields a healthy return (2.11.4).

The gift, in economic terms, is analogous to a loan.[8] As with a loan, the giving of a gift places the recipient under a debt. Seneca muses on the sentiment aroused by being placed under such an obligation: "sometimes, not merely after having received benefits, but because we have received them, we consider the givers our worst enemies" (*Ben.* 3.1.1). Bourdieu notes a Kabyle proverb that expresses the same sentiment: "A gift is a misfortune," the proverb goes, because it must be repaid.[9]

However, the countergift need not be repaid with the same currency in which the original gift was made. While some types of reciprocity did proceed on the basis of an exchange of similar material goods, in other cases, a material gift was reciprocated in the form of social support or the bestowal of honor upon the gift-giver. Numerous inscriptions attest the bestowal of public honors in the form of proclamations, statues, honorific inscriptions, and the like in return for public service or material benefits bestowed.[10] Such forms of reciprocation, which do not consist of a return in kind (e.g., material good for material good), are nonetheless viewed as providing adequate recompense for the original donation.

Both ancient practice and modern scholarship have recognized that the system of reciprocity need not, and often does not, consist of exchanges in which the countergift represents a type of product identical with that of the original gift. This raises the questions: how does one determine which cultural products, in any given milieu, are accorded a value such that they might be traded within a system of reciprocal exchange, thus marking them as goods recognized within that system? Were the benefits posited by religious discourse, which existed not in material form, but in the nonmaterial forms of discourse and imagination, accorded a value that enabled them to enter, as goods, into an economic system based on reciprocal exchange? To answer these questions, we consider three letters of Paul as test cases.

Test Cases: Pauline Epistles

Paul, I argue, describes an economy of symbolic goods operative within early Christian assemblies. This economy was based on the ideals of reciprocity practiced throughout the Mediterranean region in antiquity.[11] Paul's own reliance on the ethic of reciprocity has been well established in several recent studies, including those of G. W. Peterman, Stephan Joubert, Zeba Crook, Troels Engberg-Pedersen, David Briones, and John Barclay.[12] In what follows, I explicate Paul's use of religious symbolic goods within this system of exchange.

Paul assumes that not only monetary goods, but also symbolic goods are exchangeable within the reciprocity system. He treats religious symbolic goods (e.g., promises of an ameliorated afterlife) as exchangeable with other goods recognized within the system (i.e., currency, comestibles, the mobilization of human labor, etc.). In Paul's system, the benefit (*charis*) ostensibly granted by the god of Israel is identified with the justification of sinners resulting from Jesus' crucifixion; previous transgressions against covenantal norms are pardoned (Gal 2:19–21; 2 Cor 5:21–6:1; Rom 3:24–26; 5:15, 17).[13] This justification, Paul supposes, has stunning results, including acquittal at the god of Israel's universal judgment, an event that Paul perceived as imminent (1 Thess 4:13–18), and a home in the heavens in a glorified, or luminous, and thus godlike, body (Rom 5:2; cp. 1 Cor 15:35–57).[14] These nonmaterial benefits, construed as the direct result of a *charis,* a "gift" or "benefit" bestowed by Israel's god, exist only in symbolic form, in discourse and the imagination.[15] Paul, as we will see, accorded these discursive benefits a material exchange value.

The Collection for the Jerusalem Church

In the context of a discussion of a collection of funds from Gentile churches to be delivered to the Jerusalem church,[16] Paul formulates a principle of exchangeability between material and symbolic goods:

> For [the churches in] Macedonia and Achaia were pleased to establish a certain fellowship with the poor among the saints who are in Jerusalem. They were pleased; indeed, they stand in debt to them [*opheiletai eisin autōn*], for if they [the Jerusalem church] have shared with the Gentiles their spiritual things [*ta pneumatika autōn*], they [the Gentiles] are obligated [*opheilousin*] to render service to them even in material things [*en tois sarkikois*]. (Rom 15:26–27)[17]

According to this formulation, the members of the Jerusalem church have bestowed on the Gentiles their "spiritual things" (*ta pneumatika*). This act of gift-giving obliges the recipient to return a gift. In Paul's language, as the result of Jerusalem's gift, the Gentiles "stand in debt" to them. This debt need not be repaid in kind (i.e., "spiritual things" for "spiritual things"); material goods (*ta sarkika*) constitute a suitable return. In Paul's economy of symbolic goods, for which Rom 15:27 stands as an excellent summary, "spiritual things" and "material things" stand in a relationship of exchangeability. "Spiritual things" are accorded material value.

A year or two before penning his succinct formulation of the economy of symbolic goods in Rom 15:27,[18] Paul treated the subject of the Gentile contribution to the Jerusalem church in the "Collection Letters" in 2 Cor 8–9.[19] These letters, brought together in the canonical version of 2 Corinthians, appeal to the congregations in Corinth and Achaia (especially Cenchreae) to make weekly contributions to a fund that Paul would eventually collect and deliver to the Jerusalem church (cp. 1 Cor 16:1–4; Rom 15:25–26). As in Rom 15:27, Paul formulates a vision in which material goods (in the form of currency) are viewed as exchangeable with symbolic goods. Second Corinthians 9:6–15 illustrates the point.[20]

After giving notice that he has sent an unnamed "brother" to Achaia in order to ensure that regular contributions are being made to the collection in advance of his visit to retrieve the amassed sum, Paul assures readers that, despite this precaution, the collection is not carried out under compulsion (9:7), nor as a pretext for personal greed (8:19–21). Rather, it is undertaken as a "good deed" (*ergon agathon*)[21] grounded in the economic self-sufficiency (*autarkeia*) of the Achaian congregation. "God," after all, "loves a cheerful giver," Paul reminds his addressees (9:7, citing Prov. 22:8a LXX). But it is not only divine approval that is to motivate the Achaians' gift to Jerusalem:

> The point is this: the one who sows sparingly will also reap sparingly, and the one who sows bountifully will also reap bountifully. . . . And God is able to provide you with every blessing in abundance, so that by always having enough of everything, you may share abundantly in every good work. . . . He who supplies seed to the sower and bread for food will supply and multiply your seed for sowing and increase the harvest of your righteousness. You will be enriched in every way for

your great generosity, which will produce thanksgiving to God through us; . . . you glorify God by your obedience to the confession of the gospel of Christ and by the generosity of your sharing with them and with all others, while they long for you and pray for you because of the surpassing benefit [*tēn hyperballousan charin*] of God that he has given you. Thanks [*charis*] be to God for his indescribable gift [*tē anekdiēgētō . . . dōrea*]! (2 Cor 9:6–15)

Paul describes the principle of reciprocity using an agrarian metaphor: he who sows abundantly reaps abundantly. It is incumbent upon the Achaians to "sow abundantly" (i.e., to contribute lavishly to Jerusalem), because the material goods that Achaia has obtained are themselves gifts from God, who "supplies seed to the sower and bread for food." The Achaians' gift will not go unrewarded: God will "increase the harvest of [their] righteousness"; they will be "enriched in every way."[22] The idea expressed in Paul's agrarian metaphor parallels that of Seneca's image of the dancing Graces: the system of reciprocity "has most beauty if it is continuous and maintains an uninterrupted succession." In response to the divine benefaction of material goods, the Achaians are to donate material goods to those in Jerusalem, in response to which Israel's god will provide further benefactions.

The letter's final thanksgiving, "Thanks be to God for his indescribable gift," alludes to the Achaians' generosity, itself construed as a divine gift, as well as the *charis* constituted by Jesus' assumption of human form, to which allusion is made in 2 Cor 8:9 (cp. Phil 2:6–8), in order to mediate salvation from eschatological judgment (1 Thess 1:10; Rom 2:5). The material and symbolic benefactions ostensibly provided to the Achaians by the god of Israel are adequately recompensed by their material donations to Jerusalem; these, in turn, are rewarded with further spiritual ("the harvest of your righteousness") and material ("enriched in every way") benefits, to be provided by Paul's god. Symbolic benefactions, which exist discursively in the form of promise and assurance, are treated as exchangeable with material donations.

Paul's Letter to the Philippians

Another example of Paul's use of an economy of symbolic goods occurs in his letter to the Philippians, written in a Roman prison, perhaps in 56 or 62 CE.[23] As Paul indicates, the church at Philippi provided him with welcome, although sporadic, financial contributions (Phil 4:16; 2 Cor 11:8–9). Paul's only guarantee of food and clothing while in prison was to secure donations.[24] The Philippians had in fact sent one Epaphroditus to provide for Paul. In what might be interpreted as a thinly veiled request for further aid ("Not that I seek the gift . . ."), or as a frank admission that he had already received sufficient assistance ("I have been paid in full . . ."), Paul writes:

> You Philippians indeed know that in the early days of the gospel, when I left Macedonia, no church shared with me in the matter of giving and receiving [*logon doseōs kai lēmpseōs*], except you alone. For even when I was in Thessalonica, you sent me help for my needs more than once. Not that I seek the gift [*to doma*], but I seek the profit that accumulates to your account [*ton karpon ton pleonazonta eis logon hymōn*]. I have been paid in full [*apechō de panta*] and have more than enough; I am fully satisfied, now that I have received from Epaphroditus the gifts [*ta par' hymōn*] you sent, a fragrant offering, a sacrifice acceptable and pleasing to God. (Phil 4:15–18)

The commercial language that Paul uses in this passage is striking. He uses terms borrowed from the business sphere to refer to the Philippians' economic support: it is a matter of "giving and receiving."[25] In v. 17, Paul mixes the language of benefaction with that of business: the Philippians' "gift" to Paul accrues a "profit" to their "account."[26] Paul, having received the "gift" from Epaphroditus, has been "paid in full." The gift, however, is accorded a double signification: it serves not only to alleviate the material needs of Paul, but also as a "fragrant offering, a sacrifice acceptable and pleasing to God." Paul employs the terminology of the temple cultus.[27] A gift given to him is at the same time a sacrifice offered to the god of Israel. The cultic language is interpreted in economic terms: it results in a profit (*karpon*) that accrues to the Philippians' account (*logon*). Paul only hints at the nature of this "profit" in his closing benediction: "My God will fulfill your every need in accordance with his wealth in glory in Christ Jesus." The "wealth in glory" (*to ploutos . . . en doxē*) to which he refers may allude to the luminous (i.e., "glorious") body that, according to Paul, followers of Christ are to receive at the time of Christ's *parousia,* or return from heaven (1 Cor 15:25–57; 2 Cor 4:17; Rom 5:2; cp. 1 Thess 4:13–18), or it may hint at material riches.[28] He leaves the specific referent to the reader's imagination.

In Phil 4, benefaction and business transaction are overlapping categories. Material gifts to Paul elicit a countergift (i.e., a profit that accrues to one's account) from Paul's god. The exact nature of the countergift that proceeds from the "wealth in glory" of Israel's god is left unspecified. Whether it refers to the glorified body to be received by the followers of Jesus at the time of the *parousia* or to material wealth, as a promise of future benefaction from a divine being, it constitutes a "symbolic good." This symbolic good is held to constitute adequate recompense for the material donations of the Philippians and therefore meets the criterion of exchangeability.[29] Paul operates according to an economy of symbolic goods.

Paul's Letter to Philemon

Another of Paul's letters in which an economy of symbolic goods comes into play is that to the slave owner Philemon, written in 55–56 or 62 CE.[30] This letter was occasioned by the departure of a slave, Onesimus, who either had been providing for Paul's needs in prison or, after having angered his master, had approached Paul in an attempt to persuade him to appeal to Philemon for clemency toward the slave.[31] The letter is addressed to Onesimus's owner, Philemon, and two co-addressees, Aphia and Archippus, functionaries within the local house-church, perhaps in Colossae.[32] During the time when Onesimus had been visiting him in prison, Paul had persuaded the slave to become a convert to Paul's religious views, thus constituting him as Onesimus's spiritual "father" (v. 10). Paul's letter, to be carried by

Onesimus on his return trip, makes a request of Philemon, the exact nature of which is not specified:

> For this reason, though I am bold enough to command you to do your duty, yet I would rather appeal to you on the basis of love . . . I am appealing to you for my child, Onesimus, whose father I have become during my imprisonment. . . . I am sending him, that is, my own heart, back to you. I wanted to keep him with me, so that he might be of service to me [*hina . . . moi diakonē*] in your place during my imprisonment for the gospel; but I preferred to do nothing without your consent, in order that your good deed might be voluntary and not something forced. . . . Confident of your obedience, I am writing to you, knowing that you will do even more than I say. (vv. 8–14, 21)

It is clear that Paul wishes for Philemon to send Onesimus back to Paul while in prison.[33] Whether he is asking for Philemon to manumit Onesimus or to send him back as a slave to serve Paul has been the subject of debate.[34] Perhaps Paul intentionally framed his request ambiguously in order to leave to the judgment of Philemon how best to fulfill it ("knowing that you will do even more than I say").

From the standpoint of Paul's economy of symbolic goods, the most significant statements occur in vv. 17–20:

> So if you consider me your partner, welcome him as you would welcome me. If he has wronged you in any way, or owes you anything [*opheilei (se)*], charge that to my account [*touto emoi elloga*]. I, Paul, am writing this with my own hand: I will repay it [*egō apotisō*]. I say nothing about your owing me even your own self [*kai seauton moi prosopheileis*]. Yes, brother, let me have this benefit from you [*egō sou onaimēn*] in the Lord!

Paul uses the language of business transaction; both he and Philemon keep accounts in their dealings. Paul is willing to charge to his own account any debt incurred by Onesimus (v. 18). Paul indicates that he is creditworthy; he will repay the debt (v. 19). Philemon's account, however, stands in the red, as he owes Paul an unrepayable debt: his own life, or "self" (v. 19). Paul alludes to one of the symbolic goods provided by his preaching. In his view, a positive response to his preaching saves one from the worldwide apocalyptic judgment of God, viewed as imminent (1 Thess 1:10; 5:1–10; Rom 1:18; 2:5). Converted on the basis of this preaching, Philemon owes Paul his very life.[35] Paul's less than subtle reminder of Philemon's indebtedness serves as the basis for his final appeal: "Confident in your obedience, I am writing to you, knowing that you will do even more than I say." Paul implies that, in view of his unrepayable debt, the least Philemon can do is to allow Onesimus to serve Paul for the duration of his stay in prison (cp. v. 13: "I wanted to keep him with me, so that he might be of service to me [*hina . . . moi diakonē*] in your place during my imprisonment for the gospel").

Although Philemon owes Paul his very "self," Paul will accept Onesimus's presence as a substitute (v. 13: "that he might be of service to me *in place of you*" [*hyper sou*]).[36] Paul construes Philemon's "self" as fungible with Onesimus's. Should Philemon allow Onesimus to serve Paul, it is implied, this service would in some measure begin to repay a debt that Philemon could never fully discharge. Paul's logic rests on the principles of exchangeability and fungibility: Paul's gift of a religious symbolic good (i.e., his claim to mediate salvation from apocalyptic judgment) indebts Philemon for his very life, or "self"; Onesimus's life—or the labor value which that life embodies—may substitute for Philemon's and is credited toward discharging the latter's unrepayable debt to Paul. Paul construes symbolic goods as exchangeable for the products of human labor.

Conclusion

This chapter has shown that Bourdieu's concept of the economy of symbolic goods illuminates the system of exchanges described in Paul's letters: not only material goods and services involving human labor but also the symbolic goods described by religious discourse function within the context of a broader system that, operating according to a logic of reciprocal exchange, may be characterized as a nonmercantile economy. Paul's letters assume that nonmaterial, discursive products, such as the promise of deliverance from an apocalyptic judgment imagined to be imminent, may be accorded a material exchange value. He draws attention to these imagined benefits in attempts to motivate, on the basis of the principle of reciprocity, the transmission of material goods and labor services. In the absence of such imagined benefits, these transmissions presumably would fail to take place. These symbolic benefits, however, serve as more than a motive for exchange; they are rather a medium of it. Thus, Paul describes an economy in which symbolic goods played an integral part. There could be no better summary of the operation of this economy than that of Rom 15:26–27: if one imparts spiritual things to another, the former is entitled to a reciprocal gift consisting of material things. For Paul, such reciprocal interactions constitute the sine qua non of the spiritual enterprise.

THREE

The Benefactor's Account Book: The Rhetoric of Gift Reciprocation According to Seneca and Paul

Introduction

Since as early as the fourth century CE, comparisons have been made between Paul of Tarsus and Seneca the Younger. The two have been compared, among other things, with respect to their views of the divine, the "nature" of human beings, social ethics, and benefaction.[1] This chapter, too, participates in the tradition of comparing Paul and Seneca, albeit from a novel standpoint. Rather than focusing on major themes addressed in each author, the chapter takes as its point of departure what could otherwise be construed as an insignificant faux pas. Yet, as Pierre Bourdieu has shown, a world of meaning can reside in the simplest gesture. Bourdieu describes "an implicit pedagogy which can instill a whole cosmology, through injunctions as insignificant as 'sit up straight' or 'don't hold your knife in your left hand,' and inscribe the most fundamental principles of the arbitrary content of a culture in seemingly innocuous details of bearing or physical or verbal manners."[2] The "seemingly innocuous detail" that constitutes the focus of this investigation is an epistolary tactic Paul used that, by Seneca's standards, amounts to a shocking breach of etiquette. The significance of this breach, however, lies not in the light that it sheds on Paul's temperament, but in what it reveals about the divergent ways in which both Paul and Seneca were able strategically to manipulate elements of the Roman reciprocity system within the context of two almost diametrically opposed economic situations.

Seneca on Gift "Repayment"

Between 56 and 64 CE, Lucius Annaeus Seneca—Seneca the Younger—wrote the most extensive treatise on gift exchange to survive from Greco-Roman antiquity, *De Beneficiis*, "On Benefits."[3] Seneca describes a culturally patterned system according to which gifts given ought to be reciprocated by the return of a countergift consisting of a valued resource.[4] Countergifts could assume various forms, including material donations, wealth, social or political support, and the enhancement of prestige through public praise of the benefactor's magnanimity.[5] No legal sanction enforced the system's operation; social disapproval and approbation served as reciprocity's sanction and reward (*Ben.* 3.14.2). Although Seneca's treatise "draws heavily on specifically Stoic theories and styles of analysis,"[6] not least in his repeated adduction of Chrysippus as an authority (*Ben.* 1.3.8–1.4.1; 1.4.4; 2.17.3; 2.25.3; 3.22.1; 7.8.2), the systems of reciprocity that he both describes and advocates reflect prevailing social conventions. As Miriam Griffin puts it, "What we have here in *De Beneficiis* is not a philosophical ideal but a shared social ideal. . . . Seneca reflects the language and social etiquette characteristic of the early Principate."[7]

Seneca recognizes the strategic value of "placing" benefits wisely: wise donors make every attempt to select donees who are able to reciprocate the gifts given (*Ben.* 1.10.5; 2.11.4–5)—above all by receiving those gifts with gratitude (2.22.1; 2.24.1, 4; 2.30.2), but also by returning countergifts of value (2.35.1, 5)—although he recognizes that even the most skilled donors will occasionally miscalculate a recipient's willingness or ability to respond with gratitude (1.1.13–1.2.2). Gift-giving is likened to playing a game of pitch and catch: pitchers make judgments about the ability of catchers to receive and return the ball (2.17.3–5; 2.32.1–4).[8] The goal, for Seneca, is to sustain a protracted "game" from which both parties benefit. *De Beneficiis* serves as a strategy book for benefactors, advising them how best to "pitch" their benefits in order to maximize the chance that those benefits will be returned.

Seneca notes, however, that benefactors are motivated by various kinds of rewards: some by the desire for financial countergifts that exceed the value of the initial gift; others by the desire for political protection; and still others, including, not least, Seneca himself, by the desire for an enhancement of prestige (3.12.2). Seneca notes that magnanimity results in "prestige" (*auctoritas;* 3.14.2), "merit" (*dignitas;* 3.14.3–4), "glory" (*gloria;* 3.13.2), and "renown" (*fama;* 2.33.3) for liberal benefactors.

In keeping with his view that benefaction constituted a strategy by which skilled givers could maximize their access to valued resources, Seneca warns would-be donors against behavior that, because it humiliates donees, minimizes the chance of receiving a countergift. Donors are not to give gifts grudgingly, nor with a haughty demeanor, nor are they to seize the act of gift-giving as an opportunity to admonish donees (2.11.6; 2.13.1–3; 2.17.5). Seneca cites a precedent for this view: "Fabius Verrucosus used to say that a benefit rudely given by a harsh man is like bread with gravel in it—a hungry man has to take it, but it is hard to swallow" (2.7.1).[9] Leaving a bitter taste in the mouth of recipients, such actions threaten to undermine the efficacy of the act of gift-giving, failing either to elicit social support or to enhance prestige.

The giver, Seneca argues, should not operate like a banker, keeping books and insisting on repayment:[10] "No one records benefits in an account book [*in calendario*] and then, like a greedy collection agent [*avarus exactor*], demands payment at a set day and time. A good man [*vir bonus*] never thinks about his gifts unless he is reminded by someone wishing to repay them" (1.2.3). A "good man" never requests that his donation be reciprocated. To remind donees of a gift given constitutes shameful behavior. "It would be hard to say which is more shameful," Seneca writes, "repudiating a benefit or asking for repayment" (1.1.3). The best way to remind donees of a gift given is to shower them with additional gifts: "Is a man ungrateful in the face of the first benefit? He won't be in the face of the second. Has he forgotten them both? The third will remind him of those he has let slip" (1.2.5). Again, Seneca writes: "Someone who perseveres and heaps benefit upon benefit will squeeze gratitude even from a heart that is hard and forgetful. The recipient won't have the nerve to stare down so many benefits.... Besiege him with your benefits" (1.3.1). This advice is strategic: through multiple acts of gift-giving, donors are able to demonstrate their magnanimity and in so doing are more likely to be able to elicit countergifts in return. Seneca writes: "For benefits attend the person who asks no return and, just as glory [*gloria*] attends those who flee from it, so those who allow others to be ungrateful will receive a more grateful return for their benefits" (5.1.4). Benefactors who give under the pretense that no countergifts are expected maximize their returns.[11] Moreover, such largesse effectively mobilizes donors' larger communities to praise gift-givers for their beneficence; the benefactors' prestige is thereby enhanced: "The more and the greater [the gifts] are, the more praise [*laus*] they bring to the giver" (1.15.1).

Paul on Gift "Repayment"

Paul's letter to Philemon is a study in contrast to Seneca's advice. Paul does not follow Seneca's admonitions to benefactors never to call attention to the giving of a gift, and never to approach gift-giving as an accountant, recording profits and expenses in account books. In an epistolary attempt to persuade the slaveholder Philemon to relinquish Onesimus into his custody, Paul turns Seneca's advice upside down: he both calls attention to a gift given and raises the specter of an account book. By Paul's reckoning, Philemon owes Paul, and he owes a great deal. Paul places Philemon in debt for his very life, and he lets Philemon know it.

Although the circumstances that prompted Paul to compose his letter to Philemon from a jail cell, perhaps in Colossae, are less than clear, the most likely views, as mentioned in the previous chapter, are (1) that the slave Onesimus, having wronged his master in some way and expecting punishment, visited Paul to ask him to intercede with Philemon on his behalf with an appeal for clemency (vv. 17–19)[12] or (2) that Onesimus, playing a role analogous to that of Epaphroditus in Paul's letter to Philippi, had been sent to provide for Paul's needs during a period of imprisonment (v. 13).[13] Since vv. 17–19 are difficult to explain if Onesimus had been sent to Paul as the delegate of a house-church, the first option may be slightly more probable. Even if the occasion for the prison visit is less than clear, one event that transpired during it is almost certain: Onesimus allowed himself to be persuaded by Paul's religious views (vv. 15–16). This was perhaps a strategic move on the slave's part, as it united the two in a hierarchical bond of fictive kinship; Paul construes himself as Onesimus's "father" (v. 10).[14] As parent and guardian, Paul writes Philemon to intercede on Onesimus's behalf: "And so if there is any fellowship between us, receive him as you would me. If he has wronged you in any way or owes you, charge it to my account [*touto emoi elloga*] . . . I will repay it" [*egō apotisō*, vv. 17–19).[15]

Having raised the specter of accounts and repayment,[16] Paul paraleiptically[17] reminds Philemon of his own indebtedness (v. 19): "I need not remind you that you owe me your very self." This statement is generally understood as alluding to Paul's view—apparently shared by Philemon—that a positive response to his "gospel" entitled the respondent to salvation from eschatological judgment and eternal life in a heavenly commonwealth.[18] Paul construes his position as that of mediator of divine patronage: the god of Israel grants gifts of eschatological salvation, or the promise thereof; and these gifts are mediated through Jesus, the Christ, in particular through his death on the cross.[19] Paul, in turn, mediates these gifts by preaching the gospel of Jesus' death and resurrection (cp. Rom 10:8–9, 14–17). For gifts that the god of Israel has proleptically granted, that Jesus' death has enacted, and that Paul's gospel mediates, Paul himself, under the norms of reciprocity, lays claim to some form of gift "repayment."[20]

The gift that Paul claims to mediate is a heady one: escape from an eschatological judgment viewed as imminent (1 Thess 1:10; 5:1–10; Rom 1:18; 2:5) and, subsequently, eternal life in a heavenly home (1 Thess 4:13–18; 1 Cor 15:35–55). Inasmuch as the eschatological judgment involves the destruction of "sinners,"[21] those who, as the result of their favorable response to his proclamation of the gospel, are construed as recipients of the gift of salvation become indebted to Paul for their very lives, which, through his preaching of the gospel, Paul saves. Although Philemon owes Paul his very life, or "self," Paul is willing to accept as a substitute for Philemon's "life" the service of his slave, Onesimus.[22] As Paul writes, "I wanted to keep him with me, so that he might be of service to me in your place during my imprisonment for the gospel." The prepositional phrase *hyper sou*, "in your place," indicates that Onesimus's service constitutes a substitute for

Philemon's.[23] Paul's words contain an implicit request: "I wanted to keep him with me, so that he might be of service to me . . . but I preferred to do nothing without your consent. . . . Confident of your obedience, I am writing to you, knowing that you will do even more than I say" (vv. 13–14, 21).[24] Evidently, Paul wishes Philemon to lend him his slave for some period of time,[25] either to serve his needs while in prison[26] or to assist in his missionary endeavors.[27]

Paul's letter to Philemon breaks two of Seneca's cardinal rules of benefaction: he draws attention to a gift given, and he approaches benefaction as an accountant, asserting that Philemon "owes" him. In fact, Philemon owes a debt that he cannot repay, that is, his very life, or "self." In Seneca's terms, Paul's heavy-handed deployment of the rhetoric of reciprocity constitutes "shameful" behavior; he does not act as a "good man" should. How are we to account for Paul "shameful" behavior in comparison with Seneca's virtuous advice? Before drawing conclusions that would attribute either a dearth of virtue to Paul or a surplus to Seneca, an examination of the different economic locations of each is required.

Seneca's Economic Location

Seneca was born into an equestrian family in the city of Corduba (modern Córdoba) in the Roman military province of Hispania between the years 4 and 1 BCE.[28] In 37 CE, toward the end of Tiberius's reign, Seneca achieved senatorial status, beginning a quaestorship in that year. Exiled to Corsica under Claudius in 41 CE, he was recalled in 49 at the prompting of Iulia Agrippina, who promptly enlisted him as the tutor of her son, Nero. Following Nero's elevation as emperor in 54, Seneca was named an *amicus principis*, a "friend of the emperor." The economic advantages accompanying such a relationship were significant: according to Tacitus, Nero's gifts to Seneca included money, properties, and villas.[29] Seneca was also enriched during this period through the acquisition of legacies. Tacitus reports that Suillius criticized Seneca for amassing great wealth during the period of his "friendship with the king" (*Ann.* 13.42). Although it is difficult to assess the accuracy of the figure, Suillius estimated Seneca's worth in 58 CE at 300 million sesterces.[30]

Walter Scheidel and Stephen Friesen, in a recent study of the gross domestic product and the distribution of income in the ancient Roman economy, estimate that wealthier senatorial households—and, during his years as an *amicus principis*, Seneca would easily have fallen into that category—constituted a rarefied economic bracket that was inhabited by only six ten-thousandths to eight ten-thousandths of 1 percent (0.0006–0.0008 percent) of the Roman population.[31] At the height of Seneca's prosperity, few could have matched his wealth.

Paul's Economic Location

In stark contrast to Seneca, with his great wealth, Paul claimed to have often suffered from hunger and lack of adequate clothing (1 Cor 4:11; 2 Cor 11:27). As a leatherworking craftsman, Paul inhabited the lower end of the Roman economic scale.[32] His itinerant mission was likely a source of economic instability, as days or weeks spent on the road did not constitute productive work time.[33] Paul found it necessary to ask the communities to whom he preached to provide his travel expenses (Rom 15:24).[34] Stephen Friesen locates the itinerant preacher's income level at between five and seven on his "poverty scale" of Roman income distribution.[35] This means that at any given point in time, Paul's income fell somewhere from slightly above to slightly below subsistence level. Friesen recognizes that Paul was likely hosted at times in households that commanded access to a moderate surplus of resources (see, e.g., Phlm 22).[36] In Corinth, however, tensions within house-churches between fractions commanding a moderate surplus of resources and those existing near or below subsistence level rendered the acceptance of such forms of patronage politically unwise.[37] Paul's boast to the Thessalonians that he worked "night and day so as not to burden anyone [economically]" (1 Thess 2:9; cp. 1 Cor 4:12) is likely indicative of conditions he frequently faced, working to maintain himself near subsistence level.

Economic Location and Gift-Giving Strategy

Information on the widely divergent economic locations of Seneca and Paul allows for an explanation of their differential use of reciprocity ideals that does not simplistically attribute their differences to either a surplus or a lack of moral virtue. Seneca's access to vast amounts of economic wealth and Paul's lack of access to the same set the conditions under which each creatively deployed elements of the reciprocity system in efforts to obtain valued resources.

Seneca's great wealth inflects his description of gift exchange: it is shameful for the benefactor to call attention to the fact when a gift has been given; the "good man" does not do so. The proper means of reminding a donee that a gift has been given is to give a second or even a third gift. Following Seneca's advice could prove quite costly: the sometime donation of two or even three gifts to a single donee without the assurance of a return, when viewed in terms of the market economy, constitutes a losing strategy. Seneca, however, is at pains to point out that reciprocity does not constitute a market economy: unlike a market exchange, in which a price is decided before any transaction, gift-giving is to be carried out, as he opines, "for the sake of giving" (*Ben.* 1.2.4).

And yet Seneca's careful distinction of the gift economy from the market economy should not be mistaken for altruism.[38] The distribution of gifts, when they cannot be reciprocated on equal terms, effectively institutes an asymmetrical social relationship between gift-giver and recipient; in Richard Saller's view, that is the definitive characteristic of patronage.[39] Patronage institutes a social hierarchy in which clients are obliged continually to attempt to discharge the "debt" accrued by their acceptance of patronal gifts.[40] This may be accomplished by providing patrons with social support, gratitude, and public praise.[41] Seneca's gift-giving strategy, although economically costly, tenders social and political advantages through the production of a group of subordinates whose support could be called upon when needed.[42] It also effectively elevates the prestige of donors, who give in a manner calculated to elicit the gratitude of their clients, to be expressed in public praise.

Such declarations of praise would be expected to exert a multiplicative effect: as individuals and groups hear of a patron's beneficence, his or her reputation for unstinting giving spreads through the community.[43] This enhanced reputation, in turn, generates additional clients who imagine that they, too, may be able to benefit from the donor's largesse. Seneca's gift-giving advice may be attributed neither to extraordinary virtue nor to altruism: repeated acts of gift-giving, especially those directed toward recipients who are recalcitrant in returning countergifts, serve both to hierarchize social relationships and to enhance the prestige of the benefactor.

Seneca himself visits the question of motive in gift-giving. In a passage that is to be classed among the examples of hyperbole that admittedly pepper his treatise,[44] he writes, "the true wish to confer a benefit calls us away, drags us off to endure loss, and abandons self-interest [*utilitates relinquit*] for the supreme delight of merely doing good" (*Ben.* 4.14.4). However, when pressed by the questioning of an imagined interlocutor, Seneca admits that many advantages (*commoda*) spring from the virtue (*virtus*) of giving. These include greater security (*aetasque securior*) through the enhancement of one's ability to mobilize social support, as well as the "love and respect of good men" (*amorque et secundum bonorum iudicium*; 4.22.3). Seneca asserts that the virtue of gift-giving is to be pursued for its own sake, even as he acknowledges that "accessory advantages" (*adventiciis . . . dotibus*; 4.22.4) always accompany benefactions. Seneca devotes sustained attention to the rewards, costs, and motives involved in benefaction, an enterprise that, in his view, involves both rational calculation and risk; he operates self-consciously as a strategist.

Seneca's strategic—and costly—advice of repeated acts of giving is made possible only by his extraordinary wealth.[45] For those who, like Seneca, commanded the economic resources necessary to sustain such patronal practices, substantial noneconomic rewards beckoned.

Paul obviously did not command the economic resources necessary to sustain gift-giving practices on the lavish scale Seneca advocated. Without the economic ability to donate gift after gift to potentially "ungrateful" recipients, Paul literally could not afford to engage in such practices. This does not mean, however, that he lacked the resources necessary to derive benefit from the workings of reciprocity.

In an inversion of the normal patron-client relationship, Paul, an itinerant leatherworker commanding scant economic resources, effectively claims a role as patron, even among those who were, in economic terms, his superiors. By construing those to whom he preached as obliged to render "repayment" in return for his mediation of the gift of their very lives, Paul effectively subordinates as clients even moderately wealthy individuals such as Philemon, who is construed as bound to the apostle by an unrepayable debt.[46] Some brief remarks suffice to indicate the role of Paul's claim in v. 19 that Philemon stands indebted to him within the broader rhetorical project of the letter.

In his opening address, Paul greets Philemon as a "beloved fellow worker" (v. 1), and in his thanksgiving, he refers to the "love and faithfulness" that Philemon exercises toward "all the saints" (v. 5). Philemon's "love" was no doubt tangibly expressed in acts of *beneficium* (i.e., benefits, gifts, or services, such as those provided by a patron to clients) on behalf of the assembly.[47] In v. 1, Paul names Philemon as a "fellow worker" or "colleague" (*synergos*), lending the impression that both Paul and Philemon are united in a larger project, that is, spreading the "gospel" and "building up" the assembly (cp. Rom 14:19; 15:2; 1 Cor 10:3–24).[48] The language of shared community appears again in v. 6, where Paul mentions Philemon's "faithful partnership" (*koinōnia tēs pisteōs*) evident above all in his *beneficia* to the community, and in v. 17, which points to a "partnership" or "association" (*ei oun me echeis koinōnon*) between himself and Philemon.[49] Ideals of communal association are also evident in Paul's use of familial language: three times he addresses Philemon as "brother" (vv. 1, 7, 20); they share the same god as father (v. 3).

Paul's language of communal association, especially his depiction of himself and Philemon as "brothers," appears to imply an egalitarian social system that attempted to displace—or at least to minimize—a hierarchical social order.[50] Yet the matter is not so simple. Paul's deployment of the language of authority reflects his superior position in a hierarchical relation with Philemon.[51] "Though I am bold enough in Christ to command you to do your duty" (*epitassein soi to anēkon*), Paul writes, "yet I would rather appeal to you on the basis of love" (v. 8). By characterizing his appeal as a request based on "love," Paul provides the means for Philemon to avoid the humiliation of being publicly[52] commanded to do his "duty." The reference to his authority to command, however, carries with it the implication that, should his gracious appeal "on the basis of love" be refused, Paul stands ready to resort to his authority.[53] The parallel in 1 Cor 4:21 is instructive: "What do you wish? Shall I come to you with a stick, or in love, with a gentle spirit?" Should the appeal to love fail, Paul indicates that he is willing to resort to the "stick" of disciplinary action.

Paul's statement in v. 14, "I preferred to do nothing without your consent, in order that your good deed might be voluntary [*kata hekousion*] and not something forced [*mē hōs kata anankēn*]," employs a dialectic between volunteerism and compulsion similar to that of v. 8. Pliny's first letter to Sabianus exhibits the same dialectic: "I fear that I may seem to be applying pressure [*cogere*] rather than to be pleading [*rogare*] with you, if I join my prayers [*precibus*] to his, and I shall do this all the more fully and frankly for having rebuked him more sharply and severely" (*Ep.* 9.21).[54]

Paul again points to the asymmetry inherent in his relationship with Philemon in v. 21: "Confident of your obedience [*hypakoē*], I am writing to you" (v. 21).[55] His use of the imperative in v. 22 (*hetoimaze moi xenian;* "prepare a guest room for me") likewise indicates Paul's superior status. The issue of social stratification takes us to the heart of Paul's use of patronage motifs in his letter to Philemon.

In v. 7, Paul's characterization of the tangible "love" that Philemon extends to the members of the Colossian assembly likely refers to material benefits bestowed on the community. That, combined with the fact that the assembly met in his house (v. 2) and that his household included guest quarters that could accommodate Paul (i.e., the *xenia* requested in v. 22),[56] indicates that Philemon played a role in the Colossian assembly analogous to that of the Roman patron, providing needed goods and services to those who enjoyed less wealth and fewer political connections.[57] However, the fact that Philemon provides benefits does not, as often with patron-client relationships, lead to any suggestion that Paul, as beneficiary, occupies a subordinate social position. On the contrary, Paul treats Philemon as his subordinate. In Paul's view, Philemon owes him a debt that he cannot repay, the debt of his own "self" (v. 19); Philemon is effectively reduced to the level of client.

Although it does not, as with Paul, involve the mediation of heavenly patronage by a broker, a narrative in Apuleius of Madauros's *Metamorphoses* provides an instructive parallel regarding the nature of gift-debt and its implications for social hierarchy.[58] Apuleius's protagonist is one Lucius, who, as the result of a mishap precipitated by an excessive curiosity regarding magic, is transformed into an ass. Later, Lucius's human form is restored through the intervention of the goddess Isis. The goddess's transformation of Lucius is described as an act of heavenly patronage (*de caelo patrocinium; Met.* 11.16) and a benefaction (*beneficium;* 11.6, 12, 13, 18), to which the proper response is gratitude (*gratia;* 11.14) expressed in the following manner: "You will clearly remember and keep forever sealed deep in your heart the fact that your life's course is pledged to me [Isis] until your last breath. Nor is it unjust that you should owe all the time you have to live [*totum debere quod vives*] to her by whose benefit [*beneficium*] you return to the world of men" (11.6). As a perpetually indebted client, Lucius is to "take on the voluntary yoke of [the goddess's] service" (*ministerii iugum subi voluntarium*); he is to become her slave (*deae servire;* 11.15).[59] For the gift of a life, a life is owed; that is why Paul is able to claim Philemon's (Phlm 17).[60] In Paul's view, however, the services of Philemon's "useful" slave (v. 11), Onesimus, provided an acceptable substitute (v. 13: "in order that he might serve in your place").

Following up on a suggestion of John Barclay, David Briones has argued that in 2 Corinthians, "both Paul and the Corinthians operate interchangeably as brokers of one another"; that is, both parties mutually contribute "goods" derived from the god of Israel.[61] The situation in the letter to Philemon is similar. Philemon plays the role of patron or benefactor, offering material benefits to the assembly; Paul, on the other hand, characteristically mediates "spiritual" benefits, including deliverance from apocalyptic judgment (1 Thess 1:10) and divine "wisdom" normally inaccessible to humans (1 Cor 2:6–13).[62] However, in light of his treatment of

Philemon as a social subordinate, it is clear that Paul does not hold material and spiritual benefits as existing on a par; he accords "spiritual" benefits a greater value. On this point, Paul stands in agreement with the idea expressed in a rhetorical question attributed to Jesus in the synoptic gospels (Matt 16:26; par. Mark 8:37): "What will a person give in exchange for his life [*psychē*]?" In the view of both Paul and the synoptics, a suitable return cannot be made for the (promised) deliverance of one's life from apocalyptic judgment. Philemon's material benefactions do not adequately compensate Paul's "spiritual" contributions.

The disproportionate value of Paul's "spiritual" contributions implies a patronage relationship with Philemon. As Richard Saller points out: "the *patronus-cliens* relationship had no 'technical sense' and no formal standing in law. . . . [T]he words *patronus* and *cliens* were applied to a wide range of bonds between men of unequal status . . . Proculus' basic condition for clientage was the superiority of one party in *auctoritas, dignitas,* and *vires.*"[63] Paul's use of the language of authority is sufficient to establish his superior *auctoritas* ("authority"), *dignitas* ("rank" or "distinction"), and *vires* ("power") in his relationship with Philemon. Although the letter does not use the Greek equivalents of the terms *patronus* ("patron") or *cliens* ("client"),[64] it construes the relationship between Paul and Philemon as one "between men of unequal status"—a discrepancy brought about not least by Paul's mediation of an unrepayable gift. In that respect, Paul's relationship with Philemon mimics that of a patron and a client, even as it inverts the normal hierarchical order based on wealth.[65] In Paul's adaptation of Roman patronage practices, it is one's access to "spiritual" resources, not material wealth, that most effectively confers status.

Although Paul's claims to apostolic authority likely played a role in his construction of hierarchical relations within his house-churches,[66] the term "apostle" does not occur in the letter to Philemon. In Philemon's case, it is not least his reduction to the level of client indebted to Paul that maintains the asymmetrical relationship. And Philemon's indebtedness Paul does not hesitate to point out. In return for his mediation of the heavenly gift of eschatological salvation, Paul is able to call upon Philemon to offer as a countergift the services of his slave, Onesimus.

Conclusion

Seneca's construction of the image of the patronal "good man" who lavishes gift after gift, even upon the ungrateful, without drawing attention to the fact that gifts have been given may be attributed to virtue as little as it may be to altruism. Conversely, Paul's willingness to point to his role as mediator of divine gifts, and in that role to lay claim to a countergift, is not necessarily indicative of a dearth of virtue on his part. Each utilizes the assets at his disposal, whether vast wealth or a discursively constructed role as mediator of divine benefaction, in the manner that maximizes his chances of gaining access to valued resources. These resources include the superior social status attendant upon fulfilling the role of patron or patronage broker; enhanced prestige, brought about by the praises of grateful clients; and, in Paul's case, through an inversion of normal patron-client relations, access to the labor services of a wealthier man's slave. Like skilled players in a protracted game of pitch and catch, both Seneca and Paul used the resources at their disposal in attempts to gain access to resources they desired.

Their differential utilization of reciprocity norms does not imply, however, that Paul and Seneca functioned as purely self-motivated actors deploying gift-giving conventions to serve only their own interests. In Paul's case, his intervention with Philemon likely benefited Onesimus, if only by sparing him punishment for whatever "wrong" he had committed against his master. In Seneca's case, his largesse served as a means of support and political advancement for his clients, as both Juvenal and Martial attest. Even so, it is clear that the operations of the gift economy were heavily inflected by the material and sociopolitical interests of the principal actors. Under the best of circumstances, the interests of donors and recipients complemented one another. Inasmuch as Philemon's positive response to Paul's implicit request in Phlm 13 would have entailed a loss of his slave's labor for some period of time, however, it is evident that as with most games, the winnings and losses associated with benefaction were not to be distributed equally among all the players involved.

FOUR

Gift or Commodity? On the Classification of Paul's Unremunerated Labor

Introduction

Marcel Mauss's *Essai sur le don* (*The Gift*) has proved to be a durable point of departure for studies of gift exchange since its initial publication in *L'Année sociologique* in 1925.[1] Mauss observed a distinction between gifts and market exchanges, based on the sale of commodities. James Carrier subsequently elaborated Mauss's basic distinctions.[2] More recent studies, however, such as those by Gretchen Herrmann, demonstrate that the binary distinction between gift and commodity oversimplifies the complex data.[3] Herrmann takes examples drawn from North American garage sales to show that "transactions can fluctuate between gift and commodity, or partake of both at the same time, depending on the social relations [involved]."[4] Hermann's examples reveal Carrier's binary opposites, gift and commodity, to be unstable signifiers, each mutually transgressing its own and the other's limit, yielding hybrid forms: commodity-like gifts and gift-like commodities. William Miller shows that the classification of an exchange, whether as gift, sale, or one of the other categories recognized in medieval Iceland—loan, theft, or raid—was the subject of active negotiation before transactions.[5] The choice of category, ideally by mutual agreement, carried implications for the subsequent actions expected of both parties, the mode in which their social relations would be conducted, and the gain or loss of honor and prestige that would accrue to both parties as the result of the exchange. Miller's data suggest that the act of classifying an exchange is both the product of a complex set of sociopolitical relations and a constitutive factor in shaping those relations.

Recent discussions of gift exchange have significant implications for the interpretation of the epistles of Paul of Tarsus, who also recognizes a distinction between gift and commodity.[6] Conversely, the analysis of Paul's letters holds the potential to advance contemporary theoretical discussions by demonstrating that the very act of categorizing an exchange as "gift" or "sale" constitutes a significant sociopolitical gesture that serves the important functions of structuring the mutual expectations and social relations of the parties to the exchange. The symbolic and discursive act of categorizing an exchange, perhaps even more than the material characteristics of the goods or services involved, serves to shape and constrain future social relations between parties to a transaction.

"The Gift" According to Mauss, Carrier, Herrmann, and Miller

In his classic work *The Gift*, Marcel Mauss contrasts gifts with commodities. Gift exchange, governed by obligations to give, to accept, and to reciprocate,[7] cements social ties between groups based on kinship, physical proximity, or other factors and serves to confer status to those with the economic assets to give lavishly.[8] Gift-giving involves risk, since the possibility exists that a donee will not reciprocate a gift given, despite social pressure and moral norms designed to encourage reciprocity. Market economies, on the other hand, do not encourage group solidarity and are governed by contract rather than by moral obligation.[9] If in Mauss's work there appears to be a certain valorization of the gift economy, that is because he wrote in part to encourage programs of redistribution for the "public welfare," including health insurance provided by the state, "family assistance" to benefit industrial laborers with family obligations, and unemployment insurance, to be provided by employers.[10]

James Carrier has developed Mauss's gift/commodity distinction by enhancing and extending the list of binary oppositions assumed to distinguish gift from commodity. Carrier interprets Mauss in light of Karl Marx's analysis of capitalism as alienating labor from the products of its work.[11] In his view, "Gifts and commodity exchange may be contrasted by describing the elements that underlie the Maussian view of gifts: (1) the obligatory transfer of (2) inalienable objects or services between (3) related and mutually obligated transactors."[12] Carrier defines gifts and commodities in terms of a series of binary oppositions:

Gift	*Commodity*
Mutually obligated agents (parties obligated to reciprocate)	Free and independent agents (no obligation to sell or to buy to or from a particular party)
Relationship between parties endures over time	Relationship between parties dissolves upon payment
Inalienable: gifts bear the identity of the giver and of the relationship between giver and recipient	Alienated: commodities "bear no substantial relationship" to the people who make or sell them
Considered unique, laden with meaning and individuality	Considered generic, members of a class (e.g., candy bar, gallon of milk, etc.)
Irreplaceable	"Fungible": can be easily replaced with another member of the category or class
Evaluated in terms of relationship formed or expressed/maintained	Evaluated in terms of "money form" or the amount of money for which the commodity may be exchanged
Persons defined largely in terms of the social relations expressed/maintained in the gift exchange	Persons defined in terms of their position within a system of production of goods: division of labor and economic class

Although he defines gift and commodity in terms of a series of oppositions, Carrier cautions against an overly rigid interpretation of the binary framework: gifts and commodities are not to be viewed as exclusive categories, but as poles on a continuum: "Many gift transactions contain an element of alienation and individualism, just as many commodity transactions are tinged by mutual obligation."[13]

Despite Carrier's attempt to forestall the conclusion that gift and commodity are defined by a set of mutually exclusive characteristics, his work has drawn criticism on that very point. Gretchen Herrmann, for example, takes examples drawn from North American garage sales to show that "transactions can fluctuate between gift and commodity, or partake of both at the same time, depending on the social relations [involved] . . . [The garage sale] provide[s] the potential for actors to construct transactions that are more or less gift-like or commodity-like. Here transactors actively construct meanings that are unique to specific exchanges, often rendering items inalienable, even within the context of overtly commodified exchange."[14] Herrmann notes that sellers at garage sales often greatly reduce the prices of particular items when a buyer makes known a special need or interest in the item purchased; such "giveaway prices" may elicit gratitude similar to that displayed by the recipient of a gift.[15] At other times, sellers take the role of donors, and buyers, of donees, when the seller determines that an item will "find a good home" with a buyer who has enthusiastically "connected" with a particular item and gives it away free of charge.[16] In still other cases, sellers transmit information about the "life histories" of particular items, forging a link in the buyer's mind between an object and its past owner.[17] This practice gives rise to the paradoxical "inalienable commodity." Carrier's binary opposites, gift and commodity, are revealed by Herrmann's examples to be unstable signifiers, each mutually transgressing its own and the other's limit, yielding hybrid forms: commodity-like gifts and gift-like commodities.

Rather than deconstructing the gift/commodity dualism, William Miller's analysis of data from medieval Icelandic saga suggests that while transactions often lack essential or intrinsic qualities that would necessitate their placement within a particular classificatory category—defining it, for example, as "gift" or "purchase"—nevertheless those involved take great pains to negotiate and to label precisely the terms under which a given transaction is to be understood and conducted.[18] It is vital for the parties to a transaction to arrive at a clear understanding of the type of transaction in which they are engaged, since the classification of the exchange has important sociopolitical implications: it affects expectations regarding the nature and type of future transactions (whether by way of gift, purchase, hostile taking, legal proceeding, or physical assault) and the duration (ongoing or ephemeral) and character (sociable or hostile) of social relations, and it bears implications for the allocation of honor and prestige. Transactions in the sagas were often prefaced with prolonged negotiations between principals setting the terms and conditions under which exchanges would take place. Such precautions, however, did not prevent disagreements from erupting between parties over how prior transactions were to be categorized, nor did they prevent the occasional reclassification of a prior exchange in response to social pressure.[19]

The data that Miller collects suggest that exchanges are classified not on the basis of any single, putatively definitive characteristic of an object or service rendered, but on the basis of a number of variables, including the location at which an exchange takes place (e.g., market or home), the temporal constraints according to which the countertransfer would be accomplished (i.e., whether at a predetermined or an unspecified time), the social relations of the transacting parties (friendly or hostile, stranger or kin, etc.), and assessments of the honor and prestige that may be won or lost on the basis of the transaction. It is not simply, as Herrmann's work might suggest, that there are no clear lines of demarcation between various forms of exchange. Rather, a number of sociopolitical factors influence the choice of which category is to be applied in the context of a particular transaction; the choice of category, in turn, significantly affects subsequent interactions between the parties to the exchange. The act of classifying an exchange is both the product of a complex set of sociopolitical relations and a constitutive factor in shaping those relations.

Gift or Commodity? Apostolic Labor in the Letters of Paul

The notion that the classification of an exchange is the product of a complex set of sociopolitical relations is nowhere better demonstrated than in the epistles of Paul. As a traveling evangelist of the nascent Christian movement, Paul construes his vocation as one predicated on a set of exchange relationships. He portrays himself as the recipient of gifts from God, gifts that, through his preaching, he mediates to others who in return give thanks to the god of Israel and offer gifts to other Christian communities (cp. 2 Cor 8–9). Economic support for traveling preachers such as Paul could be understood as a countergift for the gifts purportedly mediated through evangelism (cp. Phil 4:15–20). Early Christian assemblies, however, practiced several different modes of support for traveling missionaries such as Paul.

Modes of Economic Support for Christian Functionaries

In the first century CE, at least five modes of support for representatives of various early Christian assemblies are attested:[20]

1. Hospitality (*xenia, philoxenia,* or *hospitium*). The synoptic gospels depict Jesus as enjoining itinerant evangelists to accept temporary room and board in the homes of those to whom they preached (Luke 10:1–9; Matt 10:5–13).[21] The practice has ancient roots in Greek *xenia* (cp. Homer, *Il.* 6.224–25); according to Josephus, many of Jesus' contemporaries engaged in a similar practice (*J.W.* 2.8.4, §125).[22] It is likely that Cephas (an Aramaic nickname, "Rock," for the apostle Peter)[23] was hosted in the same way during his travels (1 Cor 9:3–6).

    In a Romanized context, the practice could involve a patron-client relationship entailing hierarchical social relations between host and guest,[24] or it could involve individuals of approximately equal economic status.[25] An important factor distinguishing hospitality from patronage is that patron-client relationships involved the payment of a salary (*misthos* or *sportula*), whereas hospitality did not. There is no evidence that Paul, Peter, or other early Christian missionaries ever received a salary while staying as guests in any household.[26] For that reason, early Christian missionaries cannot without qualification be classed as clients, nor their hosts as patrons.[27]

2. Ambassadorial aid. Temporary room and board was sometimes requested for emissaries appointed to represent a local Christian assembly traveling to another city on ecclesial

business. Phoebe, a prominent figure in the assembly at Cenchreae (near Corinth);[28] Paul; and Barnabas, his early associate in Antioch,[29] were entertained as guests in this way when sent on business by the assemblies at Corinth and Antioch. This mode of support is distinguished from the preceding (no. 1) in that it applies to individuals designated by a local assembly to serve as representatives on its behalf in a matter of concern to the community,[30] whereas the defining characteristic of mode no. 1 is that individuals are engaged in no business other than the generalized and ongoing practice of evangelism.

3. Other support (funds, food, clothing). In rare instances, communities donated funds to support itinerant missionaries engaged in generalized evangelism (Phil 4:15–16) or provided them with food and clothing during periods of imprisonment (Phil 4:17–18).
4. Travel funding. Paul made requests to particular assemblies to cover his expenses while traveling. Such requests were typically euphemized with a plea to be "sent on one's way" (*propemphthēnai;* 1 Cor 16:6, 11; 2 Cor 1:16; Rom 15:24).[31]
5. Self-support through the sale of labor or goods. Paul (1 Thess 2:9), as well as the couple Priscilla and Aquila (Acts 18:1–4), labored as leatherworkers to earn money to cover their living expenses.[32] In such cases, ecclesial work and preaching took place after hours, or perhaps in the workshop or marketplace.[33]

The five modes of support[34] for ecclesial functionaries were not mutually exclusive; Paul at various times likely engaged in each of them. As traveling missionaries' relations with various assemblies grow increasingly complex, it becomes difficult in practice to distinguish modes 1 and 2, as visits to given assemblies likely included both "general evangelism" and particular items of business (as evident, for example, in Paul's epistle to the Romans).

Greek and Roman hospitality, a form of ritualized friendship, involved a mutually supportive gift-giving relation: "The forms of mutual support practiced included the exchange of valuable resources (money, troops, or grain), usually designated gifts, and the performance of important services (e.g., opportune intervention, saving life, catering for every need), usually designated benefactions."[35] In early Christian circles, however, the exchange was likely construed differently: itinerant preachers provided a message authorized by the god of Israel; hosts temporarily provided food and lodging. Note that in the Gospel of Luke (10:1–12), the missionary's pronouncement of "peace"—a statement functioning as a benediction expected to bring about peaceful affairs in the household[36]—was reciprocated when the household provided temporary food and lodging. In any case, the practice of hospitality involved what was construed as an exchange of gifts. The practice of hospitality should be clearly distinguished from patronage of the sort extended to philosophers, writers, and poets in that, unlike the former, the latter practice included a wage (*misthos, sportula*) provided to the client at regular intervals.[37]

Characterizing Apostolic Labor in 1 Corinthians

Perhaps partly because of the multiplicity of modes of economic support available to early Christian functionaries, Paul exhibited considerable flexibility in his characterizations of exchange relationships with various assemblies. In his first letter to the Corinthians, for example, he implicitly or explicitly adduces no fewer than six models to describe his exchange relationship with the members of the assembly there: manual laborer, slave, athlete, priest, prophet, and giver of gifts. Each of these roles is differentiated from the others on the basis of a number of binary classificatory schemes, including entitlement to compensation, the likelihood of compensation, the mode of compensation, the voluntary or compulsory nature of an activity or service performed, sacrality, and virtuosity of service. In contrast to the regularized negotiations characteristic of Icelandic saga, Paul appears not to have made any attempt to specify beforehand what characteristics his exchange relationship with members of early Christian assemblies, including those he had founded, would assume. Rather, he proposed various models and relied on the discretion of the assemblies to enact a mutually acceptable response.

In a defense of his credentials as an "apostle," or "sent" emissary of the early Christian movement to receive compensation for his services,[38] Paul writes the following in 1 Cor 9:4–12:

> Have we no right [*exousia*] to eat and drink?[39] Do we not have the right [*exousia*] to take along a "sister" as wife as do the other apostles and the brothers of the Lord and Cephas? Or is it only Barnabas and myself who do not have the right [*exousia*] to refrain from working? What soldier covers his own expenses?[40] Who tends a vineyard and does not eat its fruit? Or who tends a flock and does not consume some of its milk? I am not saying these things on human authority; does not the law itself say them? For it is written in the law of Moses, "You shall not muzzle an ox while it is threshing" (Deut 25:4). Surely God is not concerned with oxen; is it not entirely for our sakes that he speaks? Indeed, for our sakes it was written that the one who plows should plow, and the one who threshes (should thresh) in the expectation of receiving a share (of the harvest).[41] If we have sown spiritual things [*ta pneumatika*] for your benefit, is it a big deal [*mega*] if we harvest material things [*ta sarkika*] from you? If others claim this right [*exousia*] from you, ought not we do so all the more? But we have not made use of this right [*exousia*], but we endure everything so that we might not present any obstacle to the gospel of Christ.

Paul classifies his apostolic services as a form of compensable labor, placing it in the same category as military service, viticulture, agriculture, and animal husbandry. The principle governing these examples is that the performance of labor in the service of a particular end entitles the laborer to a share in the resulting produce. Labor is compensated, at least in part, by the produce of agricultural labor and animal husbandry; the laborer is paid in comestibles (in most cases, however, an additional wage was expected).[42] Paul attempts to legitimate his classification of apostolic labor as a form of compensable labor by citing an injunction from the law of Moses, viewed as a text endowed with the transcendent authority of the god of Israel.[43] Paul bases his conception of the divine *oikonomia* on typical human patterns of exchange, even if so describing it would, from the apostle's perspective, invert the priority. But he draws an important distinction between his own labor and that of the other professions adduced: his contributions are not material, but discursive; they constitute "spiritual things," by which he refers to the contents of the gospel that he preaches.[44] In v. 11 he suggests, as in Rom 15:27, that the "spiritual" may appropriately be exchanged with the material.[45]

Paul repeatedly asserts that, as in the other examples that he adduces, he has the "right" to claim compensation for his apostolic labor—in the form of material goods drawn from the assembly. Nevertheless, he indicates that he willingly refrains from exercising that right in Corinth. This, however, problematizes his claim to serve simply as a laborer on the analogy of the soldier, farmer, or shepherd. And so he introduces alternative models of exchange for his audience's consideration, those of priest, prophet, and slave:

> Do you not know that those who perform the sacred rites consume resources from the temple; those who serve at the altar share with the altar a portion (of what is sacrificed)? So also the Lord commanded those who proclaim the gospel to make a living from the gospel.[46] But I have made use of none of these (rights). I am not writing this that it might be so with me, for I would rather die than—no one will nullify my boast! For if I proclaim the gospel, that is not grounds for me to boast, since I am placed under constraint: woe to me if I do not preach the gospel. For if I do this willingly, I deserve payment, but if unwillingly, I am entrusted with the management of an estate [*oikonomia*].[47] What then is my payment? (Only) that, as I preach the gospel free of charge [*adapanon*], I might offer it so as not

to make full use of my right [*katachrēsasthai tē exousia mou*] in the gospel.

For although I am free [*eleutheros*] from all people, I have enslaved myself [*emauton edoulōsa*] to all, so that I might gain [*kerdainō*][48] more (of them) . . . I do everything for the sake of the gospel, so that I might be a partner [*synkoinōnos*] in it. (1 Cor 9:13–19, 23)

Paul adds to his stock of examples from the military and agrarian sectors by adducing priestly service and gesturing toward the role of prophet. These functions are distinguished from the foregoing on the basis of an opposition between sacred and profane occupations. Paul's apostleship, like priestly service, falls into the former category. The distinction, however, exists alongside a similarity in another respect. Priests, like farmers, soldiers, or pastoralists, are entitled to compensation for their labor. As shepherds drink milk from the flock or vinedressers consume the vineyard's grapes, so priests consume a portion of the sacrificial victims that they offer on the behalf of others.

Nuancing the sacred/profane dichotomy, Paul introduces a distinction between voluntary and compulsory labor. The soldier, the vinedresser, the shepherd, the farmer, and the priest labor voluntarily, in contrast to the compulsory service of the prophet and the slave, whose roles are introduced in vv. 16 and 19. He hints that his apostolic labor shares an element in common with that of prophets, who in biblical narrative are typically pressed into service, even against their will, by the god of Israel. His comment "woe to me if I do not preach the gospel" echoes a similar formulation attributed to the prophet Jeremiah in a lament over the loss of autonomy inherent in his prophetic calling (cp. Jer. 20:7–9). Paul raises the specter of slavery in v. 19: "Although I am free . . . I have enslaved myself to all." Prophet and slave are united not only by the lack of voluntarism that characterizes their services, but also by the fact that, because they are involuntarily enlisted, they are not entitled to remuneration for their labor.[49] Paul depicts his own apostolic position as hybrid in form: like soldier, shepherd, vinedresser, or harvester of wheat, he is entitled to compensation for his work, like the priest or prophet his work is sacred, and like the prophet or slave, he operates under compulsion. Unlike the prophet and slave, he is entitled to a wage, but like them, he fails to receive one. However, unlike the prophet and slave, who receive no wages because they have been involuntarily pressed into service, Paul's failure to receive a wage results from the voluntary renunciation of his entitlement to receive repayment for services rendered.

Having raised various forms of service, both sacred and profane, as potential paradigms on which to pattern the Corinthian assembly's exchange relation with Paul in his role as apostolic laborer, the evangelist introduces a related metaphor—that of the athletic competition:

> Do you not know that all the runners in the stadium run, but one takes the prize? Run so as to attain (it). And every competitor exercises self-control in all matters; they (do so) in order that they might receive a perishable wreath, but we an imperishable one. And so I myself run, (but) not as one who lacks an objective; I box, (but) not as one whose blows connect with nothing but air. Rather, I punish my body and enslave it so that, after I have preached to others, I myself might not be disqualified. (1 Cor 9:24–29)

This section introduces a distinction between labor that is rewarded by humans and that ostensibly rewarded by the god of Israel. Competitors in athletic events may receive recognition of their efforts in the form of a wreath of olive, laurel, pine, or celery bestowed by the *brabeus,* or umpire,[50] but Paul labors to receive an "imperishable wreath" bestowed by the god of Israel (v. 25). The image of the athlete's crown, it may be noted, surely resonated in Corinth, which biannually hosted the Isthmian games.[51]

Paul's introduction of the image of the athletic competitor further nuances the set of exchange relations that he had introduced prior to that point. Like priests, vinedressers, farmers, and pastoralists, athletic competitors labor in the hope of a reward for their efforts. But an important distinction is to be made: with the former, the likelihood of compensation for services rendered is high; compensation is drawn in part from the produce of the labor performed, to which workers have constant access. However, unlike those categories of labor, but like those of slaves and prophets, the athletes' likelihood of receiving compensation for their labor is low: many competitors run, but only one receives the wreath of victory. The labor of athletes thus introduces an important element not present in the previous, workaday examples: unlike most types of service, athletes are rewarded not simply for performing a particular class of labor; they are rewarded on the basis of only virtuosity. Unless athletes successfully distinguish themselves from the other competitors, no reward is forthcoming.

Paul suggests that he, like the runner crowned with victory, is characterized by virtuosity: "And so I myself run, (but) not as one who lacks an objective; I box, (but) not as one whose blows connect with nothing but air . . . I punish my body and enslave it" (9:26-27). Not content simply to compete, Paul portrays himself as one who plays to win (cp. Phil 3:12-14; 4:1; 1 Thess 2:19-20). Later in the letter, Paul again points to the virtuosity of his evangelistic labor. Comparing himself to Peter (Cephas), James, and the twelve apostles appointed by Jesus, Paul writes, "I worked harder than all of them" (1 Cor 15:10). In terms of both the success with which he expects to be crowned and the intensity with which he labors, Paul presents himself as a virtuoso apostle, as distinct from Peter, James, and "the twelve" (1 Cor 9:4-5), who are depicted by way of contrast as workaday, ordinary, and unexceptional evangelists.[52]

The image of the virtuoso athlete also introduces an important distinction not present in the previous categories of labor: the athlete typically works for compensation not in the form of comestibles, as do the priest, pastoralist, viticulturist, or for that matter Peter and the other apostles. Rather, the athlete seeks compensation in nonmaterial form, in terms of honor and prestige, of which the material substance of the victor's wreath is but a tangible sign. Paul's aposiopetic outburst in 9:15,[53] indicating that his renunciation of the right to remuneration is an act about which he could boast, is instructive: Plutarch defines boasting as an attempt to confer honor upon oneself (*Mor.* 540A, 541F).[54] By introducing the image of the athlete as a point of comparison with his own apostolic labor, Paul implies that his service is marked by virtuosity and is worthy of recognition in the form of honor and prestige. Paul's self-proclaimed repudiation of remuneration in the form of material goods entitles him, in his view, to repayment in nonmaterial, symbolic forms.

A final category—that of gift exchange—remains unmentioned in 1 Cor 9, although it appears elsewhere in the letter. In his opening benediction in 1 Cor 1:4–9, Paul presents the god of Israel as a gift-giver; he has bestowed his favor (*charis*) on the Corinthians, who are described as lacking in no gift as they await the return of Jesus from heaven. Paul, too, has been given gifts: he has been granted insight into divine mysteries (4:1), which he put to use—as an apostolic laborer—in order to found the assembly in Corinth (3:10). As he has received, so he gives: like a nursing mother, he provides spiritual "milk" for the Corinthians to drink (3:2). His apostleship itself Paul presents as a gift (*charis*) from Israel's god, in response to which he labors diligently on behalf of his divine benefactor ("I worked harder than all of them"; 15:10). Such evangelistic labor is not in vain (*ouk estin kenos;* 15:58); it will be rewarded on the day of apocalyptic judgment—a reward to which Paul refers, using the language of commerce, as a *misthos,* or "wage" (3:8, 14). The cycle of gift exchange, in keeping with the Greco-Roman image of the dancing Graces, is circular: gifts from the god of Israel elicit countergifts in the form of labor services, which may be "paid forward" to others. The countergift of labor elicits yet another gift from Israel's god, and so the cycle continues.

Although the category of gift exchange was available to Paul to apply to his evangelistic labors in Corinth, he chooses not to introduce it explicitly in 1 Cor 9, preferring instead the images of vinedresser, pastoralist, soldier, and athlete. He has good reason for avoiding the explicit use of the gift exchange model at that point in his discussion: the presentation of apostolic labor as a "gift" would undermine his central claim that he had a "right" to remuneration for his work. As Seneca points out, only in the case of market exchange does remuneration constitute a "right," guaranteed by contract and actionable in a court of law.[55] In the case of gift exchange, the reception of a countergift is not a right, but a social expectation grounded in moral and ethical rather than legal norms.[56] Paul's assertion that remuneration constitutes a "right" assumes the classification of apostolic labor as a commodity.

Paul's claim that he has waived his right to repayment, however, holds an important implication for a subsequent reclassification of his labor, at which he hints in 9:18: "What then is my payment? (Only) that, as I preach the gospel free of charge [*adapanon*], I might offer it so as not to make full use of my right in the gospel." Foregoing the right to payment characteristic of commodified labor, Paul offers his services "free of charge." A commodity freely given no longer functions as commodity, but as gift; however, he stops short of making explicit the reclassification of his labor necessitated by that comment. He cannily leaves it to his audience to classify his apostolic labor: whether as a market transaction to which Paul had the "right" to remuneration, or as a gift which, according to prevailing social norms, required that a countergift be offered in return. In either case, the Corinthian addressees could not escape drawing the conclusion that they "owed" Paul, whether in the form of payment for services rendered or in the form of a countergift.[57] The assertion that he has given away the commodity of his apostolic labor "free of charge," however, strongly suggests that his labor ought to be classified as a gift.

At issue is not only the categorization of Paul's exchange relationship with the Corinthians, but the nature of their ongoing social relations. Typically, mercantile relations are viewed as limited in duration; once payment is made, there is no necessary expectation of further social relations.[58] By way of contrast, gift exchange relations are viewed as a form of social "cement" that bonds parties through mutual obligation: the gift given elicits a return gift; that gift, in its turn, must be reciprocated, and so on.[59] At the end of his letter, Paul indicates that he would like to visit Corinth and to lodge there during the winter months (16:6-7), perhaps implying a request for room and board during his stay. In his letter to Philemon, he refers to a similar arrangement, requesting that a *xenia*, "guest room," be prepared for him. The request to be provided a guest room connotes the practice of "hospitality" (*xenia*), an arrangement involving gift exchange (cp. mode no. 1 above). Likewise, Paul's request to be "sent on his way" in 1 Cor 16:6 euphemizes a plea to be provided with funding for his subsequent travels, again implying a request for a gift. Clearly, Paul views his relationship with the Corinthian assembly as one based on the exchange of gifts rather than of commodities.

Paul's construction of a paradigm by which to categorize his exchange relations with Corinth involves a complex set of associations. The categories upon which he draws are summarized in the accompanying table. As the table indicates, in the way in which he portrays it, Paul's exchange relationship with the Corinthian assembly assumes characteristics of a market exchange, in that he claims a "right" to remuneration, and characteristics of gift exchange since, voluntarily relinquishing that right, he provides his apostolic services "free of charge" (9:18). Also characteristic of a gift exchange relation is his expectation of ongoing friendly social relations with the Corinthian association and his requests for future gifts in the form of room and board over the winter and travel funding in the spring. But Paul is no ordinary friend: his services are, like of those of the vinedresser, pastoralist, or soldier, "by right" remunerable, and his labor on behalf of the community is marked by a virtuosity that exceeds that of "workaday" apostles like Peter, James, and the twelve. He is a friend whose labor will be, like that of an elite athlete, rewarded with a wreath of victory, to be bestowed by Israel's god, rather than by any human judge at an athletic contest. His labor is sacred, like that of the prophet or priest. Like both the prophet and the slave, his labor is compelled, rather than elective: he construes himself as a slave of Israel's god.

Paul distinguishes himself from Peter, James, and other apostles primarily by his refusal to commodify his apostolic labor: rather than collecting a wage, he offers his services "free of charge." Paul is a virtuoso apostle who works harder than the rest and who will be rewarded with prestige at God's apocalyptic judgment. His apostolic labor, though remunerable, goes unremunerated—and this by his own choosing. His apostolic labor assumes the hybrid form of "gifted commodity"; he plays roles analogous to those of gift-giving friend, supplier of commodified labor, priest, prophet, slave, and virtuoso athlete.

The effect of such prolific mixing of categories, however, is not to abolish the distinctions between the various types of labor, as they are

Categorizing Paul's Apostolic Labor

Occupation/labor type	Entitlement to compensation	Electivity: labor is elective	Compensation virtually assured	Compensation primarily symbolic (i.e., prestige)	Sanctity: labor construed as sacred	Virtuosity: labor compensated only on basis of virtuoso performance	Expectation of ongoing social relation
Viticulturist	+	+	+	−	−	−	−
Agriculturalist	+	+	+	−	−	−	−
Pastoralist	+	+	+	−	−	−	−
Soldier	+	+	+	−	−	−	−
Priest	+	+	+	−	+	−	−
Prophet	−	−	−	−	+	N/A	−
SLAVE	−	−	+	−	−	N/A	−
Athlete*	−	+	−	+	−	+	−
Friend/patron**	−	+	−	−/+	−	−	+
Principal individuals or groups							
Paul	+	−	−	+	+	+	+
Peter/James/"the twelve"	+	?	+	−	+	−	?

Note: Typeface and symbols indicate categories of labor and exchange: roman typeface=mercantile/commodity exchange; italic typeface="sacred" labor; small caps=slave labor; asterisks=athletic labor (*) and gift exchange relationship (**).

carefully maintained in Paul's discourse. Rather, the effect is to suggest that his exchange relationship with the Corinthian assembly was characterized by a set of discrete traits brought into a novel configuration on the basis of his refusal to accept remuneration for his apostolic labors. And it is this refusal that distinguishes Paul from "workaday" apostles like Peter, James, and the twelve. Unlike those apostles, Paul would persuade his addressees, he works harder and does so "free of charge," thus inviting the Corinthians to reclassify his services as a gift rather than a commodity. Such a reclassification would have important implications for the Corinthians, who would then be forced by social convention to construe themselves as bound to Paul by mutual ties of friendly affection and reciprocal obligation. Indeed, he offers the assembly the opportunity to discharge themselves of their "gift-debt" by hosting him during the winter months and by supplying his travel funding on his subsequent journey to Macedonia.

Conclusions

Paul's discussion of the various categories of exchange as they pertain to his relationship with the Corinthian assembly holds considerable interest for gift-giving theory. I would suggest that the following conclusions may be drawn:

1. Static or essentialist notions about what constitutes a "gift" or "commodity" are inadequate to grasp the complexity of the data as they pertain to many types of exchange relations. What were once viewed as "gifts" may later be recategorized as "commodities," or vice versa (as shown by Miller), and the parties to an exchange may disagree about the classificatory category into which a given transaction falls (as shown by Herrmann). In Paul's case, the performance of commodified labor "free of charge" necessitates the reclassification of his labor as "gift." Moreover, in view of the likelihood that apostolic labor was generally recompensed, not by a salary or

wage, but through the practice of hospitality (cp. mode of support no. 1 above)—and so entailed gift exchange—Paul's attempt to characterize such labor as a commodity already involved significant reclassification. Entailing two classificatory reversals—gift becomes commodity that, freely bestowed, returns to the category of gift—Paul's discourse reveals the extent to which the categories of "gift" and "commodity" are unstable signifiers, subject to modification and reversal.[60]

2. The classification of an exchange as "gift" or "commodity" is not based solely on the objective features of a given transaction; the sociopolitical interests of the transacting parties play a significant role in their designation of classificatory categories. Paul's classification of his apostolic labor as a commodity given away "free of charge" implies an attempt to construct a durative, friendly relation with the Corinthian assembly—an implication congruent with his expressed desire to carry out future operations in that city.

3. The classification of exchange relations bears implications for the accumulation or loss of honor and prestige. In portraying apostolic labor as by right remunerable—and promptly renouncing that right—Paul orchestrates an opportunity for the accumulation of significant prestige. This is signaled by the statement that his renunciation, which entails the refusal to lay claim to resources of the community that are "rightfully" his, merits boasting.

4. The act of classifying an exchange is both the product of a complex set of sociopolitical relations and a constitutive factor in shaping those relations. Exchanges, social relations, and the classification of exchanges exist in a mutually generative, circular relation: social relations inflect the classification of exchanges, and the classification of exchanges inflects social relations.

Paul's notice that he performs his evangelistic labors "free of charge" engages his Corinthian addresses in the symbolic and discursive project of classifying the nature of their exchanges with the apostle; the way in which they resolve the issues that he raises will serve to condition future relations between the two parties. The act of classification is an integral feature of every exchange since, as much as the transmission of material goods and services, it conditions the character of future interactions and exchanges. The analysis of gift exchange must therefore attend carefully not only to the material aspects of the exchange, but to the symbolic and discursive aspects as well, for it is the latter that most significantly inflect sociopolitical outcomes.

FIVE

Classification and Social Relations: The Dark Side of the Gift

Introduction

Although gift exchange serves vital social functions as a "catalyst and outward sign of elective affinities,"[1] it also plays darker, socially divisive roles.[2] Natalie Zemon Davis demonstrates that "the ambiguities, dependencies, and exaggerations of unceasing obligation" entailed in gift exchange could be unfavorably compared with the clarity and impersonality of the legal contract by a Montaigne, and that gifts may serve as a form of coercion, calculated to ensure the compliance of a donee.[3] Economic anthropologist Jean-Sébastien Marcoux indicates that people sometimes turn to the market to escape the sense of indebtedness, obligation, and "emotional oppression" that may accompany gift exchange, especially in situations in which commensurability is difficult to attain.[4] According to Mauss, among Polynesians of the early twentieth century, the refusal to accept a gift was tantamount to a declaration of war.[5] For all their socially integrative functions, gifting practices also bear significant potential to effect social disintegration.

It is not, however, only modern theorists who have commented on the antisocial potentialities inherent in gift exchange. Seneca pointed to the sense of shame engendered when one was unable to reciprocate a gift[6] and the hostility that could be evoked when one was given a gift that was beyond one's means to repay, effectively reducing one's status to that of an indebted client: "sometimes, not merely after having received benefits, but because we have received them, we consider the givers our worst enemies."[7] Cicero ruminates on the fragility of friendship. The refusal to accede to the request of a friend, he observes, can quickly transform a sociable relation into one of alienation and friendly relations into open hostility. In one of Cicero's fictitious dialogues, Gaius Laelius, a Roman general of the late third and early second century BCE,[8] recounts the insights of Publius Scipio, the general who captured Carthage and Numantia and famed friend of Laelius.[9] Scipio is credited with the observation that, when one refuses to accede to the request of a friend, "it is charged by those to whom the compliance was denied that the laws of friendship [*ius . . . amicitiae*] have been disregarded. . . . By their ceaseless recriminations not only are social intimacies destroyed, but also everlasting enmities are produced."[10] It is a virtual "law of friendship" that one must accede to the request of an *amicus*; the failure to observe this law risks turning friends into enemies.

Gifts Gone Wrong in Corinth

Like Seneca and Cicero, Paul experienced firsthand the socially divisive aspects of gift exchange. Some members of the early Christian assembly in Corinth rejected the claims advanced in 1 Corinthians that Paul's mode of missionary self-support, which allowed him to preach his gospel "free of charge," rendered his missionary labor a "gifted commodity" offered freely to the assembly.[11] He was forced to defend the practice again in 2 Corinthians. Paul's mode of missionary self-support—working as a craftsman to make a living (1 Thess 2:9; cp. Acts 18:3)—entailed a refusal to accept an offer of hospitality that had apparently been extended in Corinth.[12] His refusal may be inferred from 2 Cor 11:11, where he counters the idea that he lacks "love" for the Corinthians,[13] and 12:13, where he asserts that he has not "wronged" the assembly by failing to accept its support.[14] Both references occur in contexts in which financial support is at issue. Rather than accepting Paul's suggestions in 1 Corinthians that his apostolic labor on their behalf constituted a "gifted commodity" freely offered, some members of the assembly understood Paul's refusal to accept their hospitality as an egregious breach of the laws of friendship: some, formerly friends, had turned hostile.[15] This hostility, and Paul's subsequent attempts at reconciliation, hinged on the issue of classification: was his mode of self-support a "gift" to the Corinthian assembly or a sign that he did not wish to enter into friendly relations with its constituents? Paul attempts to resolve the classificatory issues raised, and in so doing to reconcile himself to the estranged community members, in a series of letters now known collectively as 2 Corinthians.

Although 2 Corinthians now appears as a single letter, there is general—though hardly universal—agreement that it actually consists of a compilation of anywhere from two to six individual letters or letter fragments that have been stitched together by an anonymous editor of Paul's correspondence.[16] The letters were probably written sometime between 54 and 56 CE, not long after 1 Corinthians, which was written between 53 and 55 CE.[17] The bulk of Paul's references to the classification of his apostolic labor occur in 2 Cor 10-13, to which he would later refer as a letter written "with many tears" (2 Cor 2:4). This "tearful letter" was originally an independent correspondence in which the apostle portrayed in anguished terms his ruptured relations with the Corinthian community.

Paul's "tearful letter" was written as a defense against accusations raised by members of the Corinthian assembly that he lacked legitimacy as an apostle, due among other issues to an alleged dearth of skill as a public speaker, and—an unforgivable sin for an orator who would lead masses—his failure to project a commanding personal presence (2 Cor 10:10; 11:6). It is evident that the Corinthian assembly, or some of its members, were comparing Paul unfavorably to a group of early Christian missionaries who, like himself, had been active in Corinth (10:12) and whom he vituperatively labels "false apostles" and "servants of Satan" who disguise themselves as apostles of Christ (11:13-15).[18] Such overheated rhetoric can hardly be taken as an objective description. As Cicero observes, in legal proceedings, character assassination is often a more effective means of winning support for one's cause than the sober elucidation of the facts pertaining to the case.[19] Paul's self-defense operates according to the same logic: the best defense is a good offense.

Among the issues that distinguished Paul from the group of apostles vituperatively depicted in 2 Cor 10-13 was the issue of apostolic support. It appears that, unlike Paul, the missionaries with whom Paul was being unfavorably compared had accepted the hospitality of wealthier patrons within the Corinthian assembly. Since he indicates in 2 Cor 11:12 that he would continue to refuse support from the Corinthians in order to deny any opportunity to his missionary rivals to declare themselves his equals, it may be inferred that the missionary group had received support from the Corinthian assembly during their stay.[20] Larry Welborn has convincingly demonstrated that Paul depicts the principal figure among this group as a "pompous parasite," a stock character lampooned in comedy. The "parasite" is one who serves as a client in the household of a wealthy patron and is portrayed as possessed of a voracious appetite, a quick wit, cunning intelligence, and impudence.[21] The character is described as eating his fill of the comestibles offered in his host's household, taking pains to maximize opportunities to receive lavish gifts, and, in an inversion of roles evocative of the Saturnalia, attempting to elevate himself to a position of honor and authority even above that of his patron.[22] Welborn argues that Paul assimilates the leader of the rival missionary group to the pattern of the parasite in describing him as follows: "For you put up with it when someone enslaves you, when someone eats you out of house and home, when someone plunders you, when someone puts on airs, when someone strikes you in the face" (2 Cor 11:20).[23] Although obviously a caricature, such a depiction would have had little point had its object not been the recipient of the hospitality of a wealthy patron in Corinth.

The acceptance of early Christian hospitality by the missionary group in Corinth raised afresh the issue that Paul had earlier addressed in 1 Corinthians—that of his mode of self-support. But in the "tearful letter" of 2 Cor 10–13, new issues emerge. In 2 Cor 12:14, Paul assures the members of the assembly of his "love" for them, and in 11:9 he indicates the reason why such an assurance was necessary: he has refused to accept the hospitality of the patronal households in Corinth, or, as he politely phrases it, he has refused to "burden" them. The refusal of the "gift" of hospitality, however, was interpreted by some members of the community—not least the patron who had extended the offer—as a refusal to enter into the give-and-take of a friendly relationship: a refusal of friendship itself.[24]

Even as Paul asserts that he is indeed a "friend" to the Corinthians, he deflects any implication of parity that a "friendly" hospitality relation might imply. Suggesting that his relation to the Corinthian community is more intimate even than friendship, he utilizes the language of fictive kinship: Paul serves as "father" to the assembly.[25] He asserts that children need not sequester resources to be expended on their parents; parents, however, typically did so for their children.[26] As fictive parent, Paul indicates that he ought to store up and expend resources on behalf of his Corinthian "children" and not the other way around: "Look, this third time I am ready to come to you, and I will not burden you [*ou katanarkēsō*], for I seek not what is yours [*ta hymōn*], but you. For children ought not store up [*thēsaurizein*] for their parents, but parents for their children" (2 Cor 12:14). By invoking the fiction of his parenthood with respect to the Corinthian assembly, he both counters the charge that he has rejected friendly relations by rejecting the "gift" of hospitality from the assembly and discursively constructs an asymmetric relationship between himself and the assembly, placing himself in the superior position.[27] Although it was a "law of friendship" that one ought not refuse a gift offered in good faith, it was not standard practice for parents to squander their children's resources. In cases in which filial gifts would deplete household resources, it would only be fitting, Paul suggests, for parents to refuse such gifts. By analogizing himself to a parent in such a situation, he effectively exonerates himself for refusing the Corinthian offer of hospitality.

Although it comes from a letter that was originally independent of 2 Cor 10–13, Paul's notice in 2 Cor 2:17 that he is not to be characterized as a "huckster of God's word" portrays remunerated apostolic labor—even though that remuneration generally took the form of the "gift" of hospitality—as a commodity.[28] Paul's attempt to distance himself from "the many" who, in his view, "sell cheaply" or "huckster" (*kapēleuein*) the gospel may be directed at the group of missionaries otherwise in view in 2 Cor 10–13.[29] Echoing a theme of 1 Cor 9:18, he indicates in 2 Cor 11:7 that, unlike those who receive remuneration for their preaching, he himself "proclaimed the gospel of God free of charge" (*dōrean to tou theou euangelion euēngelisamēn*).

To the theme that Paul's mode of self-support, which allowed him to donate his missionary labor "free of charge," functioned as a "gifted commodity," he adds another: that of intimate relations who do not wish to impose a financial "burden" on those to whom they are related, whether by bonds of friendship or by blood. The metaphorical use of terms denoting "burdens," heavy weights that must be carried by human or beast, to refer to significant financial obligations is common in Greek and Latin literature.[30] Two representative examples may be cited. In response to a request to the Senate by Marcus Hortalus, grandson of the orator Hortensius, for funds to cover his family's living expenses, the emperor Tiberius reportedly stated: "The deified Augustus gave you money, Hortalus; but not under pressure, nor with the proviso that it should be given always. Otherwise, if a man is to have nothing to hope or fear from himself, industry will languish, indolence thrive, and we shall have the whole population waiting, without a care in the world, for outside relief, incompetent to help itself, and a burden to us [*nobis graves*]."[31] In the *Lives of Eminent Philosophers* (5.4.65), Diogenes Laertius quotes a maxim attributed to the third-century BCE orator Lyco, son of Astyanax of Troas: "A heavy burden [*bary gar phortion*] to a father is a girl, when for lack of a dowry she runs past the flower of her age."[32] Lacking a dowry and past her prime, such a girl is construed as a burden inasmuch as ideally, she would have been married and transferred to the virilocal household, where her sustenance would have been provided. Conversely, the woman with no marriage prospects continues to consume the resources of the paternal household. Financial obligations, especially those that divert resources that would otherwise be utilized for the maintenance either of the body politic or of one's immediate household, are often compared to a heavy load, difficult to bear. Paul's letter in 2 Cor 10–13 draws on the same metaphor.

In 2 Cor 12:13–16, for example, he writes:

> In what way have I slighted you[33] in comparison with the other assemblies, except that I have not burdened you [*egō ou katenarkēsa hymōn*]? Forgive me this wrong! Look, this third time I am ready to come to you, and I will not burden you [*ou*

katanarkēsō], for I seek not what is yours [*ta hymōn*], but you. For children ought not store up [*thēsaurizein*] for their parents, but parents for their children. But I will gladly spend and be spent [*dapanēsō kai ekdapanēthēsomai*] on your behalf. If I love you more lavishly, am I to be loved the less? Let it be so: I have not burdened you [*egō ou katebarēsa hymas*].

Paul likens the financial obligation that would be incurred by the Corinthian assembly offering him hospitality to a "burden" that he spares the assembly having to bear on his behalf. He assures members that he does not seek access to their resources ("what is yours") and points to the expense that would be incurred if the community were to support him. He indicates that, instead of having the community spend for him, he would rather "spend and be spent" in their service. Although the terms *katanarkan* and *katabarein* (both translated "to burden") are generally held to be synonymous,[34] the use of the former term may indicate that Paul's acceptance of Corinth's financial support would "disable" or "knock out"[35] his addressees by diverting for his sustenance the resources that would otherwise contribute to their own welfare.[36]

The line that opens the quotation above, "In what way have I slighted you in comparison with the other assemblies,"[37] indicates that Paul's actions in Corinth were being assessed in relation to his practices in other locales. It had apparently been revealed that, unlike his practice in Corinth, Paul did accept economic support in various forms from the assembly at Philippi, in eastern Macedonia (cp. 2 Cor 11:8–9). In a letter to the assembly there,[38] he recounts in glowing terms a relation of friendly gift exchange. He indicates that he views himself as existing in a "partnership" (Phil 1:5) with the assembly; it is only the Philippians, he writes, with whom he shared a relationship of "give and take" (*dosis kai lēmpsis*) in the earlier phases of his itinerant mission (4:15).[39] Although the phrase that he uses to characterize the exchange relationship is borrowed from the mercantile sphere, it was often used among friends to describe ongoing relations of mutual gift exchange.[40] He refers to goods that he had received from Philippi, whether in the form of currency or food and clothing he does not say (4:18), during one of his stints in prison.[41] He also mentions "gifts" that were sent to support him as he preached in the city of Thessalonica (4:16–17).[42] His depiction of a friendly "partnership" based on the "give-and-take" of gift exchange in Philippi contrasts sharply with his refusal to "burden" the Corinthians by acceding to their own offers of hospitality. It was likely his refusal to enter fully into "partnership" with Corinth that was perceived as a "slight" to the assembly there (2 Cor 12:13).[43]

An equally sharp contrast is to be made between Paul's characterization of his exchange relations with Philippi in his letter to that assembly and the characterization of the same in 2 Cor 10–13, where he ironically depicts the relation, not as one of "partnership," but of theft. He writes, "I robbed other assemblies [*allas ekklēsias esylēsa*] when I received a wage [or 'provisions': *opsōnion*] in order to serve you, and when I was present with you and was in need, I did not burden anyone, for the brothers who had come from Macedonia supplied what I needed" (2 Cor 11:8–9). The unnamed "brothers" had likely been sent as a delegation from the Macedonian city of Philippi.[44] The eleven-hundred-kilometer journey from Philippi to Corinth required nine to fourteen days of sailing and overland travel.[45] In light of the time involved, it seems likely that the *opsōnion*—the "wage" or "provisions" that Paul received—was sent in the form of currency rather than comestibles, which would have been bulky and subject to spoilage.[46] This was probably not a regular, scheduled wage, however, but a series of sporadic "gifts" offered to meet his needs.[47] Paul's ironic reclassification of the Philippian "gift" as "theft" is to be viewed alongside his redescription of hospitality as a "burden" to the community (2 Cor 11:9; 12:13, 14, 16) and his invocation of the parental duty not to squander household resources (2 Cor 12:14). In each case, he portrays the expenditure of community resources for the maintenance of missionaries in quite negative terms in an attempt to persuade the members of the Corinthian assembly that he had not "wronged" them by refusing to accept their support (2 Cor 12:13).

But the classification of Paul's mode of support and the discrepancies in his practices in different communities were not the only items on the Corinthians' list of grievances. It appears that some members of the assembly had accused him of malfeasance in the matter of a collection of funds that he had organized. As early as 1 Corinthians, he had asked members of the assembly to set aside weekly donations that were eventually to be collected and transported to Jerusalem to be presented to the assembly there (1 Cor 16:1–4). The early Christian assembly in Jerusalem was an influential one, as the apostle Peter and Jesus' brother, James, were stationed there (cp. Gal 1:18–19). Before writing 2 Cor 10–13, Paul had sent to Corinth his assistant, Titus, along with an unnamed "brother" to oversee the collection efforts (cp. 2 Cor 8:16–24), and in 2 Cor 12:16–18 he alludes to that event, now past:

> Let it be so: I did not burden you—but, crafty man that I am, I took you by deceit. Surely I did not defraud you through any of those whom I sent to you, did I? I urged Titus and sent along the brother; surely Titus did not defraud you, did he? Have we not conducted ourselves in the same spirit? Have we not followed in the same footsteps?

Through the use of an ironic statement ("crafty man that I am, I took you by deceit"), Paul appears to respond to a charge lodged against him in Corinth that he had "deceived" and "defrauded" the assembly there. Welborn has recently argued that this accusation was made by the patron Gaius and constituted the painful "wrong" that Paul had suffered during his second visit to Corinth (cp. 2 Cor 7:12).[48] Alfred Plummer colorfully elucidates the charge: "[Paul] and his friends collected money for the poor saints [in Jerusalem], and some of it stuck to his fingers."[49] Paul was apparently accused of misappropriating funds earmarked for use by others. In this way he appeared "crafty" and "deceitful" to at least some of his Corinthian addressees: while on one hand, assuming the posture of an adult with his children, he refused the support and hospitality of the Corinthian assembly, on the other, he allegedly planned to divert funds from their "gift" to Jerusalem for his own personal use. Paul was caught in a web in which transactions involving material and monetary resources, as well as the terms used to classify those exchanges, were weighed in the balance: was he friendly or hostile, a magnanimous giver or a deceitful fraud? Exchange, classification, and social relations had become inextricably tangled. Should he fail in his epistolary attempts to define the terms under which his affairs in Corinth were to be understood, he risked provoking the ongoing hostility of the assembly there and suffering the loss of that site as a base of his continued operations in the region of Achaia.

The Corinthian Reception of Paul's "Tearful Letter" (2 Cor 10–13)

The "tearful letter" now contained in 2 Cor 10–13 was transmitted to Corinth by Paul's emissary, Titus (cp. 2 Cor 7:6–8).[50] The arguments contained therein appear to have had an effect on his addressees. Their response is characterized in a subsequent letter, written by Paul after Titus had left Corinth and returned to Macedonia to report the outcome of his visit. Like 2 Cor 10–13, it was later incorporated into the "letter collection" of 2 Corinthians. The contents of the epistle, sometimes referred to as the "letter of reconciliation," appear in 2 Cor 1:1–2:13; 7:5–16; 13:11–13. The letter indicates how the assembly received Titus, "with fear and trembling," and declared their "zeal" for Paul (2 Cor 7:7, 12, 15). The ringleader of the Corinthian opposition to Paul had been subjected to disciplinary action by the assembly (2 Cor 2:5–7). The remaining members wished to reconcile themselves with Paul (2 Cor 7:5–16). Paul warmly accepts the assembly's overtures at reconciliation, declaring again his "abundant" love for its members (2 Cor 2:4).

But it is not only Paul's "letter of reconciliation" that testifies to the restoration of positive social relations between Paul and the Corinthian assembly. The concerns that he may have planned to embezzle funds from the collection for Jerusalem were apparently assuaged, as he is emboldened at a later date to write another letter, now contained in 2 Cor 9, calling for the resumption of efforts to complete the project (2 Cor 9:1–5). Additional evidence for the restoration of positive social relations occurs in Rom 16, which commends Phoebe, a patroness from Corinth's port city of Cenchreae,[51] to the early Christian assembly in Rome and includes greetings from the notable Corinthians Gaius and Erastus. On the basis of the references to known individuals, it is generally inferred that Paul's letter to the

Romans was written in Corinth, perhaps in 57 CE, not long after the crisis in his social relations with the assembly had erupted and had subsequently been resolved.

But it was not only the Corinthians who made significant changes to their practice in order to restore ruptured relations with Paul; he appears to have made concessions of his own. In 2 Corinthians (54–56 CE), he had adamantly declared that he had not accepted support from Corinth in the past, nor would he do so in the future (2 Cor 11:9–10, 12):

> When I was present with you and was in need, I did not burden anyone, for the brothers who came from Macedonia supplied what I needed, and in every way I kept myself from being a burden to you, and I will continue to do so [*kai en panti abarē emauton hymin etērēsa kai tērēsō*]. As the truth of Christ is in me, this boast of mine will not be silenced in the regions of Achaia. . . . And what I do, I will also continue to do.[52]

However, the situation appears to have been quite different in 57 CE, when Paul wrote his letter to the Romans from Corinth. By that time, he appears to have reversed his policy of refusing Corinthian support, as he indicates in Rom 16:23 that the wealthy paterfamilias, Gaius, was at that time functioning as his host: "Gaius, host to me and to the whole assembly [*ho xenos mou kai holēs tēs ekklēsias*], greets you." It is generally agreed that Gaius's role as *xenos*, "host," implies that he provided food and lodging for Paul and that his household served as the meeting place for the "whole assembly" in Corinth.[53] According to Acts 20:2–3, Paul overwintered for three months in Greece in 56–57 CE, and it is usually inferred that the precise location was Corinth.[54] It is likely during those months that he wrote his letter to the Romans and stayed as a guest in Gaius's household. Gaius's role as "host" (*xenos*) parallels Philemon's, whom Paul asks to prepare him a "guest room" (*xenia*) in his household (Phlm 22). Despite his protestations throughout 1 and 2 Corinthians that he would not accept the hospitality of the Corinthian assembly (1 Cor 9:1–18; 2 Cor 11:7–11), that his refusal of support gave him a competitive advantage over rival missionaries who accepted it (2 Cor 11:12; cp. 2 Cor 11:20–21), and that his self-support constituted positive grounds for boasting (1 Cor 9:15; 2 Cor 11:10), Paul seems to have reversed his position, finally accepting the hospitality of a relatively wealthy member of the assembly in Corinth as he had already done in other communities.

The restoration of friendly social relations between Paul and the Corinthian assembly entailed more than the community's commitment to subject itself to the apostle's authority, as the "letter of reconciliation" might imply (cp. 2 Cor 2:9; 7:15). Paul himself made significant concessions in the interest of *amicitia,* or "friendship," not least by ceding the ground for boasting constituted by his earlier refusal to accept hospitality in Corinth. Paul's classificatory endeavors in the "tearful letter"—his attempts to portray himself as magnanimous donor of commodified labor, parent who does not wish to squander household resources, and friend who does not wish to burden the community—apparently exerted some effect on the Corinthian assembly, as the "letter of reconciliation" attests. Even so, friendship's insistence that it be instantiated not only in discursive, but also in material form—in the form of the unreserved "give-and-take" of goods and services—could not be ignored. And it seems to be a friendship consisting both of discursive (i.e., classificatory) and of material elements that finally prevailed in Paul's relations with the Corinthian assembly.[55] In the end, he seems to have conceded that a one-sided friendship in which one party continually plays the role of donor and the other, chronic recipient, is no friendship at all. Despite his earlier protests, the apostle was finally persuaded to enter fully into the dance of the Graces by accepting the hospitality of a wealthy member of the Corinthian community.[56]

Recapitulation

As Margaret Mitchell has recently pointed out, Paul's letters were not simply "witnesses to" ongoing social relations in Corinth, but themselves constituted attempts to influence those relations.[57] As much as the sending of his envoy, Titus, and his own periodic visits to the city, Paul's letters played a significant role in shaping sociopolitical relations within the assembly, as the Corinthians' reaction to Paul's "tearful letter" (2 Cor 10–13) suggests. Issues of classification played a central role at each stage of Paul's dealings with the Corinthians: whether he was to be classed a friendly partner in gift exchange (1 Corinthians) or a hostile individual who refused reciprocal ties with Corinth and used trickery and deception to defraud them (2 Cor 10–13). By the same token, the leading figure among the group of missionaries with whom Paul compares himself in 2 Cor 10–13 was subject to similar classificatory quandaries. Was he, as his patron likely perceived, a friendly individual who had graciously accepted an offer of hospitality in keeping with Jesus' missionary injunctions or, as Paul would have it, a "pompous parasite" who was eating his patron out of house and home? In both cases, the classification of exchange held significant social consequences: charges that Paul had refused to enter into friendly exchange relations by refusing to accept hospitality and, worse, charges of financial fraud with respect to the collection classed Paul as a hostile individual, to whom the appropriate response would entail the cessation of friendly relations. Conversely, Paul's self-portrayal as magnanimous giver of gifts, providing his apostolic labor "free of charge," and fictive "parent," both "spending and being spent" on behalf of his Corinthian "children," depicted him as a social intimate, to whom the appropriate response would be the resumption of positive social relations. The anticipated response to Paul's depiction of his missionary rival as a "pompous parasite" would entail the cessation of the community's friendly relations with that individual and the group headed by him,[58] an outcome not incompatible with Paul's own claims to serve in a unique leadership role as "father" of the Corinthian assembly (cp. 1 Cor 4:14–15; 2 Cor 12:14–15).

Conclusions

The series of letters that Paul wrote to the assembly in Corinth attests to the uncertainties and ambiguities inherent in gift exchange. They also attest to the importance of cognitive and discursive acts of classification; at stake in each of the letters, from 1 Corinthians to the "letter of reconciliation," is the way in which Paul's mode of apostolic self-support is to be categorized, with all of the attendant implications for subsequent social interaction—or its cessation. The data of the Corinthian correspondence support the following conclusions:

1. The classification of an exchange is an integral part of the exchange process.
2. Subject to dispute, modification, and reclassification, the assignation of classificatory category rests not solely on purportedly "objective" features of the goods or services exchanged nor the manner in which they are exchanged, but is based instead on an interaction between the "objective" features and the subjective interests and sociopolitical goals of the classifiers. The "objective" features of exchange—the material aspects of goods or services rendered, and the circumstances under which they are transmitted—may suggest, but do not determine, classificatory categories. Categories are assigned on the basis of negotiation and consensus.
3. Gift exchange involves the potential for the development and maintenance of durable social bonds of friendship and mutual affection as well as hostility and mutual recrimination. When hostility ensues, attempts may be made to restore friendly social relations.

Two further conclusions also seem warranted:

4. Since the classification of exchange carries significant implications for social interaction (whether friendly or hostile, durative or ephemeral), attempts to classify a given exchange cannot be disassociated from attempts to orchestrate sociopolitical relations and, in fact, always serve sociopolitical functions. Orchestration of this sort may or may not entail the conscious recognition of the actors involved that a correlation exists between the classification of exchange and sociopolitical relations; the social effects persist in any case.

5. Since Paul's relations with the Corinthian assembly apparently remain unstable throughout the Corinthian correspondence, and appear to have normalized only by 57 CE, when he wrote his letter to the Romans while the recipient of Gaius's hospitality, it may be suggested that friendly social relations are facilitated by a significant material component: the mutual "give-and-take" of goods and services. Assertions of friendship, love, and paternity, when not accompanied by the mutual exchange of goods and services, fail to generate consent. To return again to the statement of Jacques Godbout and Alain Caillé with which this chapter opened, gifts constitute a "catalyst and outward sign of elective affinities." In the absence of the "outward sign" of mutual gift exchange, assertions of love, friendship, and so on remain just that. In order to be credible, the assignation of a classificatory category must be corroborated by the material form and "outward sign" most appropriate to it. And it is perhaps this recognition that finally prompted Paul to relinquish his stance of self-sufficiency in order to enter fully into the dance of the Graces with the assembly in Corinth.

SIX

The Gift of Status

Gift and Status

It has long been recognized that gift exchange has implications for the negotiation of relative status. The descriptions of putatively "archaic" precapitalist societies that characterized studies of gift exchange following Marcel Mauss's seminal work provide ample evidence that clan chiefs, "big men," and elders were accorded a greater share than others in distributive schemes based on gift exchange.[1] The result was the unequal distribution of material resources. Possessing a greater share of resources, "big men" were able to give lavishly to other members of the community or to engage in the practice of potlatch—the public destruction of wealth that showcases an individual's surplus.[2] Recipients of gifts who were unable to return something of equal or greater value were burdened by a "gift-debt." The result was a diminution in status and a concomitant elevation in the status of the lavish donor.[3] The asymmetric distribution of material goods reinforced the superior status of the "big man" and confirmed the status of his subordinates. Status is the corollary of gift exchange because the latter objectifies the differential access to economic resources of the parties involved. In such cases, wealth constitutes the basis from which prestige is derived.[4]

Mauss also described another form of giving with implications for the negotiation of relative status: the potlatch, a curious case of giving in which there is no evident recipient. Stated otherwise, the potlatch involves the intentional destruction of property. Mauss describes the potlatch as practiced by indigenous peoples in the American Northwest in the early 1900s:

Consumption and destruction of goods really go beyond all bounds. In certain kinds of potlatch one must expend all that one has, keeping nothing back. It is a competition to see who is the richest and also the most madly extravagant. Everything is based upon the principles of antagonism and rivalry. The political status of individuals in the brotherhoods and clans, and ranks of all kinds, are gained in a "war of property," just as they are in a real war. . . . Whole boxes of olachen (candlefish) oil or whale oil are burnt, as are houses and thousands of blankets. The most valuable copper objects are broken and thrown into the water, in order to put down and "flatten" one's rival. In this way one not only promotes oneself, but one's family, up the social scale.[5]

More recently, C. A. Gregory has made use of the idea of the potlatch—an intentional destruction of property meant to showcase one's unhampered access to material resources and thereby to accrue honor and prestige as the concomitants of wealth—in his analysis of giving to churches in Melanesia.[6] Various clans compete to offer the largest donation to the church, which subsequently removes those assets from local circulation in a metaphoric "destruction" of property. In this system, gifts to the church are construed as gifts to God.

In the mundane sphere of interpersonal relations, status is attained on the basis of donations; gifts of goods and services that cannot be reciprocated on an equal basis are characteristic of patron-client relations. During the Roman period, clients unable fully to repay the gifts of their patrons were reduced to subordinate status and were obliged to render service through actions calculated to enhance the status of their donors: publicly praising their magnanimity and attending them on morning walks (the *salutatio*) or at public events.[7]

Although the close connection between gift—whether potlatch, "gifts to God/gods," or gifts between human parties—and status has been thoroughly documented, a related point has not yet been generally recognized. Status is accorded not only as a corollary of exchanges that manifest the differential access to economic resources of the parties involved, but certain types of status may be granted by highly placed political figures in the form of patronal gifts. In such cases, the negotiation of status does not occur as a sociopolitical *effect* of the gift; status itself *constitutes* the gift. The letters of Paul, too, attest "gifts of status," and such "gifts" bear significant implications for the sociopolitical organization of early Christian assemblies. Before turning to examine Paul's statements on the topic, however, a definition of the multivalent term "status" is required.

Defining "Status": Positional and Accorded Types

"Status" is an English loanword from Latin, where the term literally denotes bodily posture or physical stature and by extension refers to one's political or social situation.[8] The term also denotes public rights and civil situation, particularly regarding citizenship and legal status as slave or free, as well as one's social position defined in terms of political office, trade, reputation, or character.[9] Taking the formulations of Max Weber as a point of departure, John Scott understands status as a correlate of the stratification present in complex societies; it refers to the relative rank that one holds within a hierarchically ordered social system. Conceptually distinct from economic class (although often correlated with it),[10] status is derived from "the [unequal] distribution of prestige or social honour within a community."[11] Prestige is allocated on the basis of communal judgments concerning the degree to which an individual or group conforms to the evaluative criteria for exemplary behavior recognized by the community. Those whose behavior is deemed to conform to the values and norms promoted by the group are accorded honor and prestige.[12] Status refers to one's relative ranking with respect to the degree of honor and prestige accorded one by the community; it is one's "standing or reputation in the eyes of others."[13] Lorne Tepperman and James Curtis offer a similar definition: "Status reflects an individual's position in society according to the relative prestige, esteem, or honour they are afforded."[14]

Not all sociologists accept this definition, however. In contrast with both Scott and Tepperman and Curtis, John Macionis asserts that "sociologists do not use the term 'status' in its everyday meaning of 'prestige'"; rather, it refers to "a social position that a person occupies," such as sister, daughter, friend, or parent.[15] Having defined "status" in terms of social role or position, Macionis distinguishes two types: "ascribed status," which refers to "a social position a person receives at birth or assumes involuntarily later in life," and "achieved status," which refers to "a social position a person assumes voluntarily and that reflects personal ability and effort."[16]

Other researchers define the term "status" differently. Beth Vanfossen identifies as many as six distinct usages of the term, which may refer to: "1) position in society; 2) position in a hierarchy; 3) any social category; 4) any quality indexed by objective characteristics such as income or occupation; 5) prestige; and 6) a collection of rights and duties."[17]

The discrepant definitions invite elaboration and clarification. For the purposes of this study, clarity may be achieved by distinguishing two types of status. *Positional status* is that associated with the fulfillment of a particular position or role within a sociopolitical field that is often organized hierarchically (e.g., father/daughter, senator/equestrian, citizen/alien, master/slave). This is the sense in which Macionis uses the term "status." Each role is associated with particular rights, duties, and obligations. Roman fathers, for example, were expected to discipline their children[18]—although not too harshly[19]—while children were expected to obey their parents.[20] In the imperial period, Roman citizens held rights not accorded aliens, such as enhanced legal protections and exemption from certain types of taxation. Slaves had different obligations, and far fewer rights, than did their masters. Note that Macionis's "ascribed" and "achieved" types of status both fit easily within the broader category of positional status.

The second type, *accorded status,* is that which is allocated on the basis of communal assessments regarding the excellence or exemplary manner in which one fulfills the duties and obligations associated with a particular social position.[21] Accorded status is thus synonymous with "prestige" or "honor"; this is the sense in which Scott as well as Tepperman and Curtis use the term "status." Note that although positional and accorded status may be distinguished for analytical purposes, in practice they are closely linked: with few exceptions, Roman senators were accorded greater social prestige than equestrians, masters greater prestige than slaves, husbands greater prestige than wives, and so on. Despite this close association, it is important to distinguish the two types of status: Rome had a share of dishonored emperors, senators, and fathers. In such cases, the individual's positional status often was retained, while accorded status was diminished. An example is that of Claudius, who, although emperor, was not held in high social esteem. Suetonius recounts an episode in which a litigator in court dishonored Claudius with the remark, "You are both an old man and a fool!"[22] Conversely, it was possible for those inhabiting relatively low stations of positional honor (slaves, women, or children) to be held in esteem and thus to achieve high accorded status.[23] Junia Theodora, honored in a number of Corinthian inscriptions, is an oft-cited example.[24]

To summarize: both positional and accorded status are relational categories. Positional status entails the fulfillment of a particular position or role within a sociopolitical field; each position is associated with particular rights and obligations. The various roles that constitute a given social system are hierarchically ranked: in the Roman context, for example, parents rank more highly than children, senators more highly than equestrians, citizens more highly than aliens, and so on. Accorded status ranks individuals or groups with respect to the degree of honor and prestige assigned to each. Both positional and accorded status presuppose hierarchical ranking systems.

The Gift of Positional Status in Rome

Whereas accorded status results from the aggregate judgment of the community and cannot be conferred by an individual,[25] positional status may be granted by an individual or group endowed with the requisite legal authority. Official positions, titles, and offices—each constituting a particular positional status—may be granted by a governing official or legislative body. In the Roman imperial context, three types of positional status were typically granted by individuals endowed with the requisite legal authority: citizenship, rank or order (Latin *ordo*), and office. This list, it may be noted, is meant to be illustrative, not exhaustive.

Pliny the Younger, a senator with access to the emperor Trajan, was instrumental in brokering grants of political office and *ordo* (status as senator or equestrian) for his clients. In a letter to Trajan written in 110 or 111 CE, Pliny makes a request on behalf of Rosianus Geminus, who had served as Pliny's consular quaestor in 100. The letter reads in part:

> So I am requesting your personal indulgence that you should take to your heart his high status [*dignitas*]. You will also, if you repose any trust in me, grant him your favour [*indulgentiam tuam dabis*]. He himself will ensure, in the tasks that you enjoin on him, that he is deserving of greater things.... I beg you, my lord, to assent at the earliest possible moment to my joy at the illustrious standing [*dignitas*] of my quaestor, which through him affects my own.[26] (*Ep.* 10.26.2–3)

Although it is unclear exactly what Pliny seeks from Trajan, his repeated reference to Geminus's "high status" or "worthiness" (*dignitas*) hints at political advancement.[27] As P. G. Walsh notes, "Pliny does not specify a particular role for his friend, for fear of twisting the emperor's arm, but perhaps he hopes for the governorship of a province for him."[28] The use of the terms *dare* ("to give, grant") and *indulgentia* ("favor, fondness, indulgence") indicates that Trajan's ability to grant a political office is understood along familiar lines as a patronal donation, in return for which the emperor could expect Geminus's exemplary fulfillment of official duties and, if his behavior toward Pliny was any indication, "informal gestures of service" as well (*publicae necessitudinis pignera privatis cumulat officiis*).[29] Pliny requests for his client the gift of positional status, in this case likely in the form of public office.

In another of his letters to Trajan, Pliny requests that the freedman physician Harpocras of Alexandria be granted citizen status. The request is couched in the language of reciprocal gift exchange typical of patron-client relationships. The relevant portion of the letter, written in 98 CE, reads:

> Last year, my lord, I was afflicted by an illness so serious that my life was in danger. So I called in a physiotherapist, whose concern and attentiveness I can repay with equal gratitude only by your gracious kindness [*cuius sollicitudini et studio tuae tantum indulgentiae beneficio referre gratiam parem possum*]. I am therefore asking you to award him Roman citizenship [*des ei civitatem Romanam*], for he is a foreigner, manumitted by a foreign mistress. His name is Harpocras, and his patroness Thermuthis, wife of Theon, is long dead.[30] (*Ep.* 10.5.1-2)

Pliny attributes his recovery from what he describes as a potentially life-threatening illness to the "concern and attentiveness" (*Ep.* 10.5.1) of Harpocras. As the result of the physician's services, Pliny incurs a debt of gratitude (10.5.1), which he hopes to discharge with the help of the "gracious kindness" (*indulgentia*) of Trajan, who, as we learn in a subsequent letter, grants a "speedy award" (*sine mora indulsisti*) of the right of citizenship to Harpocras. In return, Pliny acknowledges that he has incurred a gift-debt to the emperor (10.6.2). Emboldened by his success, he further requests that Trajan grant Alexandrian citizenship to the physician and describes the anticipated positive response as a "kindness" or "benefit" (*beneficium;* 10.6.2). Pliny is not disappointed; Trajan "grants" (*dare*) Harpocras the Alexandrian citizenship (10.7). Trajan's "grant" of citizenship to Harpocras is a "kindness," not only to the physician, but also to Pliny who acts as his spokesperson. Pliny, for his part, incurs a gift-debt as the result of the imperial award.

On behalf of his client Voconius Romanus, Pliny orchestrated gifts of status on several occasions. Probably before the death of Nerva in 98 CE,[31] he wrote to Javolenus Priscus, the legate of Syria sometime between 95 and 101 CE, to recommend Romanus for an army post (*Ep.* 2.13). In the letter, Pliny refers to a change in status that he had earlier orchestrated on behalf of his client, acquiring for him the "right of three children" (*ius trium*

THE GIFT OF STATUS 83

liberorum)—a right that exempted wealthy fathers from *munera* entailing the obligation to fund public works at one's own expense and that allowed married women to remain free of legal guardianship.[32]

Pliny also requested that Nerva elevate the equestrian Romanus's *ordo* to that of senator. In a letter written to Nerva's successor Trajan in 98 or 99 CE, Pliny indicates that legal necessity involving a transfer of four million sesterces to Romanus's account had prevented Nerva from immediately granting his elevation in status. The requisite legal "business" having been completed, Pliny writes to Trajan:

> Your kindness [*indulgentia*], best of emperors, which I experience in fullness, encourages me to presume to beg you to be bound by it on behalf of my friends. Among them, Voconius Romanus claims a quite outstanding place, for he has been a fellow student and a bosom friend from our earliest years. This is why I petitioned your deified father [Nerva] also to advance [*promoveret*] Romanus to our august order [*in amplissimum ordinem*]. However, this wish of mine was held back to await your favour [*Sed hoc votum meum bonitati tuae reservatum est*]. . . . So now that the business which was delaying my hopes has been completed, with some considerable confidence I give you my guarantee of the good character of my friend Romanus. [Pliny then enumerates the qualities that render Romanus fit for senatorial status, including his good character, his love of learning, his filial piety, and the "prestige of his birth."] Therefore, my lord, I ask that you grant me this happy outcome which is my dearest wish, and that you indulge what I hope are my honourable sentiments, so that through your adjudication I can take pride [*gloriari*] not only in myself but also in my friend.[33] (*Ep.* 10.4.1–6)

Romanus's elevation from equestrian to senatorial status is described using the circumlocution "our august order" to designate the latter rank. Pliny indicates his wish that his client[34] "advance" to the senatorial order, indicating the hierarchical ranking system upon which such distinctions were based. Pliny's mention of Trajan's "kindness" (*indulgentia*) serves as a form of *captatio benevolentia,* a bid for his goodwill, and places the request within the register of gift-giving.[35] The close connection between *indulgentia* and gift exchange is established by Seneca, who in a discussion of the "gifts of the gods" (*divinorum munera; Ben.* 2.29.1), adduces several divine benefactions: humans' dominion over animals, food, wealth, crafts, and comprehending minds (2.29.4–5). Analogizing the gods to nature, Seneca writes, "But if you assess nature's generosity [*naturae indulgentia*] properly you will have to admit that you have been her darling" (2.29.5).[36]

Similarly assimilated to the paradigm of gift exchange is Pliny's request to Vibius Maximus, prefect of Egypt from 103 to 107 CE,[37] that the latter grant a post to Pliny's client Arrianus Maturus. Pliny's letter to Maximus reads as follows:

> The favour which I myself would have extended to your friends, if the same opportunity were available to me, I now appear justified in begging from you for mine. Arrianus Maturus is a leading citizen of Altinum [a city in northeastern Italy. Pliny describes Maturus's merits, including his wealth, integrity, sense of justice, wisdom, business acumen, and loyalty.] He does not canvass for office [*caret ambitu*], and he has accordingly confined himself to his equestrian rank [*se in equestri gradu tenuit*], though he could easily rise to the very top [*facile possit ascendere altissimum*]. None the less, I must see to his ennoblement and further progress [*Mihi tamen ornandus excolendusque est*]. So I regard it as important to advance his distinction [*magni aestimo dignitati eius aliquid adstruere*] without his expectation or knowledge—perhaps indeed against his will. But that advancement is to be one which brings glory, yet without being burdensome [*splendidum nec molestum*]. I beg you to bestow on him [*conferas in eum*] something of this kind at

your first opportunity. Both he and I will be most gratefully in your debt [*habebis me, habebis ipsum gratissimum debitorem*], for though he does not seek the favour, he will accept it as thankfully as if he eagerly sought it [*tam grate tamen excipit, quam si concupiscat*]. Farewell.[38] (*Ep.* 3.2.1–6)

As is customary in such letters, Pliny does not point to a particular post or station that he would like Maximus to grant to Maturus, asking only that he grant "something of this kind"—apparently one that brings "glory" but "without being burdensome." Regarding the post referred to by the vague phrase "something of this kind," Adrian Nicholas Sherwin-White opines, "probably a military tribunate or prefecture is meant."[39] Again pointing to stratification in the political system, Pliny indicates that Maturus had "confined himself to his equestrian rank" only because he did not actively promote himself. Otherwise, "he could easily rise to the very top." Pliny refers to Maximus's potential gift of a position for Maturus as a form of "advancement" for the latter, indicating that gradations of status were recognized even within the equestrian rank. Pliny's mention of the "distinction" and "glory" that accompany office indicates the extent to which positional status and accorded status are related; prestige is depicted as a concomitant of political office. Finally, Pliny's notice that both he and Maturus would find themselves burdened by a gift-debt and his references to gratitude and thanksgiving in the final lines indicate clearly that Maximus's appointment of Maturus to an office would be construed as a gift.

To summarize our findings thus far: in the Roman context, certain types of positional status, including public office and citizenship, could be received as a gift. Each position carried particular obligations, rights, and duties: in the case of provincial governorship, the right to oversee public building projects and hear legal cases; in the case of citizenship, the right to legal protection and exemption from some taxes. The reception of such gifts of status burdened the recipient with a "gift-debt," which could be discharged, at least in part, through "gestures of service" performed for the patron's benefit.

The Gift of Positional Status in Paul's Letters

Like Pliny, Paul understood that positional status could be received as a gift. However, unlike his Roman contemporaries, he recognizes positional status as a grant extended not by well-placed political figures but by the god of Israel. When Paul wrote his letter to the early Christian assembly at Rome, likely during the winter of 55–56 or 56–57 CE, Nero was de facto the agent with the most power to grant positional status. Paul's letter, however, does not mention the *princeps,* but instead attributes the positional status of Roman "governing authorities" to Israel's god:

> Let every person be subject [*hypotassesthō*] to the governing authorities. For there is no authority [*exousia*] except from God, and those who are authorities are appointed by God [*hypo theou tetagmenai eisin*]. So the person who resists authority opposes the ordinance of God [*tē tou theou diatagē*]. And those who oppose will bring punishment on themselves. For rulers are not a terror to good conduct, but to bad.[40] And if you wish not to be afraid of the one who is in a position of authority [*exousian*], do what is good, and you will receive praise from him, for he is an agent [*diakonos*] of God so that you may do what is good. But if you do what is bad, be afraid, for he does not bear the sword in vain. For he is the agent of vengeance for the punishment of the one who acts badly. Therefore it is necessary to be subject [*hypotassesthai*], not only because of punishment, but also because of conscience. For this reason, then, pay tribute, for they are God's public service providers[41] [*leitourgoi*], engaged in their duties for this very reason. Pay to all what you owe: to whom you owe tribute, pay tribute, to whom you owe taxes, pay taxes, to whom you owe respect, pay respect, to whom you owe honor, show honor. (Rom 13:1–7)

Those occupying positions within the Roman imperial order, Paul asserts, have been granted authority by Israel's god, who has "appointed" authorities to regulate the behavior of the populace. The possibility of being punished by the "sword"—a metonym for all types of penal authority—is sufficient to encourage "good" behavior and to discourage the "bad." The positional status granted Roman authorities by Israel's god not only entitles those authorities to govern the behavior of the populace, but to extract from it tax and tribute.[42] The governing agents within the Roman imperial system were, Paul asserts, "appointed" by Israel's god: "there is no authority except from God." Authority figures are God's "public service providers," orchestrating a divine moral order in the world. To resist such people is to oppose the "ordinance" of God. Not only obedience, but "honor" and "respect" are due God's Roman "service providers." Such deferential attitudes call upon Paul's addressees to recognize and perpetuate the hierarchical sociopolitical organization of the Roman empire.

On the other hand, the discourse departs significantly from typical Roman perceptions in that it legitimizes the imperial sociopolitical organization by locating its origin and authority in the will, not of the deities of the Roman pantheon, but of Israel's god. Paul clearly viewed the Roman imperial order as of limited duration: in the not-too-distant future, he thought, Christ would be granted the status of God's vice-regent and executive power on earth. Envisioning an apocalyptic scenario labeled in early Christian parlance as "the end,"[43] Paul writes: "Then comes the end, when he [Christ] hands over the kingdom to God the father, when he will destroy every ruler, and every authority and power. For he himself must rule until he [God] places every enemy under his feet" (1 Cor 15:24-25). The "rulers, authorities, and powers" that, in Paul's imaginative scenario, were to be destroyed by Christ, constituted both human rulers and their heavenly counterparts, the gods and goddesses of Greco-Roman antiquity, who in Paul's view were nothing more than *daimonia*, divine beings of a lower order than the god of Israel.[44] Paul again refers to both human and divine beings when, in a letter to an early Christian assembly in Philippi perhaps written in 54-55 CE, he predicts, "every knee will bend—of those in heaven, on the earth, and in the chthonic regions—and every tongue will confess that Jesus Christ is the lord" (Phil 2:10-11). Although in Paul's view Israel's god had granted Roman functionaries—and their gods—temporary governance, in the apocalyptic future that he envisioned they would all bow in subjection to the very "lord" who had been crucified by Rome's penal authority (cp. 1 Cor 2:8). In the meantime, however, the empire's human functionaries were to be respected.

But it is not only the positional status of Roman officials that, in Paul's view, was granted by the god of Israel. The status of members of the early Christian assemblies was likewise "arranged" by God and is in some cases described as a divine gift. Foremost among the recipients of "gifts of status" within the assemblies were those recognized as apostles.

Paul frequently points to his status as an "apostle"; he applies the designation to himself in five of the seven extant letters that he likely wrote.[45] The English term "apostle" is a loanword from the Greek *apostolos*, literally, "one sent" to deliver a message.[46] Paul indicates that he has been "sent" by the god of Israel to proclaim the "good news," that is, his "gospel" message concerning Jesus, the Christ, or kingly messiah whom Paul saw prefigured in Judean scriptures (e.g., 1 Cor 15:4; Rom 10:6–7; 15:12). He views himself as responding to the dual commission of the god of Israel and the risen Jesus: "Paul, an apostle, not from men, nor through human agency, but through Jesus Christ and God the father, who raised him from the dead" (Gal 1:1). Apostles, in Paul's view, receive their position through divine appointment: "God has appointed [*etheto*], first apostles" (1 Cor 12:28). He construes his appointment as a gracious gift: "For I am the least of the apostles—I, who am unfit to be called an apostle, because I persecuted God's assembly—but by the beneficence of God [*chariti de theou*] I am what I am, and the favor that he has shown me [*hē charis autou hē eis eme*] has not been in vain, but I have worked harder than all of them—not I but the favor [*charis*][47] of God that is with me" (1 Cor 15:9–10; cp. also 1 Cor 3:10).[48] Connoting both a gift given and the favorable disposition that might result in the giving of a gift, his repeated use of the term *charis* indicates that Paul construes his apostolic appointment as a divine benefaction.[49] Similarly, in Rom 1:5, he writes that, in order to bring about "faithful obedience among all the nations," he had "received favor[50] and apostleship" (*charin kai apostolēn*) from God. The latter phrase may, however, employ hendiadys: Paul received "the favor (or 'gift') of apostleship."[51] Later in the same letter, he voices a similar sentiment: "I have written to you rather boldly, in part as one who reminds you through the favor shown me by God [*dia tēn charin tēn dotheisan moi hypo tou theou*] that I might become a steward of Jesus Christ to the nations, serving the gospel of God as a priest" (15:15–16). Paul's "stewardship" is depicted as a result of the favorable attitude or disposition of Israel's god toward him; appointment to office is both a sign and an act of divine favor. The use of *charis* in this sense corresponds with Pliny's term *indulgentia:* the "kindness" or "favor" shown by a benefactor.

Paul also describes his prophetic call—closely related to his apostolic status—as an act of divine beneficence: "When God, who separated me from the time I was in my mother's womb and, through his beneficence[52] [*dia tēs charitos autou*], called me,[53] was pleased to reveal his son to me, so that I might preach him among the people of the nations" (Gal 1:15–16a; cp. Gal. 2:9). With its language of "separation" for cultic service even before birth, Paul's statement echoes prophetic call narratives (Isa 49:1; Jer 1:5). The emphasis of God's beneficence (*charis*) is not present in the earlier biblical exemplars; it is Paul's own innovation and indicates his investment in the discourse of gift exchange.

The language of "appointment," "gift," "beneficence," and "favor" indicates points of contact between Paul and the broader Roman context of imperial appointments and the patron-client networks that they involve. Just as, in the examples cited earlier, Trajan was able to confer the gift of status upon Pliny's associates Rosianus Geminus and Harpocras of Alexandria, the god of Israel, as a beneficent gift-giver, had bestowed apostolic status upon Paul. And just as Pliny assured Trajan that Geminus would certainly fulfill his services in exemplary fashion, Paul, too, as a good client claims to have "worked harder" for God, his divine patron,[54] than all the apostles who had been commissioned before him. The client's diligent service reciprocated patronal donations—a logic as at home with Paul as it was in Rome, as Zeba Crook has convincingly demonstrated.[55]

Apostleship and Hierarchical Organization

Just as positional status in Pliny's Roman context was evaluated within a hierarchical system, Paul construed the early Christian assembly as hierarchized space. At the pinnacle of the assembly's hierarchized social space stood the figure of the apostle.[56] Commenting on the stratified organization of the assemblies, Robert Grant wrote:

> [Paul's] worldview is hierarchical and, in the local church, monarchical. By the time of Ignatius, the bishop will be the local monarch, but for Paul it is the apostle who rules. God himself set apostles first in the church, locally as well as universally (1 Cor 12:28), and Paul is the one apostle to the Corinthians (9:2).[57]

As Grant indicates, his view is based in part on 1 Cor 12, where Paul ranks various types of positional status—each associated with particular responsibilities—in the Corinthian assembly. Various types of positional status are recognized in Paul's letters, including familial roles (father/mother, son/daughter), marital status (married/formerly married/unmarried), citizenship, region of origin, ethnicity (Jew or Judean/non-Jew), and status based on the disposition of the male foreskin (circumcised/uncircumcised). Of these roles, only marital status is identified as a gift from God (1 Cor 7:7), although it is possible that circumcision may be implied in Paul's mention of "the gifts and the calling of God" in Rom 11:28–29.[58] Additional types of positional status, including those of apostle, prophet, teacher, and glossolalist (i.e., one who "speaks in tongues"), Paul also construes as gifts of God, as indicated in 1 Cor 12.

The text to which Grant pointed, 1 Cor 12,[59] includes important gift exchange motifs. It is located at the beginning of a section that stretches from 1 Cor 12:1 to 14:40, prefaced with the heading "concerning spiritual matters" (*peri de tōn pneumatikōn*).[60] The "matters" of Paul's interest pertain to the disposition of various *charismata,* "(spiritual) gifts"—a noun formed from the verb *charizomai,* "to give graciously," "to bestow." He describes these "gifts" as ones that proceed from Israel's god. Paul's words address the Corinthian assembly:

> But you are the body of Christ, and individually members of it. And (concerning) those whom God has appointed in the assembly: first apostles, second prophets, third teachers, then miracles, then gifts of healing, helpful deeds, acts of guidance,[61] types of tongues [i.e., glossolalia]. Not all are apostles, are they? Not all are prophets, are they? Not all are teachers, are they? Not all are miracle-workers, are they? Not all have gifts of healing, do they? Not all speak in tongues, do they? Not all interpret, do they? But eagerly desire the greater gifts. (1 Cor 12:27–31a)

Paul lists a series of more or less clearly defined roles encountered in the assembly in Corinth. These roles, which constitute different types of positional status, are ranked hierarchically, as indicated by the use of ordinal numbers: "first" are apostles, "second" prophets, and "third" teachers. The ordinals soon give way to a series of temporal adverbs, "*then* miracles, *then* gifts of healing"; these, too, give way to an asyndetic series ("helpful deeds, acts of guidance, types of tongues"). Their association with ordinals clearly distinguishes the first three items in the list. The fact that subsequent items lack ordinal markers, as well as the fact that "miraculous deeds" and "gifts of healing" appear in reverse order in 1 Cor 12:9–10, suggests that Paul is not concerned to place those items firmly within his ranking system.[62] With regard to the first three items, however, "the numbering undoubtedly is meant to indicate an order of importance."[63]

The first three roles listed—apostle, prophet, and teacher—as well as the roles of miracle worker, healer, one who speaks in tongues (i.e., engages in glossolalia), and one who interprets the glossolalist's utterances, constitute types of positional status recognized in Paul's Corinthian assembly. It is doubtful whether any particular role was associated with the "helpful deeds" and "acts of guidance" mentioned in v. 28; the plural nouns apparently refer to specific acts, rather than to discrete social roles within the assembly. It is, however, possible that "helpful deeds" refers to patronal donations within the assemblies, as Bruce Longenecker has suggested.[64] If so, Paul may be intentionally minimizing the role of the patron by failing to designate explicitly that position, in conjunction with apostles, teachers, and so on.

The fact that Paul lists apostles as "first" among the positions recognized within early Christian assemblies is not mere ornamentation. Indicating a preeminent positional status within the assembly, the ordinal "first" connotes a position of relative authority over other members of the assemblies. Paul expresses the same relation in other images, each of which both reinforces and nuances the connotation of relatively high positional status indicated in the ordinal. These include his use of paternalistic images to depict himself as a father to the members of the local assembly who provides an authoritative model for the Corinthians to imitate (1 Cor 4:14–16; Phil 3:17)[65] and who may, if necessary, brandish a metaphorical "rod" of discipline (1 Cor 4:21) with which to "punish every act of disobedience" effected by assembly members (2 Cor 10:6; cp. 13:2); his use of maternalistic images likening himself to a mother nursing her young (1 Thess 2:7–8);[66] his depiction of the Corinthian assembly as "infants" in need of his care (1 Cor 3:1–2); and his depiction of himself as a "master builder" and the Corinthians as his construction (3:10–15).

Paul's images depicting himself as one in a position of relative authority over other members of the assemblies was further reinforced by the particular set of obligations, privileges, and rights that he associated with the positional status of apostle. The primary obligation of the apostle is to "proclaim the gospel" (1 Thess 2:4; 1 Cor 1:17; Rom 1:1, 9) of Jesus' crucifixion, resurrection, heavenly exaltation, and imminent return to earth to gather his faithful.[67] Apostles, in Paul's view, are granted special privileges, including the authority to command subordinate assembly members (Phlm 22), anticipating their obedience (2 Cor 7:15; 10:6; Rom 1:5; 15:18; Phlm 21),[68] and to "build up and to tear down" assemblies in the manner in which they see fit (2 Cor 10:8)—an image that refers to instruction and exhortation (1 Cor 3:10–15), on one hand, and vehement opposition to rival discourses and practices, on the other (2 Cor 10:4-5). Similarly, apostles are privileged in their ability to commend or to withhold commendation regarding local assemblies (1 Cor 11:2, 17) and their "right" (*exousia*) to receive room and board at the expense of those to whom they preach (1 Cor 9:3-12)—even if in some instances they politely refrain from making use of such "rights" (1 Cor 9:12b-15; Phlm 8-9). Finally, the apostle claims the right to exercise penal authority within the assemblies, pronouncing judgment in the name of Jesus (1 Cor 5:3-5; 2 Cor 13:2-4)—even if, in practical terms, he realizes that no penal measures will be enacted without the support of important constituencies within the local assembly: "We are ready to punish every act of disobedience, *when your obedience is complete*" (2 Cor 10:6, emphasis added). Unlike the Roman administrators appointed by Trajan, Paul had at his disposal no external apparatus (such as courts and military might) to enforce his policies. These rights and privileges were not accessible to other members of the assemblies; they were the prerogatives solely of those who claimed the positional status of apostle.[69]

Closely related in function to the role of apostle, although distinct from and subordinate to it as a form of positional status (i.e., "second"), is that of the prophet. Not necessarily entailing either prediction of the future or ecstatic states, prophecy is defined by Paul as a form of speech "to other people for their upbuilding and encouragement and consolation" (1 Cor 14:3 NRSV) for the purpose of "building up the assembly" (1 Cor 14:4). Paul attributes to prophets an ability that is generally reserved for the god of Israel and his Christ: the capacity to "disclose the heart's secrets" (1 Cor 14:25; cp. Rom 8:27; 1 Cor 4:5). This is likely because he views prophets as endowed with the divine spirit, which itself possesses and makes available insight into the mind of both God and humans (1 Cor 2:9-12). This view may be compared with a statement recorded in Lucian of Samosata: "Prophecy is a piece [*aporrhōx*] of the divine mind" (*Alex.* 40).[70] Prophets are granted the right to address the assembly; when multiple prophets are present, they must take turns speaking (1 Cor 14:29-33). In his discussion about the propriety of women's veiling during assembly meetings, Paul indicates that both women and men were able to assume the prophetic role in the Corinthian assembly (1 Cor 11:4-5). This practice would seem to be contradicted by a prohibition of women's speech in the assembly in 1 Cor 14:34–35: "Let women be silent in the assemblies, for they are not permitted to speak, but let them be subject, as indeed the law says. But if they wish to learn something, let them ask their own husbands at home, for it is shameful for a woman to speak in the assembly." The passage, however, may well have been inserted by a later editor of Paul's epistles; in some manuscripts, the verses appear in a different location in the letter—often a sign of editorial tampering.[71]

Paul construes the positional status of prophet as one of the "spiritual gifts." In a section of 1 Corinthians describing the "varieties of gifts" (*diaireseis de charismatōn;* 12:4–11), Paul writes, "now to one is given through the spirit the utterance of wisdom . . . to another, prophecy" (1 Cor 12:8, 10). Similarly, in his letter to the early Christian assembly at Rome, Paul writes, "We have gifts [*charismata*] that differ according to the grace [*tēn charin*] given to us: prophecy, in proportion to faith, ministry, in ministering" (Rom 12:6 NRSV). In Corinth, he recommends that assembly members "strive for spiritual things [*zēloute de ta pneumatika*], but especially that you should prophesy" (1 Cor 14:1). Paul's depiction of prophecy as a gift for which one could "strive" may indicate that in his view, it could be granted in response to eager petitions, as was clearly the case with another of the "spiritual gifts," the ability to interpret glossolalic utterances: "Let the one who speaks in a tongue pray that he might interpret it" (1 Cor 14:13). Paul's god, like Rome's emperors, is portrayed as amenable to granting requests.

Although Paul classified prophets as "second"—outranked only by apostles—in the social hierarchy of the assemblies, they clearly surpassed glossolalists in rank: "The one who prophesies is greater than [*meizōn . . . ē*] the one who speaks in tongues" (1 Cor 14:5). "Speaking in tongues," or glossolalia, consists of the utterance of a series of unintelligible phonemes that, in the context of Greco-Roman religions, were construed as the "language of the gods."[72] In Paul's Judaic perspective, however, such utterances constituted the "language of the angels" (1 Cor 13:1).[73] There is a notable caveat to Paul's subordination of "tongues" to prophecy; the prophet is granted superior status "unless someone interprets, so that the assembly might receive edification" (*oikodomēn*). Paul holds open the possibility that the ranking system could be modified; in this case, the value of glossolalia—if interpreted, or rendered as intelligible speech—could rival that of prophecy, as both modes of speech deliver to the gathered assembly messages that claim a divine origin and authority. Both, he reasoned, are useful for "building up" or "edifying" only to the extent that they were intelligible to the gathered assembly (1 Cor 14:6–25). Both types of speech, however, claimed as their sources agencies that transcended human authority: Paul construed prophecy as a mode of speech inspired by the spirit of God and glossolalia as the "language of the angels." In contrast, the "merely" human speech of the teacher qualified that position for a ranking third in importance, just below prophecy and twice removed from apostleship.

Like apostleship and prophecy, Paul construed the role of the teacher as a gift from Israel's god (Rom 12:6–7). He assumes the role of the teacher to include ethical instruction, of both children and adults, particularly through the inculcation of Mosaic law (Rom 2:20–23). Inasmuch as instruction in Mosaic law presupposes literacy, the role of teacher would not, like prophecy, have been one to which the majority of people within the early Christian assemblies could aspire. Since Paul says so little about the role, the extent of its associated prerogatives and duties is not known.

"Anti-Status" Views of Paul

In light of the argument advanced here that Paul advocated a hierarchical sociopolitical organization within the assemblies, a brief discussion of the contrary position is required. Let me begin, however, with a digression on the "politics of interpretation" of Pauline texts at work within both the academy and religious organizations. There is often resistance to interpretations of Paul that view him as promoting hierarchical relations within early Christian assemblies, and for understandable reasons. The contemporary academy tends to prefer "egalitarian" social systems over hierarchical ones. Hierarchical organization is often associated with forms of oppression that the academy wishes to escape: most notably, racism, sexism, classism, and discrimination based on sexual identity—problems that continue to plague contemporary cultures. Second is the fact that Paul's letters are often made to function as "charters" for the ideologies and practices advocated by contemporary religious groups, some of which are loath to attribute to Paul the acceptance of patriarchalism, heterosexism, or slavery, for example. The predilections of the modern academy and of progressive religious organizations ought not divert us, however, from the properly *historical* enterprise of adequately describing the discourse of Paul's letters or the sociopolitical organization of the assemblies that he founded. As Bruce Lincoln reminds us, the critical scrutiny of ancient religious texts hones skills that can be "put to good use at home" in contemporary contexts.[74] It is only after regimes of discourse and practice have been subjected to critical scrutiny that oppressive practices may be recognized, opposed, and then replaced with practices that entail a greater degree of equality and social justice. For that reason, the critical analysis of Paul's letters is not inimical to contemporary concerns to promote just social and religious systems, but rather is a prerequisite to their formation.

Now to our theme: although Robert Grant's statement that Paul's "worldview is hierarchical and, in the local church, monarchical" has much to commend it, Edwin A. Judge has been an advocate of the contrary view in which Paul renounces status. Judge argues that Paul rejects a "notable aspect of classical ethics, their emphasis on status—the concern with relations between people and the appropriate ordering of them as between greater and lesser."[75] This, Judge asserts, is due to Paul's "fascination with the self-abasement of Christ,"[76] a fascination manifested in "servitude to the interests of others."[77] He notes that Paul construes his role as one of "ministry" and "stewardship," rather than "the theory of leadership which one would expect to see in his counterparts on the classical side of the fence."[78]

Others scholars since Judge have added to the arguments in favor of the view that Paul did not engage in the "appropriate ordering of [people] as between greater and lesser." Each of the arguments, however, rests on misperceptions concerning the relevant information in Paul's letters. When the letters are understood correctly, it becomes evident that even the apparently "egalitarian" material in Paul supports and reinforces the hierarchical ranking system that Paul would promote in his assemblies. The most significant arguments against the view that Paul ranked positions within the assemblies include the following:

1. Judge correctly notes that Paul's self-descriptions as a "servant" portray him in a subordinate position. He is generally portrayed as subordinate, however, not to other human members of the assemblies, but to Christ, whose servant he proclaims himself to be (Rom 1:1; Gal 1:10; Phil 1:1). With respect to other humans associated with the early Christian assemblies, Paul resists the implication that he should be seen as subordinate even to authoritative figures such as James (the brother of Jesus), Peter, and John, the "pillar apostles" active in the early Christian assembly in Jerusalem (Gal 2:6–9).
2. As Dale Martin has shown, the status of slaves, former slaves, and clients is linked to that of their patrons or masters.[79] Subordinates of high-status figures basked in a measure of the reflected glory of their superiors:[80] imperial slaves and former slaves were frequently accorded a status above that of most freeborn citizens. To portray oneself as a slave of Christ, the exalted "lord," is therefore not to portray oneself as an individual of low status.
3. In some instances, Paul even asserts that he is a slave to other members of the assembly (1 Cor 9:19; 2 Cor 4:5) or a steward on their behalf (1 Cor 4:1). However, Judge makes a false assumption in viewing service as incompatible with hierarchical preeminence. By way of comparison, Dio Chrysostom argues that kingship is a form of stewardship (*epitropē*) given as a gift (*dōrea*) by Zeus (*Or.* 1.45–46). Similarly, Dio writes: "Then, the care bestowed on his subjects he [the king] does not consider an incidental thing or mere drudgery . . . [but] it is only when he helps people that he thinks he is doing his

duty, having been appointed to this work by the greatest god. . . . No indeed, the king does not object to toil and discomfort in behalf of others, nor does he deem his lot any worse simply because he has to face the most tasks and have the most troubles" (*Or.* 3.55–57).[81] And as Paul Veyne has shown, liturgies and public benefaction were forms of service to the public that enhanced, rather than undermined, one's status and prestige.[82]

4. Judge's apparent assumption that self-interest and interest in others are mutually exclusive options involves a false dichotomy.[83] Dio Chrysostom indicates that the good king is concerned for the welfare of subordinates, "not divorcing his own interest from that of his subjects, but rejoicing most and regarding himself as most prosperous when he sees his subjects prosperous too" (*Or.* 3.39).[84] Paul's construction of a role of authority over other assembly members is not incompatible with genuine concern and positive regard for those construed as subordinates.

5. Paul's use of the language of fictive kinship (i.e., members of the assembly are "brothers and sisters") is sometimes viewed as undermining hierarchical ranking systems.[85] However, as every ancient commentator indicates, the domestic space of family and household was highly stratified. Aristotle writes: "the male is by nature better fitted to command than the female . . . and the older and more fully developed person than the younger and immature. It is true that in most cases of republican government the ruler and ruled interchange in turn . . . but the male stands in this relationship to the female continuously. The rule of the father over the children on the other hand is that of a king" (*Pol.* 1.1259b).[86] Despite Elizabeth Schussler-Fiorenza's now classic arguments to the contrary, Paul's position was not fundamentally different.[87] We need only point to a few passages to substantiate this view: "I write these things not to

shame you, but to admonish you as my beloved children" (1 Cor 4:14); "I want you to recognize that Christ is the head of every man, man is the head of his wife, and God is the head of Christ" (1 Cor 11:3);[88] Paul claims to have behaved toward the Thessalonian assembly blamelessly, "as a father encouraging his own children" (1 Thess 2:11–12). Note that Paul's ultimate authority figure, the god of Israel, is construed as "father" (e.g., 2 Cor 6:18; Gal 4:6); second in authority is Jesus, God's "son" (e.g., 1 Cor 15:28; Rom 8:32). No transcendent authority figure is classified as female.[89]

6. As Bruce Lincoln, Margaret Mitchell, Dale Martin, and others have shown, in Greco-Roman antiquity, the description of the corporate entity (whether empire, city, or local assembly) as a body was often deployed in calls for civic unity.[90] Such calls for unity, however, were accompanied by pleas in support of hierarchical leadership (i.e., the body politic never lacks a "head"). In 1 Corinthians, the metaphor of the body is accompanied by an ordinal system ranking certain members.

7. Paul could at times resort to the language of "equality," but contrary to the contemporary use of the term, Greco-Roman discourses of equality both recognize and perpetuate systems of economic, political, and social stratification.[91] According to Aristotle's classical view, "equality" entailed the notion of proportionality: to each a share "'according to merit;' for all people agree that what is just in distribution must be according to merit in some sense. . . . This, then is what the just is—the proportional; the unjust is what violates the proportion. Hence one term becomes too great, the other too small, as indeed happens in practice; for the person who acts unjustly has too much, and the person who is unjustly treated too little, of what is good" (*Nic. Eth.* 5.3.7, 14–15).[92] Aristotle's view of "proportional equality" did not entail numerically equal distribution of goods between all parties;

rather it entailed a "just" distribution proportional to the "merit" of each.[93] "Injustice" resulted only when the disparity between the various parties became too great. Paul's advice concerning the distribution of economic resources between various early Christian assemblies adopts the notion of proportional equality. As part of his plea to the assemblies of Achaia to contribute to a collection that was to be delivered to Jerusalem, he cites Exod 16:18 as an example of proportionally equal distribution: "The one who had much did not have too much, and the one who had little did not have too little" (2 Cor 8:15 NRSV).[94] Paul's advice was not designed to bring about numerically equal distribution among the assemblies, but to avoid the "injustice" evident when some enjoy an overabundance "of what is good," even as others suffer deprivation. The ideal of proportional equality does not seek to eradicate socioeconomic stratification, but to attenuate it; it seeks only to avoid extreme disparities in distribution.

None of Judge's observations contradicts the overwhelming evidence that there existed in the early Christian assemblies hierarchized social relations and that Paul himself was a primary agent in the construction and perpetuation of those hierarchical relations. When understood correctly, Paul's statements that might at first glance seem to undermine hierarchical relations actually serve to maintain them. Nor were the forms of sociopolitical organization that Paul deployed in the assemblies far removed from "the theory of leadership" espoused by his "counterparts on the classical side of the fence." Paul, like Aristotle, understood that extreme disparities in the distribution of material goods were not conducive to the harmonious operation of the body politic. And like Dio, he understood that the effective leader needed to be able to generate the assent of subordinates and that domineering and overbearing tactics were not the most effective methods to accomplish that goal. But if his tacit admission that his methods were at times perceived as authoritarian offers any indication, it appears that this lesson may not have been learned with alacrity. Paul concedes: "Now if indeed I boast somewhat excessively about our authority, which the Lord has given for building up and not for destruction, I will not be ashamed of it. I do not want to seem as though I am trying to terrify you with my letters" (2 Cor 10:8–9). Negative reactions to similar statements may have precipitated his denial that he "acted as master" (*ouch hoti kyrieuomen*) over the faith of members of the Corinthian assembly (2 Cor 1:24). For Paul, the negotiation of a "middle way" between tyranny and anarchy required frequent course corrections, and the way forward was not always self-evident.

Summary and Conclusions

In light of the fact that sociology works with multiple, sometimes contradictory, definitions of "status," we have identified two distinct usages of the term: positional status refers to the fulfillment of a particular position or role within a sociopolitical field, and accorded status accrues on the basis of communal assessments regarding the excellence or exemplary manner in which one fulfills the duties and obligations associated with a particular social position. As Pliny the Younger's letters amply attest, in the Roman context certain types of positional status, including citizenship and political office, were regularly conferred as patronal donations. In his letters, these donations were orchestrated by Pliny himself as "broker" between client and emperor.

In Paul's letters, several types of positional status are described as "gifts" from Israel's god: foremost among these are the positions of apostle, prophet, glossolalist, and teacher. Like various positions within the Roman *cursus honorum*, Paul ranks hierarchically the various types of positional status that he identifies as active within early Christian assemblies. Of the positions named in 1 Cor 12, Paul construes that of apostle as preeminent among the members of the assembly. Corresponding with the priority of rank claimed by the apostle are rights and privileges not available to other members, including the "right" to room and board at the expense of the assembly within which the apostle is active, and the right to make demands of subordinate members, to threaten to deploy penal authority, and to "build up and tear down" assemblies as the apostle saw fit. In terms of both rank and rights, the apostle claimed a preeminent position among the membership of the early Christian assemblies. Although some New Testament scholars have propounded views in which Paul eschews status in its various forms, such views misconstrue the available evidence and are contradicted by Paul's clear statements promoting a hierarchical organization within the assemblies.

Some clear consequences of Paul's discourse on the "gift of status" may be identified. First, Paul's discourse, to the extent that it was accepted as authoritative, effectively orchestrated a hierarchical organization within early Christian assemblies, with the role of apostle inhabiting the superior position. Second, the discourse more or less effectively naturalized the hierarchical organization that Paul proposed. He did not claim authority for his views as an itinerant leatherworker, but as one who had been commissioned as an "apostle" by the god of Israel; and it was this god who, in Paul's discourse, "appointed" the hierarchical order of the assemblies. Although he claimed that the sociopolitical organization of the assemblies was "arranged" by God, it is clear that Paul's own discourse and management practices were instrumental in promoting the organizational structure that he envisioned.

In addition to the mechanisms of gift-debt typically associated with the development of hierarchical social relations in the anthropological literature since Mauss, the study of Paul adds another mechanism by which the discourse of "the gift" affects sociopolitical organization. Perhaps taking his cues from the practice whereby a highly placed political figure bestows political office as a patronal gift, Paul construes certain aspects of the social organization of the early Christian assemblies—notably the positions of apostle, prophet, teacher, and glossolalist—as gifts from Israel's god. In the case of such gifts, it is not the failure of one party to reciprocate on equal terms that effects a social hierarchy, as in Mauss's examples; instead, it is the discursive claims that "gifts of status" had been granted by Israel's god that serve to structure sociopolitical relations.

There is a distinction to be made between the "gifts of status" described in Paul's letters and Pliny's. Whereas in Rome, those who held positions granted as the result of patronal or imperial assignation could expect to demonstrate their positional status through legal documentation, titles, and decrees, Paul was unable to call on such forms of legitimation to demonstrate his position as "apostle." Unlike Harpocras of Alexandria or Voconius Romanus, who could anticipate legal documents to attest to their newly bestowed positional statuses, Paul could adduce only his own claims to have received apostolic status as a gift of God. The gifts of emperors are more readily demonstrable than those of gods. To the extent to which his claims were recognized as legitimate by his auditors, Paul could invoke rights and privileges that he associated with apostolic status, not least of which was a preeminent position within early Christian assemblies. His discourse concerning divine gifts, therefore, carried significant implications for the orchestration of sociopolitical relations within those groups, even in the absence of external legal or martial support.

Paul's practical and discursive construction of a preeminent positional status within the assemblies, however, by no means ensured that all parties involved would accept his suggestions. On the contrary, there is ample evidence that he was engaged in a nearly continual struggle to achieve and maintain a privileged status within some assemblies. In this struggle, too, the discourse of the gift played a decisive role. But that story must await our next chapter for its telling.

SEVEN

Spiritual Gifts and Status Inversion

Introduction

In his letters, Paul proposes a hierarchical ranking system to organize the early Christian assemblies. As we have seen in chapter 6, occupying the position of preeminence within the proposed organizational structure is the figure of the apostle. Israel's god, Paul claimed, had assigned to each person his or her own particular position within the assembly. However, Paul's proposals were not always accepted, his attempts to ground them in the transcendent authority of the god of Israel notwithstanding. Other culturally prominent principles of organization lay close at hand. Among them were the assignation of status based on wealth and skill in declamation. Both of these principles appear to have been utilized by some parties within the Corinthian assembly. Paul, however, did not accept those ranking systems, as both tended to devalue the characteristics and qualities that he himself claimed or appears to have possessed. In place of those culturally prevalent systems of evaluation, Paul proposed other evaluative schemes that privileged qualities and characteristics associated with the "gifts of God" in assignations of hierarchical preeminence—such gifts as Paul claimed to have received. His proposals effectively called for an inversion of schemes of hierarchical ranking with respect to evaluations of both positional and accorded status. Enlisting Carole Crumley's notion of heterarchy, moreover, facilitates the critique and elaboration of Wayne Meeks's now classic formulations on "status" and "status inconsistency."

In his seminal work *The First Urban Christians: The Social World of the Apostle Paul,* Meeks argued that status ought not be viewed as a single point on a one-dimensional scale of measurement, or even as the average of measurements on several different scales.[1] Instead, it results from the interaction of social evaluations made in several salient areas, including—in Paul's Romanized context—"ethnic origins, *ordo,* citizenship, personal liberty, wealth, occupation, age, sex, and public offices or honors."[2] Meeks points out that since status is a "multidimensional phenomenon," in order to "describe the social level of an individual or group, one must attempt to measure their rank along *each* of the relevant dimensions."[3]

In any given social context, it is possible, even likely, that people will be ranked more highly with respect to some variables and less highly with respect to others. The result is the situation of status inconsistency, which is uncomfortable both socially and psychologically. Meeks notes that many members of early Christian groups likely experienced this condition,[4] and Paul was certainly no exception: was he to be assigned a social rank based on his role as a leatherworker, his public speaking skills—which by some accounts were less than impressive—or his claims to apostolic status?

Meeks's analysis represents an advance over earlier views that tended to "regard an individual's status as a single thing. One is high or low or middle or perhaps somewhere in between, but still measured along a single scale."[5] Correcting this "single scale" model, Meeks notes that "most sociologists have come to view social stratification as a multidimensional phenomenon."[6] Meeks's formulations abandoned the "single scale" model in favor of what was in essence one based on multiple scales, such that he could write, "The generalized status of a person is a composite of his or her ranks in all of the relevant dimensions."[7] What is lacking in this formulation, however, is the notion that one's rank could change over time or be subject to contest and negotiation.[8] Meeks's metaphors of "scale" and "measurement" need to be augmented through the addition of the categories of time, change, and contestation.

Meeks's formulations remain valuable some thirty years after the publication of *The First Urban Christians.* We can, however, elaborate and refine those formulations by supplementing them with theoretical perspectives developed in the social sciences, particularly anthropologist Carole Crumley's notion of "heterarchy," which she introduced in 1979 in response to what she viewed as an overreliance on the concept of hierarchy in the study of complex societies.[9] She writes: "Hierarchies (as opposed to other kinds of structured relations) are composed of '... elements which on the basis of certain factors are subordinate to others and may be ranked.' ... Yet many structures, both biological and social, are not organized hierarchically."[10] To account for "patterns of relations that are complex but not hierarchical," Crumley enlists the notion of heterarchy, which "may be defined as the relation of elements to one another when they are unranked or when they possess the potential for being ranked in a number of different ways."[11] Heterarchy, however, does not necessarily connote the absence of systems of hierarchical ranking, inasmuch as it involves "the relation of elements to one another ... when they possess the potential for being ranked in a number of different ways." Rather, as Mark Mosko notes, it may entail "a multiplicity of 'hierarchical' or asymmetrical oppositions."[12]

The distinction between hierarchy and heterarchy is to be drawn not on the basis of the presence or absence of hierarchically ranked elements, but on the basis of the stability and fixity with which those hierarchies persist. Heterarchy emphasizes aspects of process, modification, and change involved in sociopolitical systems. Distinct from hierarchical models in which elements are ranked in a fixed or static manner, heterarchy queries the "*dialectical relation* between ranked and counterpoised power."[13] It is in this dialectical relation that one apprehends *process,* as opposed to fixity, stability, and inflexible *structure.* Crumley calls for an examination of "the play between hierarchy and heterarchy: across space, through time, and in the human mind."[14] As Alison Rautman notes, the notion of heterarchy does not function as a precise analytical tool; it serves instead as a heuristic device that presses the researcher to "examine the specific social relationships among individuals and/or groups (or sites) to establish the way(s) in which power is constituted in that society, and how the definition and distribution of power(s) might have changed over time."[15]

It is precisely the elements of process and dialectical "play," and the examination of the ways in which "the definition and distribution of power(s) might have changed over time," that are missing from Meeks's notion of status inconsistency. Citing the work of Elizabeth Brumfiel,

Rautman notes that heterarchy could take one of several possible forms in a given context, including systems in which elements within the sociopolitical aggregate (1) "operate independently of one another," or (2) belong to "many different unranked interaction systems," or (3) constitute "members in 'many different systems of ranking' such that the same element might occupy a different rank in each different system."[16] Clearly, the third possibility describes the situation of "status inconsistency" discussed by Meeks; it is the result of a system in which individuals and groups may be ranked in a number of different ways. According to Meeks's formulation, status is a "multidimensional phenomenon," and in order to "describe the social level of an individual or group, one must attempt to measure their rank along each of the relevant dimensions."[17] Meeks does not, however, address the issues of process and change that its proponents identify as the chief advantage of employing the notion of heterarchy.

In what follows, I elaborate and refine Wayne Meeks's discussion of status inconsistency by drawing attention to the elements of process, change, and "the play between hierarchy and heterarchy" to which Carole Crumley's writings have pointed. I accomplish this goal by analyzing the discourse that Paul uses in his attempt to invert two systems of sociopolitical ranking that effectively subordinated him to other individuals and groups within early Christian assemblies. In his letters to various early Christian assemblies, particularly that in Corinth, Paul crafts discourses that seek to invert systems of rank that tended to disadvantage him in relation to other influential agents within the assemblies. He seeks to overturn systems for the evaluation and assignment of rank pertaining to both positional status, which is associated with the fulfillment of a particular position or role within a sociopolitical field, and accorded status, or honor and prestige. In these discourses, the processual quality of the "play" between hierarchy and heterarchy is evident.

The discourse of gift exchange is, moreover, a fundamental element in the evaluative systems that he proposes. Paul's claim to mediate gifts from the god of Israel, and a concomitant valuation of "spiritual" goods over material ones, enables him to orchestrate inversions of positional status. His claim that the "gift of the spirit" facilitates an inner transformation resulting in divine "glory" and an attendant devaluation of external characteristics in favor of internal ones is instrumental in his attempts to effect inversions of accorded status. His discourse on "the gift" bears important implications for the sociopolitical organization of the assemblies.

Heterarchy: The Contested Ranking of Patrons and Apostles

Paul's promotion of a system of rank in which apostles were granted preeminent positional status (i.e., they rank "first"; 1 Cor 12:27–31) was no guarantee that his proposals would be accepted by all parties. Within the social milieu of the early Christian assemblies, other possibilities existed for the hierarchical ranking of positions. As Meeks indicated, wealth was a primary criterion by which status was assigned.[18] This was true of Greco-Roman society in general. The first-century CE rhetorician Aelius Theon lists several characteristics that constitute suitable grounds for praising an individual: "good birth . . . education, friendship, reputation, official position, wealth, good children, a good death" (*Exercises*, 109–10).[19] In the first century CE, individuals such as Seneca the Younger could achieve renown as lavish benefactors through distributions of their great wealth (Martial, *Ep.* 12.36; Juvenal, *Satire* 5.107–11).[20] The fact that the moneyed Trimalchio was the object of satire in Petronius's *Satyricon* indicates that wealth interacted with other factors in evaluations of prestige: most notably Trimalchio's freedman status, his unrefined tastes, his evident lack of a formal education, and above all his penchant for ostentatious display.[21] Although individuals had the potential to be ranked in a number of ways, wealth was an important criterion.

Under the influence of studies by Edwin Judge, Peter Lampe, Gerd Theissen, Peter Marshall, John Chow, and others, a consensus has emerged that patronage was operative in early Christian assemblies.[22] Moreover, it is widely accepted that the standard system of ranking which elevated wealthy patrons over the recipients of their largesse, construed as clients, was operative there as well. The use of the criterion of wealth in assignations of rank, however, stood in direct contradiction to Paul's own vision for the organization of the assemblies, with apostles assigned preeminent position. It is within this heterarchic situation, with all of its potential for instability, conflict, and change, that Paul deployed one of the classic tools for the mobilization of sociopolitical forces: discourse, and in particular, the rhetoric of inversion.[23] Moreover, Paul strategically deployed the language of gift-giving in his proposal to invert the criteria used in assigning rank within the assemblies. A brief examination of Paul's relations with two of the named patronal figures serves to illustrate the point.

Positional Status Inversion: Patron and Apostle

Philemon

Paul's relationship with his patron Philemon, perhaps in the city of Colossae,[24] represents a hierarchical inversion of the typical patron-client relation in which it is the wealthier party who enjoys a higher status. In his relationship with Philemon, it is not material wealth but purported access to "spiritual goods" that is most significant in defining the nature of the hierarchical relation.

It is clear that Philemon functioned economically as a patron to Paul. Philemon was the wealthier of the two, owning at least one slave (Phlm 16) and a "guest room" in which Paul requests temporary lodging on an impending visit (Phlm 22). Paul, on the other hand, claims often to have suffered indigence, going underclothed and underfed (1 Cor 4:11–12; 2 Cor 11:27), working night and day to meet his basic needs (1 Thess 2:9). His own economic position likely varied, at times slipping just below subsistence level, and at other times, rising near or slightly above it.[25] Philemon clearly controlled greater economic resources than did Paul. Likewise it is clear that he put those resources—both his guest room and his slave—at Paul's disposal. Normally, this state of affairs would indicate a patron-client relationship, with Philemon, as patron, in the dominant position. But Paul's language in his letter indicates that this relational pattern had been inverted: the economically poorer Paul ranked higher than the wealthier Philemon.

The hierarchical relation is indicated by Paul's use of the language of command, in terms of both grammatical structure (i.e., his use of imperatives) and expressions euphemizing demands.

In several instances, Paul uses imperative verbs when addressing Philemon. As linguist F. R. Palmer notes of the imperative mode, "In fact it is the strongest of the directives, one that emanates from someone in authority, which, therefore, does not expect non-compliance."[26] Paul assumes a position of authority over Philemon when he commands him: "prepare me a guest room" (Phlm 22). The command occurs immediately following a reference to Philemon's "obedience": "Confident of your obedience, I am writing to you, knowing that you will do even more than I say" (v. 21). Paul presumes the compliance of Philemon in granting his request.

In other cases, the implications of the imperative for the authority structure involved are softened somewhat; one is preceded by a wish formula, and two occur in conditional statements. Regarding his implied request to be accompanied by Philemon's slave, Onesimus, Paul writes, "Yes, brother, let me have this benefit from you in the Lord; refresh my sentiments in Christ!" (v. 20). The polite request to "let me have this benefit" (optative) is followed by the more forceful imperative: "refresh my sentiments!"

The final two examples occur in the context of conditional statements: "If you hold me as your associate, receive him as you would me. And if he has wronged you or owes you, charge it to my account" (vv. 17-18). In both cases, the fulfillment of the imperative in the apodosis is framed as contingent on the fulfillment of the condition expressed in the protasis. Like the use of the optative, this softens somewhat the authority structure implied in the imperatives, but does not remove it. Paul presents himself as using "soft power," exercising an authority that obtains its desires by making polite requests rather than brusque demands. Nonetheless, the compliance of the subordinate Philemon is assumed throughout, as signaled above all by the reference to his "obedience" in v. 21.

The relevance of gift exchange to the hierarchical relation between Paul and Philemon is evident in vv. 18-19, where the former writes: "And if he [Onesimus] has wronged you or owes you, charge it to my account. I,

Paul, write this with my own hand: I will repay it—not to mention that you owe me your very self." Paul introduces the notion of gift-debt through his use of the rhetorical technique of *paraleipsis,* adducing information that might be painful or socially damaging to the addressee under the pretense of omitting it.[27] In Paul's view, Philemon "owed" him his "very self." This statement is generally taken to be an allusion to the supposed effects of the preaching of Paul's gospel, a positive response to which is purportedly able to save one from imminent apocalyptic judgment, or "destruction" (Rom 9:22–24; 1 Thess 5:3).[28] As the Gospel of Mark indicates, life is a resource for which there is no adequate exchange: "What can people offer in exchange for their lives?" (Mark 8:37). Similarly, it would be impossible to render adequate compensation for the double favor not only of sparing life, but of prolonging it indefinitely in a future, heavenly existence, such as Paul's gospel promised (1 Thess 4:15–17; 1 Cor 15:49–55). Although it is the god of Israel whom Paul represents as the ultimate provider of such gifts, under the conventions of patronage, those who brokered or mediated benefactions functioned as patrons to those whom their mediation benefited.[29]

The patronal logic that subordinated Philemon to Paul entails an inversion of normal patron-client relations. Normally, a patron offers material or monetary donations to the client, who responds with the linguistic countergifts of thanksgiving and praise, as well as personal services of various sorts. In such cases, it is material goods that are valued more highly. In the case of Paul, however, the situation is reversed: his linguistic goods in the form of preaching "the gospel," since it entails promises of deliverance from apocalyptic "destruction" and eternal, heavenly life, are valued more highly than Philemon's material goods (a guest room and a slave's attendance). According to a materialist evaluation of the situation, Paul ought to be Philemon's obedient client. Instead, he plays the role of authoritative patronage broker. In accordance with the logic of the patronage system, this role implies that he also served as patron to Philemon, to whom he had mediated benefactions.

It is difficult, however, to disaggregate Paul's role as mediator of heavenly gifts from his claimed status as an apostle. Although the term "apostle" does not occur in the letter, it would be rash to conclude that Paul's claims to apostolic authority played no role in the construction of the hierarchical relation between himself and Philemon.[30] His claims to apostolic authority undoubtedly intersected with and reinforced the patronal logic evident in the letter. Both his role as mediator of heavenly gifts and his role as apostle effectively elevated his status in relation to other members of the assemblies. In both cases, the discourse of gift exchange was central: apostolic status was construed as a gift (1 Cor 3:10; 15:9–10; Rom 1:5) that entailed the role of mediating God's gifts to others—with all of the ramifications for relative status implied therein.

Phoebe

A similar inversion of hierarchical preeminence occurs in Paul's relation with Phoebe of Cenchreae, who by most accounts functioned as a patroness to the assemblies. Paul refers to her as *prostatis,* "patroness" to "many" within the assemblies, including Paul himself (Rom 16:1–2).[31] He does not indicate what form her patronage took: perhaps she opened her home for assembly meetings, provided food for the Lord's supper, donated funds, or hosted traveling emissaries from other assemblies. It seems likely that it is she who delivered Paul's letter from Corinth to the early Christian assembly in Rome in 57 CE.[32] Of interest is the fact that Paul recommends Phoebe to the assembly at Rome: "I recommend to you Phoebe, our sister, who is also a servant of the assembly in Cenchreae, that you might receive her in the Lord in a manner worthy of the saints, and that you might provide for her whatever she might need from you. For indeed, she has been a patroness [*prostatis*] of many, including myself." Peter Lampe notes the incongruity:[33]

> On the one hand, Phoebe was a "patroness" for Paul (16:2c). On the other hand, Paul was an apostle, the founder of the Corinthian church, and, in Rom 16:1–2, he writes a short letter of recommendation in favor of Phoebe. That is, *he* assumes the role of patron here, wanting to make sure that the Roman Christians receive her well and support her in all that she needs during her

visit in Rome. Thus, the roles of patron and client were not static, vertical-dependency relationships in early Pauline Christianity, but could even be reversed.

Indeed, the reversal of status roles seems to have been prevalent in the assemblies connected with Paul. But the extent to which hierarchical relations were "not static" should not be exaggerated. In both of the examples we have considered, the positional status of apostle outranked that of patron or patroness: spiritual resources were evaluated more highly than material ones. Paul appears to have been consistent in his attempts to impose a social hierarchy that corresponded with this inverted evaluative system. Although the possibility for individuals to be "ranked in different ways" was endemic to the early assemblies, Paul seems actively to have encouraged one possible ranking system—that which privileged himself and those styled "apostles"—at the expense of another, based on wealth. He exploited a potentiality inherent in the heterarchic situation of the assemblies.

Patrons in Corinth and Philippi

The situation is equally complex in the letters to Corinth and Philippi. Scholars have often postulated that in both cities, Paul faced systems of status evaluation in which material wealth constituted the privileged criterion (i.e., the "standard" patronage model). In this scenario, Paul sought to resist the implication that patronal donations of material goods carried any implication that he, as their recipient, should fall in status to the level of client. Peter Marshall has championed this idea with respect to Corinth, and Gerald Peterman with respect to Philippi.[34]

Briefly stated, Marshall argues that Paul resisted the demotion in status potentially entailed in the reception of hospitality in the form of room and board in the homes of wealthier patrons in Corinth. He did so, in Marshall's view, by refusing to accept the hospitality of patrons in the assembly, incurring their social hostility as a result: it is bad form to refuse a gift, including hospitality freely extended. Thus in 1 Cor 9, Paul defends his "right" to receive room and board in particular households but gallantly refuses to "make use" of that right, preferring to work to cover his expenses instead.

Peterman argues that in Philippi, Paul resisted the implication that patronal donations could reduce him in status to the level of client, not by refusing to accept patronal gifts, but by asserting that the gifts were in fact "gifts to God," rather than to Paul, and that God's countergifts would more than recompense the Philippians' material donations. In this scenario, Paul is construed as a proxy or broker between human donors and Israel's god. On the basis of the logic that the "gifts of God" are of greater value than those of humans, Paul, as God's proxy, is never reduced to the status of client vis-à-vis his human patrons in Philippi.[35] The logic of Paul's position is evident in his letter to the assembly at Philippi acknowledging his receipt of their gift—perhaps consisting of food, drink, and clothing—during a stint in prison in 54 CE:[36]

> But you have done well by sharing in my distress. And you indeed know, Philippians, that at the beginning of the good news, when I came from Macedonia, no assembly shared with me in an account of giving and receiving except you alone, because even in Thessalonica you sent for my need more than once. Not that I seek the gift, but I seek the fruit that increases to your account. But I have received everything in full, and I am overflowing! I am filled up, having received from Epaphroditus the things that you sent: a sweet scent, an acceptable sacrifice, pleasing to God. And my God will fulfill your every need in accordance with his wealth in glory in Christ Jesus. (Phil 4:14–19)

In all likelihood, the donation that Paul had received in prison provided for his physical needs, as basic necessities in Roman prisons were often provided by friends, family, and supporters, not by jailers.[37] He describes the donation in a manner analogous to sacrifices and offerings made in the Jerusalem temple: "a sweet scent [of roasting sacrificial meat], an acceptable sacrifice, pleasing to God." Paul presents himself as a proxy or broker between the Philippians and Israel's god; as a recipient of metaphorical sacrifices, he portrays himself in a role analogous to that of priests in the Jerusalem temple (e.g., Lev 2:1–2). By portraying gifts to himself as gifts to God, Paul evades any implication that donations made to him should reduce him to the level of a client or dependent. Paul is not reduced in status because he stands under no obligation to provide a reciprocal donation of goods or services: "my God will fulfill your every need in accordance with his wealth in glory in Christ Jesus" (v. 19). It is God himself who will provide the countergift, in Paul's view. Although often, in a gesture of solidarity, he uses the first-person plural possessive pronoun when referring to God ("our God"; cp. Phil 4:20; 1 Cor 6:11; Gal 1:4), here he uses the first-person singular form ("my God"), indicating a proprietary claim, in the sense not of ownership, but of exclusive rights and privileged relations with Israel's god. He portrays himself in the position of mediator in exchanges between humans and the divine.

The standard asymmetric relation, whereby donors whose gifts cannot be reciprocated by a (material) gift of equal or greater value are accorded a high status relative to that of the indebted recipient, is reversed in Paul's scheme. Whereas the Philippians were able to provide for *some* of Paul's material needs,[38] Paul's God is able to "fulfill your *every* need in accordance with his wealth in glory." God is construed as a more lavish donor than the Philippians. An asymmetric relation is implied in Paul's description of the exchange, and it is God, the lavish giver, who inhabits the position of relatively high status. Paul, as the mediator or "broker" in exchanges between God and humans, stands in an analogous position of relatively high status. According to the logic of the Roman system, patronage "brokers" are likewise construed as patrons to those to whom they mediate gifts. The members of the early Christian assembly in Roman Philippi cannot have missed the implication for Paul's status in relation to their own.

The Gift of the Spirit and the Inversion of Accorded Status

Just as Paul was able to orchestrate inversions of positional status whereby wealthier patrons were effectively subordinated to less wealthy apostolic figures, he also attempted to orchestrate inversions in his accorded status, that is, with respect to the honor and prestige in which he was held. Attempts to effect inversions of his accorded status are most evident in the Corinthian correspondence, in which he proposes that the "gift of the spirit" potentially bestows cognitive faculties by which the typical criteria for the assignation of honor and prestige—criteria based on access to monetary wealth, freedom from the necessity of manual labor, and the display of superior oratorical skills—might be overturned and others, associated with the "gift" of access to supernatural wisdom and inner, spiritual transformation, set in their place. Deploying rhetoric of status inversion, Paul attempts to counter evaluations by which he was accorded shame and dishonor in Corinth.

It is clear that there were significant challenges to Paul's honor in Corinth. First, his positional status as a craftsman, earning a living through the performance of manual labor, was a cause of offense for some wealthier members of the early Christian assembly in the city. Ronald Hock has noted the negative evaluations of artisans encountered in ancient sources, which reflect the elevated socioeconomic positions of their authors: "Stigmatized as slavish, uneducated, and often useless, artisans, to judge from the scattered references, were frequently reviled or abused, often victimized, seldom if ever invited to dinner, never accorded status, and even excluded from one Stoic utopia."[39] In 2 Cor 11:7, Paul tacitly admits that he had, in the perception of his auditors,[40] "debased himself" (*emauton tapeinōn*) by working as a craftsman in Corinth.

Second, in a context in which wealth was an important criterion for the assignation of prestige, Paul, as an impoverished and homeless itinerant, was accorded shame and dishonor (1 Cor 4:10–12). Third, his activity as a traveling speaker "proclaiming the good news" invited evaluations of his oratorical skills. These evaluations were apparently quite negative.[41] Some members of the Corinthian assembly reportedly complained that "his letters are weighty and strong, but his bodily presence is weak and his oratory is to be despised" (2 Cor 10:10). Lacking a vigorous "bodily presence" and impressive oratorical skills, Paul failed to garner prestige as an effective declaimer.[42] Instead of being esteemed, his oratory was "despised."

Portrayals of Paul as Lacking Prestige

Examples in which Paul portrays himself as an individual accorded scant honor and prestige are not difficult to find in the Corinthian correspondence. A particularly striking example occurs in 1 Cor 4:10b–13:

> We are weak, but you are strong; you are honored, but we are dishonored. Until the present hour we hunger and thirst, we are poorly clothed, we are slapped around[43] and homeless, we labor, working with our own hands. . . . We have become like the world's dirty dishwater, everyone's soap scum until now.[44]

In this passage, evaluative criteria for the assignation of prestige based on access to wealth play a prominent role. Paul associates his economic position, which at times fell below subsistence level, with material implications including homelessness, hunger, thirst, and a lack of adequate clothing, and social implications including dishonor and physical abuse: he is "slapped around" by others, who do not expect him to be able or willing to retaliate. He depicts himself as socially debased, lacking all prestige: "like the world's dirty dishwater, everyone's soap scum." Clearly, he depicts himself as one who is accorded a low status, in terms of honor and prestige, by some in Corinth.

Paul likewise describes himself as a figure lacking honor and prestige in 1 Cor 4:9: "For it seems to me that God has displayed us apostles last, as people sentenced to death, because we have become a spectacle to the world, both to angels and to humans." Henry Nguyen has convincingly located the cultural context of this passage in the Roman amphitheater, where condemned criminals (*noxii*), whose "fate involved some form of humiliating and aggravated death: by the sword [*ad gladium*], thrown to wild beasts [*ad bestias*], crucifixion, or being burnt alive [*ad flammas* or *crematio*]."[45] As their deaths were often displayed in public forums, the bodies of the condemned functioned as "spectacles," serving both to entertain the body politic and (paradoxically, to twenty-first-century sentiments) to preserve the "moral order" by displaying the swift and ineluctable outcome of transgressing publicly sanctioned norms.[46] Nguyen also draws attention to the *infamia* ("ill repute") associated with "subjecting [one's body] before the gaze of others."[47]

Similarly, when he catalogs a long list of infamies in 2 Cor 11:23–33, he portrays himself as someone who is accorded a low status on the basis of prevailing social standards. In a lengthy *synkrisis,* or comparison between himself and other traveling evangelists in Corinth,[48] he writes:

> Are they ministers of Christ? I am talking like a fool—I am a better one: with far greater labors, far more imprisonments, with countless floggings, and often near death. Five times I have received from Jews [or "Judeans"] the forty lashes minus one. Three times I was beaten with rods. Once I received a stoning. Three times I was shipwrecked; for a night and a day I was adrift at sea; on frequent journeys, in danger from rivers, danger from bandits, danger from my own people, danger from people of the nations, danger in the city, danger in the wilderness, danger at sea, danger from false brothers and sisters; in toil and hardship, through many a sleepless night, hungry and thirsty, often without food, cold and naked. And, besides other things, I am under daily pressure because of my anxiety for all the churches. Who is weak, and I am not weak? Who is made to stumble, and I am not indignant?
>
> If I must boast, I will boast of the things that show my weakness. The God and Father of the Lord Jesus (blessed be he forever!) knows that I do not lie. In Damascus, the governor under King Aretas guarded the city of Damascus in order to seize me, but I was let down in a basket through a window in the wall, and escaped from his hands. (NRSV, modified)

The passage reads as a perverse encomium, consisting not of praiseworthy deeds, but of situations of shameful treatment (imprisonment, flogging, beatings with rods, stonings) and humiliating misfortunes (being shipwrecked, suffering hunger and thirst, being underclothed).[49] Paul boasts,[50] not of experiences that signal his "strength," or sociopolitical efficacy and influence, but the opposite: his "weakness," or sociopolitical inefficacy.[51]

The passage continues as Paul recounts an episode in which he was secretly lowered in a basket to the bottom of the city wall of Damascus in order to avoid capture by the local ethnarch under the Nabataean monarch Aretas IV (2 Cor 11:32–33).[52] Edwin Judge has argued that the passage should be read as an inversion of the noble achievement, accompanied by glory and renown, of being the first to scale the city wall during a siege.[53] Paul flaunts experiences by which he ought to have been accorded shame and disrespect according to prevalent evaluative criteria.

Inversions of Criteria for the Allocation of Prestige

Paul, however, was not content to let evaluations by which he was accorded shame and disrespect stand as authoritative accounts of his worth. He crafted discourses in which he suggested that those who would unfavorably judge him ought to invert their evaluative criteria. Such an inversion occurs in 1 Cor 1:20–25, where he distinguishes the "wisdom of the world" from the "wisdom of God"; the two types of "wisdom" entail diametrically opposed standards for the assignation of honor and prestige:

> Where is the wise person? Where is the scribe? Where is the debater of this age? Hasn't God made the wisdom of the world foolish? Since in the wisdom of God, the world did not know God through wisdom, God saw fit to save those who are faithful through the foolishness of our proclamation, and since Judeans ask for signs, and Greeks seek wisdom, but we proclaim Christ crucified, a scandal to Judeans, and foolishness to the people of the nations—but to those who are called, both Jews and Greeks, it is Christ, the power of God and the wisdom of God, because the foolishness of God is wiser than human wisdom and the weakness of God is stronger than human strength.

In Paul's view, God is not apprehended through "human wisdom." The "wisdom of God," which subverts (or "makes foolish") human wisdom, is manifested above all in the "foolishness" and "scandal" of Paul's proclamation of a crucified messiah. The scandalous character of this proclamation is indicated by a statement of the Roman senator and orator Cicero, who opined, "the very word 'cross' should be far removed not only from the person of a Roman citizen but from his thoughts, his eyes, and his ears.... The mere mention of such a thing is shameful to a Roman citizen and a free man."[54] But for those who are being saved, Paul writes, such proclamation represents "the power of God and the wisdom of God." Proclamation concerning a crucified man, viewed from the perspective of the "wisdom of the world," is both shameful and scandalous, but viewed from the opposed perspective of the "wisdom of God," it is the "power of God," mediating salvation from apocalyptic judgment to those faithful to its message.

The passage implies the need to invert typical evaluative schemes in two respects. First, the honor and prestige that were associated with powerful oratory and its concomitant, elite education, are reevaluated. Instead of elevating the "wise person" and "debater" in status, Paul asks rhetorically "Where is the wise person?" (i.e., of what value is he?) and suggests that "God made the wisdom of the world foolish." Elite education, entailing training in the art of declamation[55] and, in some cases, instruction in philosophical traditions,[56] is devalued: "the world did not know God through wisdom." Paul suggests an inversion of schemes in which rhetorical skill, education, and philosophical reasoning are highly valued: God has "made the wisdom of the world foolish."

Paul's inversion of the criteria for determining what constitutes "wisdom" is nuanced and elaborated in a discussion of the qualities associated with "strength" and "weakness." Greco-Roman literature typically indicated that it was the wealthy, educated, and politically connected who constituted the "strong" of society; the poor, the uneducated, and those lacking any political office constituted the "weak."[57] Paul indicates that he approached the Corinthians "in weakness and fear, and with much trembling" (1 Cor 2:3). He mixes irony with a sober assessment of his lack of honor among some Corinthians when he writes: "We are fools for the sake of Christ, but you are wise in Christ. We are weak, but you are strong. You are held in honor, but we in disrepute" (1 Cor 4:10). Depicting himself as socially "weak," Paul seeks, "like a Greek politician of old, to 'bring the *dēmos* into his faction,'"[58] by portraying the majority of the Corinthian community in similar terms:

> Consider your calling, brothers and sisters: not many of you are wise according to human standards, not many are powerful, not many are high-born. But God selected what is foolish in the world in order to put the wise to shame; God chose what is weak in the world in order to put the strong to shame; God chose what is low-born and despised in the world—the "nobodies"—in order to reduce the "somebodies" to nothing,[59] so that no one might boast in the presence of God. (1 Cor 1:26–29)

He suggests an inversion of criteria used to assign honor and prestige: the socially "weak," generally denied honor, are those whom God has "selected" or "chosen" to be honored more highly: "God selected what is foolish in the world in order to put the wise to shame; God chose what is weak in the world in order to put the strong to shame." The standard criteria for assigning honor are inverted.[60]

The Gifts of the Spirit and Shifting Evaluative Criteria: Internal/External, Weakness/Strength

Paul's reversals entail shifts in the criteria used to apportion honor. He suggests that the "gift of the spirit" carries the potential to effect a perceptual shift in the minds of its recipients. This perceptual shift entails a rejection of standard criteria for the allocation of prestige based on the world's "wisdom" (i.e., philosophy) and eloquent public speech, and an adoption of criteria based on access to revealed wisdom. Two types of "wisdom" are distinguished, that "of God" and that "of the world" or "of this age." Paul elaborates on the two types of "wisdom" in 1 Cor 2:6–9, where he states:

> But we do speak wisdom among the initiated, albeit a wisdom not of this age nor of the leaders of this age, who are doomed to perish, but we speak God's wisdom, hidden away in mystery, which God designated before the ages for our glory. . . . But as it is written: "Things that no eye has seen, nor ear heard, and have not occurred to the heart of humans; these things God has prepared for those who love him."

Paul employs the language of mystery initiation, such as would be familiar to his Corinthian audience.[61] The "initiated" were those who had undergone a ceremony, often nocturnal, in which a sacred drama was enacted for the initiates, whose perceptions and present state of being were purportedly transformed as the result of the experience.[62] Through their participation in the drama, they came to identify themselves more closely with a particular god or goddess. After the ritual, initiates were forbidden to reveal to "outsiders" what they had seen. Paul's presentation, however, is inflected by motifs from Jewish apocalypticism, where "mystery" may refer to secret knowledge about the apocalyptic judgment (cp. 1QpHab VII.5, 8, 14) or the suprahuman, immortal existence that was expected to become available following it (cp. 1QS IV.6–7; XI.3–9a). Paul's apocalyptic wisdom was of a type "not of this age nor of the leaders of this age, who are doomed to perish," but "God's wisdom, hidden away in mystery," which "no eye has seen, nor ear heard."

Knowledge of God's inaccessible wisdom could be granted only through divine revelation, as Paul opines in 1 Cor 2:10–13:

> God has revealed to us through the spirit, for the spirit searches all things—even the deep things of God. For who knows more about a person than the spirit that is in him? Likewise, no one knows more about God [literally, "the things of God"] than the spirit of God. And we have received [*elabomen*], not the spirit of the world, but the spirit which is from God, so that we might recognize the things bestowed on us [*charisthenta hēmin*]

by God, and what we speak is not in words taught by human wisdom, but in words taught by the spirit, judging spiritual matters on the basis of spiritual criteria.

Paul reasons that a person's "spirit" has unmediated access to information about that person and, by analogy, God's spirit has unmediated access to information about God. Those who have "received" the "spirit of God" are capable of understanding things about God that are not accessible to human beings generally.

The "spirit" is portrayed as a gift: it can be "received" only from God. Paul frequently speaks of the spirit as a gift: it is "given" (Rom 5:5; 2 Cor 1:22; 5:5), "supplied" (Gal 3:5), or "sent" (Gal 4:6) by God (1 Cor 6:19) and "received" by humans (Rom 8:15; 2 Cor 11:4; Gal 3:2). The gift of the spirit enables humans to perceive "the things of God"—including the "deep things of God" mentioned in 1 Cor 2:10 and the "mysteries of God" in 1 Cor 4:1 (cp. 1 Cor 15:51). Similar knowledge of things divine is not available to those who have received only the "spirit" of the world: "in the wisdom of God, the world did not know God through [merely human] wisdom" (1 Cor 1:21).

The "gift" of the spirit, in Paul's view, bears important implications for the evaluative schemes that one might bring to bear in assessments of status:

> But the unspiritual person [*psychikos anthrōpos*] does not receive the things of the spirit of God, for they are foolishness to him and he is not able to understand them, because they are judged spiritually. The spiritual person judges everything, but himself is judged by no one. For "who has known the mind of the Lord, in order to instruct him"? But we have the mind of Christ. (1 Cor 2:14–16)

The "unspiritual person" is unable to understand "the things of the spirit of God, for they are foolishness to him." Conversely, "the spiritual person judges everything"—a panoptic vision permits judgment by one who is not susceptible to being judged.[63] The "spiritual person," in Paul's view, possesses nothing less than "the mind of Christ."

Aware that he has been the subject of negative evaluations in Corinth, Paul addresses the competence of those who would "judge" him. In 1 Cor 4:3-4, he writes: "It is insignificant to me, that I might be judged by you or by any human court—but I do not even judge myself. I am not aware of any strikes against me, but I am not thereby acquitted, for the Lord is the one who judges me." He likens the judgment of his Corinthian detractors to that of a "human court." According to the criteria he outlines in 1 Cor 2:14–16, however, merely human judgments hold no weight. Lacking the perceptual capacities endowed by the spirit and lacking too "the mind of Christ," who stands as the prototypically competent judge ("the Lord is the one who judges me"), merely human tribunals are incompetent to evaluate "spiritual persons" such as Paul: "the spiritual person judges everything, but himself is judged by no one."

It is such "unspiritual" judges, Paul implies, who attribute to him the sociopolitical "weakness" associated with his poverty, manual labor, and poor speaking skills and who believe, falsely, that "strength" is associated with wealth, wisdom, and eloquence. Such incompetent judges fail to recognize the reversal that Israel's god has effected: "God chose what is low-born and despised in the world—the 'nobodies'—in order to reduce the 'somebodies' to nothing, so that no one might boast in the presence of God" (1 Cor 1:28).

The series of inversions that Paul suggests in 1 Cor 1–4 subordinate the "wisdom of the world" to that of God, sociopolitical "strength" to sociopolitical "weakness," impressive oratorical skills (cp. "the debater of this age") to Paul's "foolish" preaching, the high-born who are associated with inherited wealth to the low-born who live in poverty, politically connected "somebodies" to politically powerless "nobodies." Under the terms of the inverted honor system that Paul suggests, the foolish "put to shame" the world's wise, the weak "put to shame" the strong, and the nobodies "reduce the somebodies to nothing."[64]

Moreover, Paul attempts to add legitimacy to the inverted honor system by identifying Israel's god as its source and origin: "God chose what is weak." Paul (mis)represents his proposed evaluative system as divine and transcendent in origin, thus attempting to place it beyond scrutiny or reproach.[65] Conversely, he delegitimizes the evaluative system utilized by his Corinthian detractors by situating its sources and origins firmly within "the world." The difference between the two systems, Paul implies, is analogous to that between heaven and earth, the divine and the (merely) human.

Paul is not content, however, simply to assert that Israel's god had inverted the standards for assigning prestige and honor. He suggests additional criteria that ought to be taken into account in allocations of honor. Rather than viewing him from "the world's" perspective, by which Paul appears as a poor, abused, and homeless vagrant, he suggests another way in which he might be viewed. He writes:

> Let a person consider us as Christ's attendants and stewards of God's mysteries. In this case, moreover, it is desirable that stewards be found trustworthy [or "faithful"]. But it is an insignificant thing to me, that I might be judged by you or by any human court—but I do not even judge myself. I am not aware of any strikes against me, but I am not thereby acquitted, for the Lord is the one who judges me. Therefore, let no one judge prematurely, before the Lord comes, who will shine light even on things hidden in darkness, and who will make known the counsels of hearts—only then will each person receive praise [or "recognition"] from God. (1 Cor 4:1–5)

Paul's invitation to "let a person consider us as Christ's attendants and stewards of God's mysteries" raises the issue of the evaluative standards by which Paul was being "judged" in Corinth. He suggests a paradigm for his detractors to consider, that of the "faithful" (or "trustworthy") servant. As Paul is an "attendant" of Christ, it is only Christ who is qualified to render judgment on him, his subordinate: "the Lord is the one who judges me."

Unlike Paul's detractors, who judge him on the basis of his "external" attributes, Christ judges on the basis of "internal" characteristics: he "will shine light even on things hidden in darkness, and . . . will make known the counsels of hearts." On the basis of Christ's evaluation, God himself will subsequently allocate praise (or "recognition"; 4:5) for "faithful" service. The possibility of divine "recognition" renders the merely "human" judgment of Paul's Corinthian detractors insignificant by comparison: "it is an insignificant thing to me, that I might be judged by you or by any human court."

Although Paul's description of himself as an "attendant" implies a subordinate position, and "stewards" in many cases were slaves or former slaves, nonetheless those positions are not devoid of honor: he is the attendant *of Christ* and steward *of the mysteries of God*. As Thomas Schmeller notes, some of the prestige of patrons (or, we may add, masters) "rubs off" onto their subordinates.[66] And Paul's superiors bask in glory: the god of Israel, as the preeminent power in the cosmos (Rom 1:20), and Christ, as his second in command (1 Cor 15:24–28), through whom apocalyptic judgment will be meted out (Rom 2:16; 2 Cor 5:10). "Glory," in the sense of honor and prestige, characterizes both Israel's god (e.g., Rom 3:23; 4:20; 5:2; 11:36) and Christ, whom Paul describes as the "lord of glory" (1 Cor 2:8). Israel's god can confer glory upon his human subordinates (Rom 9:23; 1 Cor 2:7; 2 Cor 4:17), provided they "patiently do good" (Rom 2:7, 10) or offer "faithful" service to God (cp. 1 Cor 9:24; 2 Cor 6:4; Phil 3:14).

In Paul's view, Israel's god accords glory (i.e., honor and prestige) according to criteria other than those typically used by human beings. Factors such as lack of wealth or of rhetorical prowess, which would lead to negative evaluations according to the "wisdom of the world," run counter to the criteria used by Israel's god. Distinguishing internal and external factors, Paul asserts that Christ, the agent of God's judgment, assesses the inner human being, examining "things now hidden in darkness" and "the purposes of the heart." Humans, in contrast, are consigned to judge by external appearances, such as Paul's apparent lack of wealth and his amateurish declamatory style.[67]

The negative evaluations of Paul's honor by some members of the Corinthian assembly, however, do not seem to have been ameliorated by the arguments that Paul presented in 1 Corinthians. On the contrary, the fact that he revisits many of the same issues with intensified sarcasm and irony in the later letters now known collectively as 2 Corinthians suggests that his arguments may have served only to embolden his critics. Salient among these developments are Paul's comments in 2 Cor 4:7–18 and 12:9–10.[68]

In a perverse encomium similar to that in 1 Cor 4:10b–13, Paul lists characteristics by which he would be accorded scant honor on the basis of the evaluative standards of "the world" (i.e., those likely utilized by his detractors). But he adds an important element not present in his earlier catalog of hardships. Developing the external/internal dichotomy, he suggests that the internal should be accorded greater weight than the external in allocations of honor and likens his own external afflictions to the suffering of Jesus:

> But we have this treasure in clay jars, so that it may be made clear that this extraordinary power belongs to God and does not come from us. We are afflicted in every way, but not crushed; perplexed, but not driven to despair; persecuted, but not forsaken; struck down, but not destroyed; always carrying in the body the death of Jesus, so that the life of Jesus may also be made visible in our bodies. . . . So we do not lose heart. Even though our outer nature is wasting away, our inner nature is being renewed day by day. For this slight momentary affliction is preparing us for an eternal weight of glory beyond all measure, because we look not at what can be seen but at what cannot be seen; for what can be seen is temporary, but what cannot be seen is eternal. . . . We are not commending ourselves to you again, but giving you an opportunity to boast about us, so that you may be able to answer those who boast in outward appearance and not in the heart. (2 Cor 4:7–10, 16–18; 5:12 NRSV)

Paul likens the human being to a clay jar; the "outer nature" is subject to decay (cp. "wasting away"), while the "inner human being"—provided one possesses the gift of God's spirit (2 Cor 3:17-18)—is "being renewed day by day."[69] The afflictions, perplexity, persecution, and experience of being "struck down" echo his list of ignominious experiences in 1 Cor 4:10-13. But, Paul suggests, to contemplate his dishonor is only to apprehend the "outer nature"; his "inner human being," in contrast, is being prepared "for an eternal weight of glory beyond all measure, because we look not at what can be seen but at what cannot be seen." The "eternal weight of glory" for which Paul asserts that both he and his auditors are "being prepared" plays on the dual connotations of "glory," which refers both to honor and prestige and to the luminescence characteristic of supernatural beings—a luminescence that he assumes will characterize God's elect in the postapocalyptic, heavenly kingdom no less than it does the "glorious body" of the risen Christ (1 Cor 15:35-57). The "glory" for which Paul's "inner human being" is being prepared is the counterpoint to the ignominious appearance of his "outer nature."

The inner/outer dichotomy enables Paul strategically to draw an analogy between himself and Jesus. Paul's "outer nature," which he declares is "wasting away," as evidenced by his afflictions, perplexity, and persecution, recapitulates the suffering of Jesus: he is "always carrying in [his] body the death [literally, "the process of dying"] of Jesus." The external "process of dying" conceals the power and glory of God at work within both Jesus and Paul. In 2 Cor 13:4, he writes, "For indeed, he [Jesus] was crucified in weakness, but he lives by the power of God." Paul claims a "power" analogous (albeit subordinate) to that of Jesus: he asserts that his implausible proclamation demonstrates the "spirit and power" of God (1 Cor 2:4)[70] and that, even when absent bodily, his own "spirit" is present, mediating the "power" of Jesus during meetings of the Corinthian assembly (1 Cor 5:4). The "good news" that Paul preaches carries the "power of God for salvation" (Rom 1:16); he claims to have exhibited the "power of signs and wonders" in his itinerant mission (Rom 15:19).

The attribution of "weakness" to Jesus in his crucifixion, Paul suggests, rests on a misperception. Earlier, in 1 Cor 2:7-8, he had noted that "we speak God's wisdom, hidden away in mystery, which God designated before the ages for our glory—a wisdom which none of the leaders of this age recognized. For if they had recognized it, they would not have crucified the lord of glory." The "leaders of the age" failed to "recognize" the "wisdom of God," to wit, that Jesus was the agent through which the apocalyptic judgment would be carried out (2 Cor 5:10) and that all beings would eventually be subjected to him (1 Cor 15:24–27). He whom the "leaders of this age" misperceived as "weak" was actually the "lord of glory" to whom "every knee will bow" (Phil 2:9–11) at the time of the apocalyptic judgment.

The implications of the parallel that Paul draws between himself and Jesus are clear: just as Jesus should not have been judged on the basis of his apparent "weakness" in being subjected to crucifixion, neither should Paul be judged on the basis of his apparent lack of wealth, his homelessness, or his amateurish declamatory skills. Instead, he should be evaluated on the basis of the "glory" that was manifested in his "inner human being." In 2 Cor 3:18 he opines: "And we all, with unveiled face, perceive as in a mirror the glory of the lord, while we are transformed by successive stages of glory into the same image, just as from the spirit of the lord." The "inner human being" of those who have received the "gift of the spirit" is "transformed by successive stages of glory" into the luminous image of the risen Jesus (cp. 1 Cor 15:35–57). Paul's external image was characterized, in the eyes of his detractors, by "weakness" and ignominy, but his "inner human being" was undergoing a process of transformation into the image of Christ, the "lord of glory." Although Paul's "outer nature" manifested the "death" of Jesus, his "inner human being" mirrored the glory of the risen Christ.

Just as Paul developed and further nuanced in 2 Corinthians the external/internal dichotomy introduced in 1 Corinthians, he likewise developed the weakness/strength dichotomy. He develops the theme by connecting it with the language of benefaction. In 2 Cor 12:9–10, he reports a divine response to prayer in which God answers,

> "My favor [*charis*] is enough for you, for [divine] power is perfected in [human] weakness." Thus, I will instead gladly boast

of my weaknesses, so that the power of Christ may dwell in me. Therefore I revel in my weaknesses, when I am treated with insolence, in my calamities, when I am persecuted and in distress for Christ's sake: for when I am weak, then I am strong.

In Paul's view, divine power is "perfected" in human weakness. The implication, which Paul makes explicit, is that the very situations that result in his loss of social honor (insolent treatment, calamity, persecution) are those in which divine "power" is the most effectively present.

The paradox entailed in the notion of "strength in weakness," however, is only apparent: two sets of evaluative criteria are at work in the formulation. The "weakness" attributed to both Paul and Jesus characterizes the faulty perception of "the world"; those who hold to such modes of vision, which apprehends only the "external nature" of the human being, are "doomed to perish." Conversely, those whose perceptions have been transformed as the result of the "gift of the spirit" are capable of apprehending the "inner human being," whose glory recapitulates that of Christ, the "lord of glory." People capable of perceiving the "treasure in clay jars" exhibit the perceptual apparatus of "those who are being saved"; they have "the mind of Christ." The two evaluative paradigms are not accorded equal legitimacy. The former constitutes a type of self-deception (cp. 1 Cor 3:18); the latter constitutes the perspective of transcendent beings: Israel's god, Christ, and the "spirit."

Through the skillful exploitation of dichotomies involving the external and internal, weakness and strength, Paul is able to suggest evaluative criteria for the allocation of honor and prestige that privilege the characteristics with which he was most closely associated in Corinth: lack of wealth, the performance of manual labor, physical abuse, itinerancy and homelessness, and apparent lack of skill in the art of declamation. Such marks of "weakness," Paul proclaims, are the very ones that signal divine "power" at work within his "inner human being." Moreover, by attributing to transcendent beings—God, Christ, and the spirit—the evaluative criteria that privileged characteristics that he appeared to possess, he effectively claims a more-than-human authority for his views.

Some evidence suggests that Paul's rhetoric was effective in causing his detractors to abandon their perception of him as characterized by shame and dishonor. The "letter of reconciliation" in 2 Cor 1:1–2:13; 7:5–16, which many scholars take to be an originally independent letter stitched together with others to form canonical 2 Corinthians, indicates a period of détente between Paul and his detractors.[71] This thawing of frosty relations likely persisted at least until 56–57 CE, when he wrote his letter to the Romans as a guest in the house of Gaius (Rom 16:23). However, in the realm of sociopolitical interaction, structure rarely triumphs fully over process: evaluations of Paul may have continued to occasion contest and disagreement, in the first century no less than in the twenty-first.

Summary and Conclusions

Paul consistently opposed the "standard" patronal paradigm that assigned relative rank in patron-client relationships on the basis of access to material wealth. In its place, he proposed an evaluative system in which spiritual rather than material resources constituted the more highly valued assets. A corollary of this evaluative system, both intersecting with and reinforcing it, was Paul's scheme of hierarchical ranking in which apostles were construed as "first" in the assemblies. Paul consistently promotes an organization within the assemblies that recognizes apostles as having the preeminent rank and authority among evident participants. Peter Lampe's conclusion regarding patronage within the assemblies bears consideration: "To summarize, in early Pauline Christianity, there were no clear-cut and rock solid static vertical relationships. Things were more dynamic."[72] The situation that Lampe describes is one of heterarchy: there certainly existed "the possibility of elements being ranked in multiple ways." However, we should note that in every case recorded in Paul's epistles, he actively resisted any implication that he, as an apostle, should accept a status subordinate to that of patrons or patronesses. On the contrary, there is every indication that he actively promoted an inversion of the "standard" patronal model. As he saw it, apostles should be ranked "first." Paul was therefore an active agent both in exploiting and in suppressing the "dynamic" possibilities of heterarchy. He promoted a stable—and self-serving—model of sociopolitical relations, with apostles at the top of the hierarchy. Paul's formulations were inflected by his own sociopolitical interests.

The discussion of the heterarchic possibilities endemic to early Christianity provides a vantage point from which Wayne Meeks's notions of status inconsistency may be clarified and extended. When describing the "multidimensional phenomenon" of status, it is not sufficient simply to "attempt to measure their rank along each of the relevant dimensions," as if such measurements and rankings might yield fixed and stable results. Rather, we see in Paul's letters an intense contest and negotiation in which various parties attempted to promote evaluative systems based on the sorts of assets that each typically had at its disposal: the wealthy proposed systems of rank based on wealth; the evangelist proposed a system based on the "spiritual gift" of apostolic status. Each party attempted "to set the specific capital, to which it owed its position, at the top of the hierarchy of the principles of hierarchization."[73] The "multidimensional phenomenon" of status inconsistency was not simply the result of a number of "measurements" of fixed values, but a field in which both the systems of ranking and the values to be assigned constituted the subject of conflict, contest, and negotiation. Before we can attempt to "measure their rank," we must carefully attend to the processes by which systems for the evaluation and assignation of rank were negotiated and contested.

Similarly, the evaluative systems involved in communal assessments of the honor and prestige of members were subject to negotiation and contest. Even while Paul prominently displayed himself as an individual lacking honor in the Corinthian correspondence, he actively sought to undermine the evaluative criteria by which he was assigned scant honor. In their place, he proposed a system in which the weak of the world—as he himself appeared to be—were accorded higher honors than the world's "strong," or sociopolitically dominant. Paralleling and nuancing the weak/strong dichotomy, Paul proposed that evaluations based on external appearances (e.g., wealth, oratorical skill) were inadequate, misleading, and merely "human," whereas those based on knowledge of the "inner human being" were adequate, legitimate, and divine.

In Paul's formulations, the notion of the gift plays an important role. The inversions of positional status in which wealthier patrons were subordinated to less wealthy apostolic figures such as Paul were based on three factors: (1) his claim to have received the "gift" of his status as an apostle; (2) his claim to mediate gifts from Israel's god; and (3) the valuation of claimed spiritual resources more highly than material ones. The inversions of accorded status (i.e., honor and prestige) were likewise based on several factors: (1) the claim that the "gift of the spirit" facilitated an enhancement of evaluative capacities enabling its recipients to perceive supernatural qualities otherwise unrecognized; (2) the association of the "spirit" with divine "power" and "glory" not available to merely human agents devoid of the spirit; and (3) a valuation system that privileges claimed "divine" or "supernatural" characteristics over those characterized as merely "human."

The data in Paul's letters indicate that discourses of gift exchange provide linguistic resources of potential value for the orchestration of sociopolitical relations through the strategic manipulation of claims to mediate or possess gifts ostensibly transmitted by supernatural agents. When combined with the postulate that "spiritual" resources are more valuable than material ones, discourses of gift exchange provide "religious" agents with a means of access to enhanced social rank and prestige that rivals, and in some cases exceeds, that provided by material wealth. Theories of gift exchange thus do well to attend closely to the inversions of social rank and prestige made possible when "the gift" and "religion" intersect.

EIGHT

Summary and Conclusions

Recapitulation

This book has attempted to delineate some of the material implications of "spiritual," or religious, discourse in the letters of Paul of Tarsus. The opening chapter addressed two fundamental issues that constitute a prolegomenon to that which follows. First, the notion of the "free gift," common in Christian theological constructions, indicates that the gift is not transmitted under the conditions of mercantile exchange, but does not imply that it bears no reciprocal obligations. As a "catalyst and an outward sign of elective affinities,"[1] the "free gift" is laden with the obligation of reciprocal interaction: to offer one's time, one's goods, and one's services for the construction and maintenance of ongoing social relations. The refusal of reciprocity is tantamount to a rejection of the social relation of which the gift is an "outward sign." Second, it is noted that the "irreducible heterogeneity" of human exchanges and the roles of agents in classifying those transactions disallow any unproblematic definition of "gift." Nevertheless, some typical characteristics are identified for their heuristic value in distinguishing gifts from other types of exchange. Finally, a brief summary of each of the book's chapters is offered.

On the basis of the principle that the "spiritual" and the material stand in a relation of exchangeability within an economy of symbolic goods, Paul developed notions concerning reciprocal transaction such as were common in his Roman context and modified them in the service of his own agenda, namely, that of preaching his version of the "gospel" throughout the northern Mediterranean region, as argued in chapter 2. Portraying himself in the role of broker or mediator of spiritual gifts, some of which are made available on the basis of a positive response to his evangelistic proclamation, he utilizes the discourse of the gift to motivate the exchange of goods and services within early Christian communities. These were at times directed toward Paul, in the form of a slave's occasional service, monetary donations to cover living and travel expenses, or food and clothing during his stays in prison. In the case of his collection of funds to be contributed to the early Christian assembly in Jerusalem, monetary goods were transmitted in interassembly exchanges. In each case, the notion that Israel's god had first provided gifts of various sorts was instrumental in motivating agents to offer their own currency, goods, or services, which were construed in the role of countergifts for God's benefactions.

Chapter 3 considers Paul's (strategic) faux pas of calling attention to a gift given. This contrasts with the advice of Seneca the Younger, who admonishes his addressee(s) never to do so, as it humiliates the donee. Both Seneca's "virtuous" advice and Paul's "shameful" breach of etiquette are explicable as strategies to maximize their access to valued goods and services—whether honor, in the case of Seneca, or the services of a wealthier man's slave, in the case of Paul. The contrasting strategies of the two are inflected by their diametrically opposed economic situations.

In chapters 4 and 5, a close examination of the terms used to characterize unremunerated evangelistic labor indicates the futility of searching for "objective" criteria by which to classify that endeavor. Did Paul's performance of manual labor to support himself render his evangelistic work in Corinth, which he was able subsequently to offer "free of charge," a gift? Was his receipt of ostensible gifts from Macedonian assemblies to be classified as an act of "theft," performed for the benefit of the Corinthians? Was the acceptance of hospitality from wealthier patronal figures in Corinth to be classified as an act of "parasitism," as his caricature of one such figure suggests? The versatility that Paul exhibits in his classification of particular exchanges, his apparent use of categories to activate differential social responses (i.e., friendship or hostility), and his ability to adjust his classificatory schemes over time strongly suggest that exchanges are defined not solely on the basis of their "objective" characteristics, but are subject to a "politics of classification" whereby agents characterize transactions in the terms that best suit their sociopolitical interests.

Chapter 6 distinguishes two types of status: positional status, which refers to roles or positions within a sociopolitical system, each with its distinct duties, responsibilities, and privileges; and accorded status, which refers to honor and prestige. Whereas in the political system of the Roman empire positional status was often granted as a patronal donation by highly placed figures—Pliny's letters to Trajan offer numerous examples—in Paul's view, it was granted by the god of Israel. Paul asserts that his own status as an "apostle" is a "gift" from God. Moreover, in an attempt to naturalize his position of authority, he argues that apostles are granted a place of preeminence within the hierarchical organization of the early Christian assemblies.

Paul's attempts to orchestrate an inversion of the criteria utilized in the allocation of honor and prestige within the assembly in Corinth are addressed in chapter 7. In opposition to an evaluative scheme in which prestige was positively correlated with wealth and its concomitant, elite education as evidenced by skill in philosophical reasoning and public declamation—a scheme by which Paul, an apparently poor, homeless, and ineloquent craftsman, was accorded scant honor—he strategically deployed the notion that the "gift of the spirit" was at work within his "inner human being," transforming him into the glorious image of the risen Jesus. He posits that, to the extent that his "outer" person, lacking signs of honor and prestige, manifests the "death" of Jesus, the "life" of Jesus—his divine power and glory—was being made manifest within his "inner person." Paul's rhetoric implies a desire to be evaluated on the basis of the inner characteristics that he claimed rather than the external characteristics that were evident to his detractors. On the basis of the evaluative scheme that he proposed, the external signs by which Paul was accorded low honor and prestige were recoded as indicia of the considerable honor and prestige that accrued by association with the glorified body of Jesus of Nazareth, construed as a heavenly being.

Chapter 7 also argued that the aspects of process, contest, and change highlighted by Carole Crumley's notion of heterarchy are on display in

Paul's attempts to invert the evaluative criteria employed by his Corinthian detractors. Attending to processual aspects facilitates the development and elaboration of Wayne Meeks's notion of status inconsistency. One's status is more than a "composite of [one's] ranks in all of the relevant dimensions," as Meeks argued. Both positional and accorded status are subject to contestation and negotiation as various interested parties promote evaluative systems privileging the assets that each typically has at its disposal. Paul instrumentalizes discourses of gift exchange in contests over the definition and assessment of both his positional and his accorded status.

Additional Reflections

Although in some cases, Paul deploys the logic of the classic formulation *do ut des,* "I give so that you might give," more often he operates on the basis of a different logic: *do quia dedisti,* "I give because you have given." In the latter formulation, the temporal framing of the gift associated with the second person ("you") is shifted from that of posteriority ("I give *so that you might give*") to that of anteriority ("I give *because you have given*"). In Paul's economy of symbolic goods, it is preeminently God's gift of his son and Jesus' sacrificial gift of himself in a death by crucifixion that hold priority in the "circle" of gift exchange. The faithful give because the heavenly Father and Son, both singly and collectively, "have given."

The placement of emphasis on what is construed as the prior gift of God undoubtedly arises from the historical datum that Jesus' death by crucifixion, understood as God's gift par excellence, preceded Paul's proclamation of the crucified Messiah. Paul's emphasis on the temporal priority of the "gifts of God" bears significant implications for his economy of symbolic goods, inasmuch as it places those regarded as recipients of such gifts in the role of debtor: "you have given, therefore I should give." Considerable amounts of labor services, currency, and material goods have been transmitted, from the first century until the present day, in accordance with the logic of this symbolic economy. Unlike gift economies operating in the "secular" sphere of interpersonal relationships, which may function according to a logic of "alternating disequilibrium"[2] in which each gift and countergift respectively burdens the recipient with a perception of gift-debt, in Paul's economy equilibrium is never achieved: the human donor of countergifts in various forms can never attain parity with, nor supersede in magnitude, the gifts of the heavenly Father and Son. Agents acting within the constraints of this economy of symbolic goods may play the role of grateful recipients of heavenly gifts, responding in gratitude with gifts of their own: their lives, their service, their goods and currency. Conversely, agents may construe themselves as operating under a situation of oppressive debt, bearing in the cross of Jesus a burden that they do not have the power to remove. The former perception may engender renewed acts of service and sentiments of gratitude, whereas the latter may prompt resentment and attempts to escape the symbolic economy that generates such affects.

As the "gifts of God" cannot be reciprocated directly to their putative donors, God and/or Christ, except through "offerings" of thanksgiving and praise, material donations of labor, goods, and currency are frequently transmitted to an individual or organization claiming to function as a proxy for those divine agents. Paul himself served in that role, as today do ecclesiastical organizations and their functionaries.

Utilizing the principle of generalized reciprocity (as understood by Claude Lévi-Strauss), now popularly indicated by the phrase "paying it forward," agents might escape the circular and apparently self-serving character of the religious economy of symbolic goods by transmitting material items, foodstuffs, currency, and services outside the confines of the religious institution in acts of "charity." Such acts of generalized reciprocity may result, however, in differential effects on the continued viability of the institution: either ruining it by diverting the resources that might otherwise contribute to its maintenance, or augmenting it through the accumulation of agents who, having received goods and services mediated through it, respond by offering donations and labor services of their own on behalf of the religious organization. As Seneca already noted, all gifts assume the element of risk that characterizes investments: they may or may not be acknowledged or reciprocated.

Critical analyses of symbolic economies in which religious agents claim to mediate the "gifts of God" through their proclamation and practices need assume neither cynical manipulation nor dissimulation on the part of agents, who are likely socialized to accept the logic of the symbolic economy that they themselves are instrumental in perpetuating.

Paul's Letters and the Multidisciplinary Academy

When examined within the context of a comparative program, the letters of Paul are of considerable value to classical studies, in that they indicate strategies both for the accumulation of honor and prestige and for the securing of a positional status of some importance and authority—even if on the small scale of various early Christian assemblies—by one who identified with a colonized group (Judeans/Jews) within the Roman empire. Apparently lacking both wealth and political connections, Paul creatively modified discourses and practices of gift exchange—positioning himself as a mediator of gifts from Israel's god—in order to craft a position of influence and significance, albeit limited in scale. His letters thus serve as a counterpoint to the perspectives of the elite, wealthy, and politically connected authors whose writings constitute the majority of our sources for Roman social history.

Paul's letters are of significance to religious studies in that they demonstrate the importance of discourses and practices of gift exchange for the construction of authority: he claimed that his role as an authoritative apostle was granted as a gift of Israel's god. Similarly, claims to knowledge concerning a posited transcendent realm, and insight into the thoughts, desires, and intentions of the beings purported to inhabit that realm, may be couched in the terminology of gift-giving. Construing the "spirit" as a gift, Paul writes, "the spirit searches all things—even the deep things of God." The deployment of the language of gift-giving may hold an advantage over other modes of constructing religious authority, inasmuch as they imply that (1) the recipient stands in the goodwill and favor of the divine being or beings construed as having given such gifts, and (2) the recipient has been honored through the bestowal of a highly valued donation by a divine agent. Constructions of religious authority involving "gifts of the gods" draw on a rich set of associations involving honor, status, and the perception of divine favor. Implied in the gift itself, such associations need not be stated outright.

Moreover, Paul's preference for the *do quia dedisti* ("I give because you have given") paradigm rather than the standard *do ut des* ("I give so that you might give") pattern indicates the necessity of paying close attention to the temporal sequencing of gifts and countergifts posited within religious economies of symbolic goods. When gifts of a transcendent sort (e.g., immortal life, a heavenly existence) are posited as having been transmitted to donees or as being contingent on a gift that has already been given, would-be recipients of such benefactions are placed into the position of perpetual debtors—a position that may be exploited by those who style themselves intermediaries between the human and the divine.

Anthropological and sociological studies since Marcel Mauss have charted in detail the mechanics of gift exchange. Although such studies advert to the role of religion in gift exchange,[3] there remain lessons to be learned from transactions of a highly symbolic character, that is, when one of the parties to the exchange or the posited gifts exist purely in symbolic form, in discourse and the imagination. The introduction of such imaginary entities into the cycle of exchange provides a means by which agents who lack material goods or political connections may attempt to gain honor, prestige, and enhanced positional status by claiming a role as mediators between humans and the divine. When paired with systems that evaluate "spiritual" gifts more highly than material ones, mediatorial figures may lay claim to countergifts in the form of valued goods and services from those cast in the role of recipient of the gifts of God.

Economies in which purely symbolic goods and agents are construed as operative may produce significant material effects, such as binding parties into social units and spurring the transmission of goods, currency, and labor services. Such "spiritual economies" are no less effective in facilitating material transmissions than economies in which all participants and goods are of evident material substance. Since the "goods" postulated to circulate within "spiritual economies" are nonevident, and are to be apprehended (it is claimed) only on the basis of faith, "belief," or hope, participants have no obvious means of evaluating their worth. As a result, the agents who promote such systems are in a position to evaluate most highly the "spiritual goods" that they claim circulate within the symbolic economy in which they take part. Paul's letters thus serve as vehicles for the refinement and elaboration of theories of gift exchange, contributing (inter alia) to discussions concerning the gift/sale dichotomy, the role of the "politics of classification" entailed in agents' labeling of transactions, and the functions of (purely) symbolic goods in "religious" exchanges.

Finally, Pauline studies benefit significantly from interaction with the data, theories, and methods utilized in classics, religious studies, anthropology, and sociology. Interaction with these data and methods facilitates the historical enterprise of describing with greater precision the ideas, discursive habits, and rhetorical strategies used in Paul's letters, and of imagining with greater clarity the practices and complex sociopolitical interactions that prevailed in the communities presupposed by them. More importantly, enhanced interaction with other disciplines is the prerequisite to surpassing the somewhat insular position that biblical studies has long occupied within the contemporary academy. The present study is offered in the hope that it may facilitate that process. When utilized as exemplars in the service of a broader project of comparison and rectification, Paul's letters may yet bequeath gifts to the academy, some twenty centuries after their initial reception in Corinth, Philippi, Colossae, and Rome.

Appendix: Letters and Events Significantly Shaping Paul's Relations with the Corinthian Assembly: A Relative Chronology

Letters and Events Significantly Shaping Paul's Relations with the Corinthian Assembly: A Relative Chronology

Events: Letters and Visits	Paul's first visit to Corinth (and Cenchreae).	First Corinthians written.	Paul's second visit to Corinth.	"Tearful letter" (2 Cor 10–13) written.	"Letter of reconciliation" (2 Cor 1:1–2:13; 7:5–16; 13:11–13).	Paul writes letter to the Romans from Corinth.
Description	Founds assembly and various house-churches in homes of Gaius, Stephanas, and Phoebe.	Addresses questions about Paul's mode of self-support. Paul asserts his "right" to receive hospitality but boasts that he does not "make use" of that right.	Breach in friendly relations between Paul and assembly. Paul accused of malfeasance in his collection for the Jerusalem assembly. He withdraws, humiliated.	Letter is delivered by Titus to Corinth.	Assembly responds by punishing Paul's accuser and by committing themselves to his authority. Titus reports the news; Paul responds with "letter of reconciliation."	Paul has by this point accepted the hospitality of Gaius, who functions as his "host" during the winter of 56–57 CE.
Classification of Exchange	Paul's missionary labor classified as "gift."		Paul's collection effort classified as "fraud."	Paul's missionary labor is classified as "gift." Failure to accept support justified by parent-child relationship and refusal to be a "burden." Philippian "gift" classed as "theft."	Paul reasserts "abundant love" for assembly.	Gaius and Paul function as host and guest in a relationship of hospitality.

Abbreviations

ABD	*Anchor Bible Dictionary.* Edited by David Noel Freedman. 6 vols. New York: Doubleday, 1992.
ANRW	*Aufstieg und Niedergang der römischen Welt: Geschichte und Kultur Roms im Spiegel der neueren Forschung.* Part 2, *Principat.* Edited by Hildegard Temporini and Wolfgang Haase. Berlin: de Gruyter, 1972- .
AYB	Anchor Yale Bible
BDAG	Danker, Frederick W., Walter Bauer, William F. Arndt, and F. Wilbur Gingrich. *Greek-English Lexicon of the New Testament and Other Early Christian Literature.* 3rd. ed. Chicago: University of Chicago Press, 2000 (Danker-Bauer-Arndt-Gingrich).
BETL	Bibliotheca Ephemeridum Theologicarum Lovaniensium
BZNW	Beihefte zur Zeitschrift für die neutestamentliche Wissenschaft
EDNT	*Exegetical Dictionary of the New Testament.* Edited by Horst Balz and Gerhard Schneider. ET. 3 vols. Grand Rapids: Eerdmans, 1900–1993.
EKK	Evangelisch-katholischer Kommentar zum Neuen Testament
ICC	International Critical Commentary
JBL	*Journal of Biblical Literature*
JGRChJ	*Journal of Greco-Roman Christianity and Judaism*
JRS	*Journal of Roman Studies*
JSNT	*Journal for the Study of the New Testament*
JSNTSup	Journal for the Study of the New Testament Supplement Series
L&S	Lewis, Charlton T., Charles Short, Ethan A. Andrews, and William Freund. *A Latin Dictionary: Founded on Andrew's Edition of Freund's Latin Dictionary.* Rev. ed. Oxford: Clarendon, 1962 (Lewis & Short).
LCL	Loeb Classical Library
LNTS	Library of New Testament Studies
LSJ	Liddell, Henry George, Robert Scott, and Henry Stuart Jones. *A Greek-English Lexicon.* 9th ed. with revised supplement. Oxford: Clarendon, 1996.
LXX	*Septuaginta.* Edited by Alfred Rahlfs. Stuttgart: Deutsche Bibelgesellschaft, 1979.

MM	Moulton, James H., and George Milligan. *The Vocabulary of the Greek Testament*. London, 1930. Repr., Peabody, MA: Hendrickson, 1997.
NA[28]	*Novum Testamentum Graece*. Edited by Barbara Aland, Kurt Aland, Johannes Karavidopoulos, Carlo M. Martini, Bruce M. Metzger, Eberhard Nestle, and Erwin Nestle. 28th rev. ed. Stuttgart: Deutsche Bibelgesellschaft, 2012 (Nestle-Aland).
NICNT	New International Commentary on the New Testament
NIGTC	New International Greek Testament Commentary
NovT	*Novum Testamentum*
NovTSup	Supplements to Novum Testamentum
NRSV	New Revised Standard Version
NTS	*New Testament Studies*
OCD	*Oxford Classical Dictionary*. Edited by Simon Hornblower and Anthony Spawforth. 4th ed. Oxford: Oxford University Press, 2012.
OLD	*Oxford Latin Dictionary*. Edited by P. G. W. Glare. 2nd ed. Oxford: Oxford University Press, 2012.
PNTC	Pillar New Testament Commentary
RBL	*Review of Biblical Literature*
SBL	Society of Biblical Literature
SBLDS	Society of Biblical Literature Dissertation Series
SNTSMS	Society for New Testament Studies Monograph Series
TDNT	*Theological Dictionary of the New Testament*. Edited by Gerhard Kittel and Gerhard Friedrich. Translated by Geoffrey W. Bromiley. 10 vols. Grand Rapids: Eerdmans, 1964–1976.
WBC	Word Biblical Commentary
WUNT	Wissenschaftliche Untersuchungen zum Neuen Testament
ZAC	*Zeitschrift für Antikes Christentum/Journal of Ancient Christianity*
ZNW	*Zeitschrift für die neutestamentliche Wissenschaft und die Kunde der älteren Kirche*

Notes

Chapter 1. Introduction

1. Derrida, "Time of the King," 121–47 (128).
2. Derrida, "Time of the King," 129. Emphases, here and in subsequent citations of Derrida, are in the work cited.
3. Derrida, "Time of the King," 124.
4. Derrida, "Time of the King," 124.
5. Bourdieu, *Logic of Practice;* Bourdieu, "Marginalia; and Bourdieu, *Practical Reason*.
6. Both Pseudo-Aristotle's *Oeconomica* and Xenophon's *Oeconomicus* treat household management, including the ordering of familial relations (parents/children; husbands/wives), the management of slaves, and agriculture. Moses I. Finley argued that the ancient economy was "embedded" within social relations; that is, it neither functioned as an independent sphere nor was construed as such. See Finley, *Ancient Economy*. On the suppression of mercantile exchange within familial and close social relations, see Bourdieu, *Logic of Practice*, 112–34.
7. Petitat, "Le don."
8. Derrida, "Time of the King," 130.
9. Petitat, "Le don," 27.
10. Godbout and Caillé, *World of the Gift;* quotations on pp. 9 and 18, respectively.
11. *Ben.* 1.4.2.
12. Petitat cites the writings of Derrida and Thomas Aquinas as examples of the "utopian" view of the gift ("Le don," 17–20).
13. The fullest form of the name given in the film is Eulys F. Dewey.
14. The fictive location appears to conflate the town of "Boutte" in southeast Louisiana with a bayou ("Bayou Boutte") some eighty kilometers south of Baton Rouge.
15. On the "gift" of salvation in *The Apostle*, see also Blanton, "Gift, Film."
16. Jonathan Z. Smith, "In Comparison a Magic Dwells," in Smith, *Imagining Religion*, 19–35; Smith, *Drudgery Divine;* Smith, "The 'End' of Comparison," Smith, "Bible and Religion," in his *Relating Religion*, 197–214 (esp. 198).
17. For Smith's discussion of "definitions" of "religion," see his "Religion, Religions, Religious," in his *Relating Religion*, 179–96.

18. Smith, "Bible and Religion," 198.
19. Smith, "The 'End' of Comparison," 239.
20. "Marcel Mauss," in *Encyclopaedia Britannica;* online at http://www.britannica.com/EBchecked/topic/370263/Marcel-Mauss. See also Mauss, "An Intellectual Self-Portrait"; Mary Douglas, "Foreword: No Free Gifts," in Mauss, *The Gift*, vii–xviii.
21. Gouldner, "Norm of Reciprocity," 171.
22. So also Douglas ("Foreword," viii): "By ignoring the universal custom of compulsory gifts we make our own record incomprehensible to ourselves: right across the globe and as far back as we can go in the history of human civilization, the major transfer of goods has been by cycles of obligatory returns of gifts."
23. On the significance of gift exchange in the contemporary context marked by globalized corporate capitalism, see Godbout and Caillé, *World of the Gift*.
24. De Waal, "Chimpanzee's Service Economy"; see also de Waal's Ted Talk "Moral Behavior in Animals" at TED, http://www.ted.com/talks/frans_de_waal_do_animals_have_morals?language=en.
25. Schino and Aureli, "Relative Roles of Kinship and Reciprocity."
26. Schino and Aureli, "Grooming Reciprocation," 9.
27. Schino and Aureli, "Grooming Reciprocation," 10.
28. Schino and Aureli, "Grooming Reciprocation," 9.
29. Smith, "Religion, Religions, Religious," 193–94.
30. I am thus in agreement with the recent proposals of Brent Nongbri, who writes: "a good focus for those who would study 'religion' in the modern day is keeping a close eye on the *activity* of defining religion and the *act* of saying that some things are 'religious' and others are not. Such an approach means giving up on the essentialist project of finding 'the' definition of religion. Such a reorientation in the study of religion would also allow for a more playful approach to second-order, redescriptive usages of religion. Religion could be deployed in nonessentialist ways to treat something as a religion for the purposes of analysis" (emphases in original). See Nongbri, *Before Religion*, 155.
31. Mauss, *The Gift*, 5.
32. Said, *Culture and Imperialism*.
33. Mauss, *The Gift*, 4.
34. Mauss, *The Gift*, 7.
35. The gift, in Mauss's view, was a form of exchange that forestalled the necessity of obtaining goods through martial means: war, raids, or theft (*The Gift*, 13, 25, 41, 82).

36. Mauss, *The Gift*, 3.
37. Mauss, *The Gift*, 3.
38. Petitat, "Le don," 27: "Les échanges sociaux ne forment pas un système, mais ils s'articulent au contraire autour de l'impossibilité d'une règle des règles qui transcenderait l'hétérogénéité de base des échanges. La diversité infinie des sociétiés et des jeux de l'échange procède de cette hétérogénéité irréducible."
39. On the language of gift exchange, see Benveniste, "Gift and Exchange in the Indo-European Vocabulary"; Walter Burkert, "The Reciprocity of Giving," in his *Creation of the Sacred*, 129–55 (esp. 129–30); Barclay, *Paul and the Gift*, 575–82.
40. So, for example, Edwin A. Judge, "The Social Identity of the First Christians: A Question of Method in Religious History," in his *Social Distinctives*, 117–35 (130–31).
41. On the category "religion" as (often, but not always) involving "culturally postulated superhuman beings," see the discussion of Smith (*Relating Religion*, 160–78), who in turn cites the definition of Melford Spiro (pp. 165–66).
42. So, for example, Mauss, *The Gift*, 15–17; see also Betz, *2 Corinthians 8 and 9*, 109–17.

Chapter 2. Symbolic Goods as Media of Exchange in Paul's Gift Economy

1. Veyne, *Bread and Circuses*.
2. See, for example, Saller, *Personal Patronage*; Eisenstadt and Roniger, *Patrons, Clients, and Friends;* Garnsey and Saller, *The Roman Empire*, 148–59; Wallace-Hadrill, ed., *Patronage in Ancient Society;* Gellner and Waterbury, eds., *Patrons and Clients in Mediterranean Societies;* Gill, Postlethwaite, and Seaford, eds., *Reciprocity in Ancient Greece*.
3. On the role of social networks within the reciprocity system, see Boissevain, *Friends of Friends*.
4. The designation "religious symbolic good" depends on a definition of the term "religion." For heuristic purposes, I define "religion" as those discourses and practices that involve significant reference to supernatural beings. The problems in defining the term are discussed, *inter alios,* by Jonathan Z. Smith, "Religion, Religions, Religious," in his *Relating Religion*, 179–96, and Arnal, "Definition"; Nongbri, *Before Religion*, 15–24.
5. Bourdieu, "The Economy of Symbolic Goods" and "Appendix: Remarks on the Economy of the Church," in Bourdieu, *Practical Reason,* 92–123, 124–26, respectively.

6. Regions in which reciprocity systems have been described include the ancient Mediterranean, Melanesia and Polynesia, Southeast Asia, the Middle East, Europe, Latin America, and the United States. These and other regions are discussed in Mauss's seminal work on reciprocity, *The Gift,* and Eisenstadt and Roniger, *Patrons, Clients, and Friends.* Alvin Gouldner ("Norm of Reciprocity") regards reciprocity as a universal norm, while recognizing that its forms are culturally specific. For an overview of Seneca's views on reciprocity, see Griffin, "*De Beneficiis* and Roman Society."
7. Translations from Seneca are those of J. W. Basore, *Seneca: Moral Essays* (3 vols., LCL; Cambridge, MA: Harvard University Press, and London: Heinemann, 1935 [repr. 1964], 3:13, 15), in some cases slightly modified.
8. There are, however, distinctions to be made. Unlike loans, in the case of gifts, no written accounts are kept, no legal sanctions enforce a return, and no time limit is specified within which the return must take place. There is always a danger that, due to ingratitude, a gift may not be reciprocated.
9. Bourdieu, *Outline of a Theory of Practice,* 198, n. 7; Bourdieu, *Logic of Practice,* 298, n. 10.
10. The inscriptions assembled by Frederick W. Danker in *Benefactor* are illustrative. They attest to reciprocal interactions in which the return constitutes a medium of exchange different from that of the original donation. For example, public honors are bestowed in return for valued services of human labor (inscription nos. 3, 9, 16, 21), public honors are bestowed in return for material benefaction and (in some cases) public service (nos. 11, 12, 17, 20, 23, 24, 33, 35, 39), and divine honors (sacrifices, dedication of altars or statues in temples) are bestowed in return for military service (no. 30) or public benefaction (nos. 31, 44). Compare also Saller, *Personal Patronage,* 29.
11. Although systems of reciprocity existed in both Greece and Rome, their specific mechanisms varied. For attempts to distinguish various types of reciprocity, including patron-client relationships and "friendship" relationships, see Eric R. Wolf, "Kinship, Friendship, and Patron-Client Relations in Complex Societies," in Schmidt, Scott, Landé, and Guasti, eds., *Friends, Followers, and Factions,* 167–77; Saller, "Patronage and Friendship." On euergetism, or "civic benefaction," see Veyne, *Bread and Circuses,* 10–13; Danker, *Benefactor,* 26–55.
12. Peterman, *Paul's Gift from Philippi;* Joubert, *Paul as Benefactor;* Crook, *Reconceptualising Conversion;* Lampe, "Paul, Patrons, and Clients"; Engberg-Pedersen, "Gift-Giving and Friendship"; Briones, *Paul's Financial Policy;* Barclay, *Paul and the Gift.* David J. Downs argues that Paul's presentation of benefits as originating with the god of Israel "subtly subverts the dominant ideology of pagan benefaction by highlighting the honor, praise, and thanks-

giving due to God, the one from whom all benefactions ultimately originate" (*Offering of the Gentiles*, 143–44). However, as Apuleius of Madauros's *The Golden Ass* indicates, the construal of a divine being as heavenly patron/patroness does not subvert the "ideology of pagan benefaction," but coheres with it (11.6, 12, 13–14, 18; cp. also Seneca, *Ben.* 2.30.1–2). James R. Harrison (*Paul's Language of Grace*) views Paul as departing in significant ways from the ideal of reciprocity. For the relationship of various Jewish writers (although not including Paul) with the "Mediterranean value" of reciprocity, see Schwartz, *Were the Jews a Mediterranean Society?*

13. See Engberg-Pedersen, "Gift-Giving and Friendship," for Paul's use of *charis* in relation to his covenantal paradigm. On Paul's use of *charis*, in addition to the titles mentioned in the previous note, see Hans Conzelmann, *TDNT* 9:393–96; Klaus Berger, *EDNT* 3:457–60.

14. Although Paul describes reciprocal relationships in term of patronage, he also employs friendship *topoi* to describe such relationships. For use of friendship themes in Pauline literature, see the survey of Alan C. Mitchell, "'Greet the Friends by Name': New Testament Evidence for the Greco-Roman *Topos* on Friendship," in Fitzgerald, ed., *Greco-Roman Perspectives*, 225–62, and Fitzgerald, "Paul and Friendship." However, as Richard Saller points out, socially asymmetrical patron-client relationships were sometimes euphemized as instances of (ostensibly symmetrical) "friendship" in order to avoid shaming inferior parties by labeling them clients ("Patronage and Friendship," 49–62; cp. also Griffin, "*De Beneficiis* and Roman Society," 97, 109–12). Both patron-client and "friendship" relationships were governed by the principles of reciprocity outlined by Seneca.

15. That the divine benefits posited by Paul existed *only* in symbolic form is demonstrable. The postulated benefits rely on two false assumptions: (1) the imminence of the apocalyptic judgment (e.g., 1 Thess 4:13–18; Rom 2:5–7; 9:27–29; 12:19); and (2) a geocentric cosmological view, such that a heavenly world was construed as existing some finite distance above the surface of the earth (implied in the spatial language of 1 Thess 4:16–17; 2 Cor 12:1–4; Gal 4:25–26; Phil 1:9–10; 3:14, 20). On the importance of this cosmology for Hellenistic religions in general, see Martin, *Hellenistic Religions*, 6–9; see also Ptolemy, *Tetrabiblos;* Cicero, *Republic* 6.17. The view is parodied in Lucian of Samosata's *Icaromenippus.*

16. There are several studies on Paul's collection for Jerusalem, including Georgi, *Remembering the Poor;* Nickle, *The Collection;* Joubert, *Paul as Benefactor;* Friesen, "Paul and Economics"; and most recently Longenecker, *Remember the Poor*. Although David Downs views the collection as a response to an

economic crisis, he himself notes that the extended time span during which the collection was undertaken rendered it unsuitable as a form of emergency relief (*Offering of the Gentiles,* 25). Longenecker views the collection as an instance of an abiding early Christian concern that the economically advantaged should supply funding (i.e., alms) to the disadvantaged (*Remember the Poor,* 135–219).

17. Translation mine. All other translations of Pauline epistles used in this chapter are those of the NRSV, in some cases slightly modified.
18. Romans was written c. 56–57 CE; 2 Cor 8–9, c. 55–56 CE. On the dates, see Roetzel, *Paul,* 178–83; Meeks and Fitzgerald, eds., *Writings of St. Paul,* 44, 61.
19. I favor the theory that 2 Cor 8–9 originally represented independent letters that were brought together with other letters in the canonical version of 2 Corinthians. For overviews of various partition theories, see Thrall, *Critical and Exegetical Commentary,* 1:1–49; Reimund Bieringer, "Teilungshypothesen zum 2. Korintherbrief. Ein Forschungsüberblick," in Bieringer and Lambrecht, *Studies on 2 Corinthians,* 67–105; Betz, *2 Corinthians 8 and 9,* 3–36. None of the arguments advanced in this chapter hinge on this partition theory, or on the order in which the various parts of 2 Corinthians were written.
20. For previous discussions of the gift-giving/*charis* themes in the collection letters, see Barclay, "Manna and the Circulation of Grace"; Gaventa, "Economy of Grace."
21. Bruce Longenecker observes that the related phrase, *ergazesthai to agathon,* which Paul uses in Gal 6:10, "is (virtually) technical terminology in the ancient world for bestowing material benefits on others" (*Remember the Poor,* 163).
22. On the background of the agrarian imagery, see the excursus of Hans Dieter Betz in *2 Corinthians 8 and 9,* 98–100, where he notes that Paul construes Achaia's gift to Jerusalem in a manner analogous to a sacrifice for a god: "The gift given to the divinity represents a thank-offering for gifts received, accompanied by the expectation of future blessings" (p. 99).
23. On the issues involved in dating the letter, see Roetzel, *Letters of Paul,* 113.
24. So Rapske, *Book of Acts and Paul in Roman Custody,* 209–19.
25. Carolyn Osiek notes: "The second piece of would-be economic language, repeated at the end of verse 17, is 'in the matter of' (*eis logon*), which can technically mean 'into the account of' (NRSV: 'to your account'). The third is 'giving and receiving' (*dosis kai lēmpsis*), meaning regular exchange or debits and credits (see Sir 41:19 [42:11 LXX]; 42:7). Another is the 'profit' or 'return' or therefore 'interest' (literally, 'fruit,' *karpos*) that accrues to their account because of their gift in verse 17. Yet another is *apechō,* 'I have been paid in full,'

the language of a business receipt in verse 18. Taken all together, they present a formidable set of formal financial language, all of which is well attested in business documents" (*Philippians, Philemon,* 121). Jean-Baptiste Edart (following Wettstein) cites Cicero, *Lael.* 58, to the effect that one "popular view" of Roman friendship involved balanced, reciprocal economic relations (*L'Épître aux Philippiens,* 314–15). Cicero objects to this "popular view," not on the grounds that friendship excludes reciprocal economic exchange, but that is excludes strict accounting practices that would reduce it to a mercantile relationship. He states, "It surely is calling friendship to a very close and petty accounting to require it to keep an exact balance of credits and debits" (*ratio acceptorum et datorum;* translation of William Falconer, *Cicero: De senectute, de amicitia, de divinatione* [LCL; London: Heinemann, and New York: Putnam, 1930 [1923], 169).

26. Julien Ogereau has recently objected to the view that Paul was united in a gift exchange relationship with the Philippians, postulating instead that they had formed a *societas evangelii* in which the Philippians provided funding and Paul provided labor to perpetuate the latter's mission (*Paul's Koinonia with the Philippians*). Despite the excellent work that Ogereau has performed in illuminating the socioeconomic context of Paul's language, the thesis has serious problems: (1) in the examples that he adduces, *societas unius rei* is inaugurated in situations in which some material gain is envisioned (i.e., sale of goods or services, joint ownership of land, resources, or an estate; cp. pp. 337–38); no parallels are adduced in which the "gain" envisioned is ideological and social (i.e., spreading a message or philosophy); (2) any (necessarily unilateral, cp. p. 342) Philippian contribution to the society's joint account would have assumed the character of a donation, as it would have gone directly to Paul's own upkeep and maintenance; (3) the *karpos* ("fruit" or "profit") mentioned in Phil 4:17 is said to accrue to "your account," that is, that of the Philippians specifically, and not to a joint account as Ogereau's thesis requires (Phil 4:19, not 1:22, glosses the character of the "fruit" mentioned in v. 17); (4) the thesis does not explain why Paul should liken the Philippian contribution to a "gift to God" in the form of a sacrifice in 4:18, or why the theme of a divine countergift should be introduced in 4:19. Here as elsewhere, Paul introduces language implying obligatory payment into what in actuality were elective reciprocal exchanges (cp. 1 Cor 9:1–18; 2 Cor 8–9; Rom 15:27).

27. Downs discusses texts in which Paul uses cultic language to describe his collection of funds for the Jerusalem church (*Offering of the Gentiles,* 120–60). He views the cultic language as a means of subverting the ideology of the patronage system (pp. 134; 138; 141–43; 145, n. 84; 158). Harrison, on the

other hand, correctly notes that religious ritual (and consequently, cultic language) is built on the ideas of benefaction and reciprocity: "People initiated a relationship with the gods in the hope of reciprocal favour. By observing the proper cultic rites in honour of the gods, human beings might secure the gods' favour. A bond of mutual obligation—initially founded in the gods' acceptance of the rites—ensued, with the suppliant adopting a grateful disposition towards the gods, and the gods reciprocating with favours and gratitude to those who had demonstrated the requisite piety" (*Paul's Language of Grace,* 53). Greco-Roman religion, including that of Paul, is construed in terms of patronal reciprocity (cp. Blanton, "*De caelo patrocinium.*")

28. Gordon Fee argues that the line refers both to an "eschatological referent" and to material wealth (*Paul's Letter,* 452 and n. 19). Similarly Peter O'Brien: "By stating that God will supply the Philippians' every need, the apostle not only echoes the immediately preceding context and refers to their material needs, but also and more significantly he focusses on . . . the fulfilling of their spiritual needs" (*Epistle to the Philippians,* 543).

29. Fee aptly summarizes Paul's rhetoric: "Although he cannot reciprocate in kind, since their gift had the effect of being a sweet-smelling sacrifice, pleasing to God, Paul assures them that God, whom he deliberately designates as "*my* God," will assume responsibility for reciprocity. . . . They obviously have the better of it!" (*Paul's Letter,* 452).

30. For these dates, see Roetzel, *Letters of Paul,* 116–17; Meeks and Fitzgerald, eds., *Writings of St. Paul,* 95–96.

31. The reason for Onesimus's presence in the prison with Paul has been the subject of debate. For overviews of the discussion, see Osiek, *Philippians, Philemon,* 126–31; Barth and Blanke, *Letter to Philemon,* 141–42, 227–28; Dunn, *The Epistles,* 301–7; Thurston and Ryan, *Philippians and Philemon,* 181–82. Peter Lampe, ("Keine 'Sklavenflucht' des Onesimus" and "Paul, Patrons, and Clients") understands Philemon as a clemency letter. Sara C. Winter views the letter as a request by Paul for the manumission of Onesimus so that he might assist him in his missionary endeavors ("Paul's Letter to Philemon" and "Methodological Observations").

32. The location of the addressees cannot be established with any certainty. The mention of Onesimus in Col 4:7 has led some to the conclusion that he and Philemon were located there. However, uncertainties about the authorship of Colossians render this evidence dubious (see Meeks and Fitzgerald, eds., *Writings of St. Paul,* 95–96; Roetzel, *Letters of Paul,* 116–17).

33. Winter notes that the formula *parakalein tini peri tinos* used in v. 10 can be construed as a request for Onesimus (i.e., that he be allowed to serve Paul),

the preposition *peri* signaling the object of the request ("Paul's Letter," 6-7). Scott S. Elliott ("'Thanks but No Thanks'") takes a contrary view, arguing that, in sending Onesimus back to Philemon, "Paul is returning a gift of patronage to his would-be patron, [and] his expressions of reluctance and the wish that he could keep Onesimus for himself can be read as a rather clever way of saying, 'Thanks, but no thanks'" (i.e., he does not wish to retain Onesimus's services) (p. 59). Although I agree that Paul resists any implication that Philemon could be construed as his patron—in fact, Paul assumes the opposite (v. 19; cp. the use of the language of command and obedience in vv. 8 and 21 and the imperative of v. 22)—vv. 13-14 imply that Paul wishes to retain the slave's service in some capacity but refuses to humiliate Philemon by commanding it.

34. For overviews, see Barth and Blanke, *Letter to Philemon,* 200-224; Dunn, *The Epistles,* 299-307; Thurston and Ryan, *Philippians and Philemon,* 181-82; Callahan, *Embassy of Onesimus,* 1-19.

35. Dunn, *The Epistles,* 340, writes, "It is universally inferred that the obligation referred to is Philemon's conversion under Paul's ministry (cp. Rom 15:27)." More recently, Douglas Moo (*Letters to Colossians and Philemon,* 430-31) writes: "What Paul means by saying that Philemon owes him his very 'self' (*seauton*) is that Philemon is in debt to Paul for his eternal life. Paul was used by God in Philemon's conversion. . . . In light of this infinite debt that Philemon owes to Paul, he should have no hesitation in accepting Paul's offer to cover Onesimus' debts." It is clear, however, that the "benefit" for which Paul asks (employing the verb *oninēmi*) in v. 20 refers to more than his offer to cover Onesimus's debts. Paul's reference to his "heart" in v. 20b recalls v. 12, where he referred to Onesimus in identical terms. By implicitly recalling his affection for Onesimus in v. 20, Paul reminds Philemon of his request that Onesimus, Paul's "heart," might be allowed to serve him during his imprisonment (v. 13).

36. BDAG, s.v. *hyper,* A.1.c, supports this rendering of the prepositional phrase (cp. also Harald Riesenfeld, *TDNT* 8:512-13). Daniel Wallace (*Greek Grammar,* 384-87) adduces ample evidence for the use of *hyper* with the genitive as "bearing a substitutionary force" in Koine Greek. It encroaches on semantic territory reserved for the preposition *anti* in Attic Greek.

Chapter 3. The Benefactor's Account Book

1. The first three topics are treated in Sevenster, *Paul and Seneca.* For more recent treatments, see Vining, "Comparing Seneca's Ethics"; Malherbe,

"Hellenistic Moralists"; Hartog, "'Not Even among the Pagans'"; James P. Ware, "Moral Progress and Divine Power in Seneca and Paul," in Fitzgerald, ed., *Passions and Moral Progress*, 267–83; Horn, "Der Zeitbegriff der antiken Moralphilosophie," 132–34; Joubert, "'Homo reciprocus'"; Engberg-Pedersen, "Gift-Giving and Friendship"; Engberg-Pedersen, "Gift-Giving and God's *Charis*." On the fourth century CE pseudepigraphic correspondence between Paul and Seneca, see Cornelia Römer, "The Correspondence between Seneca and Paul," in Schneemelcher, Hennecke, and Wilson, eds., *New Testament Apocrypha*, 2:46–53; Elliott, *Apocryphal New Testament*, 547–53.

2. Bourdieu, *Logic of Practice*, 69.
3. Biographies of Seneca include Griffin, *Seneca,* and Veyne, *Seneca*. For a recent English translation of *De Beneficiis* with notes and introduction, see Griffin and Inwood, *Lucius Annaeus Seneca*. Other discussions include Griffin, "Seneca as a Sociologist"; Griffin, "*De Beneficiis* and Roman Society"; Dixon, "Meaning of Gift and Debt."
4. A small sampling of the vast literature on reciprocity in Greek and Roman societies includes Wallace-Hadrill, ed., *Patronage in Ancient Society;* Veyne, *Bread and Circuses;* Saller, *Personal Patronage;* Gouldner, "Norm of Reciprocity"; Gellner and Waterbury, eds., *Patrons and Clients;* Gill, Postlethwaite, and Seaford, eds., *Reciprocity in Ancient Greece*.
5. Compare Saller, *Personal Patronage*, 29.
6. Griffin and Inwood, *Lucius Annaeus Seneca*, 2.
7. Griffin, "Seneca as Sociologist," 115.
8. The analogy between gift-giving and the ball game, like the analogies of the Graces (*Ben.* 1.3.4–1.4.1) and the foot race (2.25.3), Seneca owes to Chrysippus, who, Griffin and Inwood note, was a long-distance runner before becoming a philosopher (*Lucius Annaeus Seneca*, 195, n. 26).
9. All translations of Seneca's *De Beneficiis* in this chapter are those of Griffin and Inwood, *Lucius Annaeus Seneca*, in some cases slightly modified.
10. The seminal article on bookkeeping in Greece and Rome is that of de Ste. Croix, "Greek and Roman Accounting."
11. Brad Inwood ("Politics and Paradox") argues that Seneca employs the paradox between the view of gift-giving as disinterested (i.e., the giver has no desire to receive a countergift) and as interested (a gift is given on the basis of calculations as to the possibility of the donee returning a countergift) as a means of mediating between the lofty moral ideals of Stoicism and the "realities of giving morally based advice to real and imperfect people" (p. 265). Inwood overlooks the fact, however, that even the lofty moral ideal of disin-

terested giving itself constitutes a gift-giving strategy designed (paradoxically) to maximize the probability of a reciprocal interaction. Thus the polarity between the disinterested ideals of the Stoic sage and the interested acts of "ordinary people" (p. 253) collapses; the disinterested ideal masks interest. On the "interest in disinterestedness" that characterizes many gift-giving systems, see Bourdieu, *Practical Reason*, 75–123.

12. As argued by Lampe, "Keine 'Sklavenflucht' des Onesimus" and "Paul, Patrons, and Clients," 501–2. Sara C. Winter argues that the letter implies a request by Paul for the manumission of Onesimus so that he might assist him in his missionary endeavors ("Paul's Letter to Philemon" and "Methodological Observations").

13. A third possibility, that Onesimus had been arrested and imprisoned in the same jail in which Paul was spending time, is impossible: had Onesimus been arrested and jailed, Paul would have lacked the authority to "send him back" to Philemon (v. 12). Nevertheless, the view still finds its supporters (Roetzel, *Letters of Paul*, 116–17). For overviews of the various possibilities, see Osiek, *Philippians, Philemon*, 126–31; Dunn, *The Epistles*, 301–7; Thurston and Ryan, *Philippians and Philemon*, 181–82. Brian Rapske critiques the various views and finds additional support to bolster Lampe's thesis ("The Prisoner Paul").

14. Paul writes: "I am appealing to you for my child" (v. 10 NRSV).

15. Translations of New Testament passages in this and subsequent chapters are my own unless indicated otherwise. Peter Müller argues that vv. 18–19 interrupt the argument in which v. 20 logically follows v. 17, and so constitute a "juristischer Einschub" or excursus (*Der Brief an Philemon*, 130–31). The digression is a well-crafted rhetorical gesture, however, as indicated by Paul's use of the figure of *paraleipsis* in v. 19 (on which, see n. 17 below). Moreover, vv. 18–19 remove a potential obstacle (i.e., Onesimus's indebtedness to Philemon) and provide positive grounds (i.e., Philemon's indebtedness to Paul) for Philemon's acquiescence to Paul's requests in vv. 17 and 20 and for Paul's "confidence" expressed in v. 21.

16. Paul's use of economic terms is discussed in Osiek, *Philippians, Philemon*, 121–22; Dunn writes of v. 17: "Somewhat surprisingly Paul now switches his appeal to a sustained commercial metaphor (vv. 17–19)" (*The Epistles*, 336). Julian Ogereau outlined the commercial context of the term *synergos* (v. 1) in his paper "Business Partnership Among the First Christians? The Funding of the Pauline Mission," delivered in the Early Christianity and the Ancient Economy section at the SBL annual meeting, San Francisco, Nov. 22, 2011; see also his massive study *Paul's Koinonia*.

17. On the rhetorical figure *paraleipsis,* see Smyth, *Greek Grammar,* §3036.
18. So Dunn, *The Epistles,* 340: "It is universally inferred that the obligation referred to is Philemon's conversion under Paul's ministry (cp. Rom 15:27)." Similarly, Douglas Moo, in *Letters to Colossians and Philemon,* 430: "What Paul means by saying that Philemon owes him his very 'self' (*seauton*) is that Philemon is in debt to Paul for his eternal life. Paul was used by God in Philemon's conversion."
19. On mediators, or "brokers" of patronage in the Roman empire, see Saller, *Personal Patronage,* 35, 43, 48–51, 59, 75–76; Andrew Wallace-Hadrill, "Patronage in Roman Society: From Republic to Empire," in Wallace-Hadrill, ed., *Patronage in Ancient Society,* 81–84. On Jesus' role as mediator of divine benefaction in the New Testament, see Malina, "Patron and Client"; Neyrey, "God, Benefactor and Patron"; Lampe, "Paul, Patrons, and Clients." On Paul's self-presentation as a mediator of divine gifts, see Jennings, "Patronage and Rebuke"; Briones, "Mutual Brokers of Grace."
20. Incidentally, Seneca warns against the use of mediators when giving gifts: "So if you want your gifts to be thought of with gratitude, take care that they get to the people to whom they are promised intact and undiminished, with no 'deduction' having been made. Don't let anyone intervene; don't let anyone slow them down. When you are going to give something, no one can earn any gratitude without reducing yours" (*Ben.* 2.4.3).
21. For the category of "sinners," see Rom 5:8, 19; Gal 2:15, 17. On the eschatological "destruction" of members of that group, see Rom 9:22; Phil 1:28; 3:19; 1 Thess 5:3. Paul apparently does not think that there is an afterlife for the wicked; they simply cease to exist—destroyed in the apocalyptic judgment (cp. Wis 5:9–14; contrast the fate of the righteous, who "live forever," Wis 5:15).
22. As noted in chapter 2 herein, "Paul is willing to charge to his own account any debt incurred by Onesimus (v. 18). Paul indicates that he is creditworthy; he will repay the debt (v. 19). Philemon's account, however, stands in the red, as he owes Paul an unrepayable debt: his own life, or 'self' (v. 19)." Dunn's (*The Epistles,* 339) assumption that Paul, although a man of "little independent means," "would be able to call on wealthy backers . . . should the IOU be called in" is unnecessary, as is the related view of Peter Müller that, since Paul had little money, his statement must have been made in jest (*Der Brief an Philemon,* 130). Paul's rhetoric effectively removes the possibility that Philemon should "call in the IOU": any amount to be charged to Paul's account on Onesimus's behalf would fall far short of the unrepayable debt that Philemon owed Paul, which amounted to the value of his very life. Carolyn Osiek ("Politics of Patronage") astutely refers to v. 19 as a "reminder that Philemon

owes Paul considerably more than Onesimus owes Philemon, or that Paul is asking of Philemon. Thus Philemon, while expected to reciprocate, remains pitiably in even greater debt to Paul, the gracious giver . . . [H]e will never catch up and attain parity with Paul, and this is the whole point" (p. 148). So also John Barclay: "The transparent rhetorical device of *praeteritio* . . . is here used to transform Philemon's position from creditor to debtor and to put him under a limitless moral obligation to comply with Paul's requests" ("Paul, Philemon, and the Dilemma," esp. 171-72).
23. So Müller, *Der Brief an Philemon,* 115-16.
24. NRSV.
25. It is possible, although less likely, that Paul was implicitly requesting the manumission of Onesimus, as argued by Callahan, *Embassy of Onesimus.* The verb phrase that Paul uses in v. 13, *hina . . . moi diakonē* ("in order that he might be of service to me") is, however, an appropriate description of a slave's labor. Moreover, in 1 Cor 7:21-24, Paul seems more interested in perpetuating the social status quo than in upsetting it. On the tensions involved between early Christian fictive kinship and the "practical reality" of slavery, see Barclay, "Paul, Philemon, and the Dilemma."
26. So Lohse, *Colossians and Philemon,* 202 and n. 49; Winter, "Paul's Letter to Philemon," 1-15; Winter, "Methodological Observations," 203-12.
27. So Dunn, *The Epistles,* 331.
28. On Seneca's biography, see Griffin, *Seneca,* 29-128; Veyne, *Seneca,* 1-29. The following discussion draws heavily from Griffin.
29. Seneca or his father owned a suburban Roman villa; later in his career, Seneca the Younger acquired estates at Nomentum, Albanum, and Egypt. Griffin cautiously accepts Rostovtzeff's conjecture that the Egyptian estates were gifts of Nero. It is certain that Seneca acquired the villa at Nomentum during Nero's reign (Griffin, *Seneca,* 286-89). Tacitus has Seneca refer to the *pecunia* and lands given to him by Nero in his resignation speech in 62 CE (*Ann.* 14.53.5-6). Seneca was further enriched by the interest he received from loans in Italy and the provinces (*Ann.* 13.42.4). On the contradictions involved in a Stoic philosopher amassing great wealth, see Griffin, *Seneca,* 286-314.
30. Tacitus, *Ann.* 13.42, discussed in Griffin, *Seneca,* 291. A word of caution is in order: Walter Scheidel argues that figures that are powers of ten and multiples of thirty and forty are best understood as "purely conventional valuations" ("Finances," 222). Suillius's figure cited by Tacitus is stereotypical (Scheidel, "Finances," see Table 2, p. 231: "Private Fortunes").
31. Scheidel and Friesen, "Size of the Economy," esp. 75-81 and Table 10, p. 85.

32. On Paul's trade as a leatherworker and the low social esteem in which craftsmen were held in the Roman world, see Hock, *Social Context of Paul's Ministry*.
33. For an attempt to reconstruct Paul's itinerary, including estimates of time spent in transit, see Murphy-O'Connor, *Paul: His Story*, passim; Murphy-O'Connor, *Paul: A Critical Life*, 1–31.
34. The verb translated "to be sent on one's way" (*propemphthēnai*), implies a request for travel funding or supplies (BDAG, s.v. *propempō*).
35. Friesen, "Poverty in Pauline Studies," 350. In a subsequent article ("Prospects for a Demography," esp. 368), Friesen categorizes Paul on the lowest economic rungs (PS6–PS7; the latter indicating an inability "regularly [to] procure the amount of food necessary to sustain the human body"). Despite some quibbles, Longenecker largely depends on Friesen's economic analysis in *Remember the Poor*, 298–332.
36. Friesen, "Poverty in Pauline Studies," 350.
37. On the problems caused in Corinth by the admixture of fractions representing differing economic levels, see Marshall, *Enmity;* Chow, *Patronage and Power;* Friesen, "Poverty in Pauline Studies," 348–50; Friesen, "Prospects for a Demography," 367.
38. Some of Seneca's statements indicate that gift-giving should be motivated by altruism: "The bookkeeping for benefits is quite simple. A certain amount is dispersed; if there is any repayment at all, then it is a profit. If there is no repayment, then it is not a loss. I gave it only in order to give" (*Ben.* 1.2.3; cp. 2.6.2; 2.9.1–2.10.3; 4.13.3). His later qualifications, however, indicate that such statements are hyperbolic: "Do you want to repay the benefit? Accept it with a kindly attitude; you have returned the favor. Not that you should think that you have paid off the debt, but so that you may be indebted with a greater sense of confidence" (2.35.5). Likewise: "And so, although we can say that he who has willingly received a benefit has returned it [i.e., through his gratitude], we nevertheless urge him to give back to the donor something similar to what he has received" (2.35.1). Griffin (*"De Beneficiis* and Roman Society," 94) views statements in the former category as examples of the Stoic rhetorical method of making exaggerated ethical demands in the hope that, although falling short of perfection, people might at least arrive nearer the goal when prompted by lofty ideals (for a similar view, see Inwood, "Politics and Paradox," 241–65). Seneca notes: "Hyperbole never expects to attain all that it aspires to; instead, it claims the unbelievable in order to secure the believable" (*Ben.* 7.23.2).
39. Saller, *Personal Patronage*, 1, 10–17; cp. also Saller, "Patronage and Friendship," 49.

40. On the socially hierarchizing function of asymmetrical gift-giving, see Blau, *Exchange and Power,* 106–12, who notes: "A person who gives others valuable gifts or renders them important services makes a claim for superior status by obligating them to himself. If they fail to reciprocate with benefits that are at least as important to him as his are to them, they validate his claim to superior status" (p. 108).
41. Arnaldo Momigliano and Tim Cornell note: "Ordinary clients supported their patron (*patronus*) in political and private life, and demonstrated their loyalty and respect by going to his house to greet him each morning . . . and attending him when he went out. The size of a man's clientele, and the wealth and status of his individual clients, were a visible testimony to his prestige and social standing" (*OCD,* s.v. *cliens*).
42. Citing Seneca's *De Vita Beata* 24.2, Saller notes: "Because friends were so strongly obliged to return favors, all *beneficia* distributed to them were felt to be insurance against misfortune since in time of need they could be called in. As Seneca says, a *beneficium* should be stored away like a buried treasure (*thensaurus*), 'which you would not dig up, except from necessity.' The recipient, on the other hand, should be content to guard the *beneficium* until a time of need" (*Personal Patronage,* 25).
43. Seneca's gift-giving strategy did prove effective; his beneficence was praised (albeit after his death in 65 CE) by both Martial and Juvenal. Martial (*Ep.* 12.36) addresses Labullus as a relatively liberal patron during times of illiberality: "To tell the truth, you're the best of a bad lot. Give me back the Pisos and the Senecas and the Memmiuses and the Crispuses, or their predecessors: you will immediately become the worst of a good lot." Translation of D. R. Shackleton Bailey, *Martial: Epigrams* (3 vols., LCL; Cambridge, MA: Harvard University Press, 1993). Juvenal (*Satire* 5.107–11) romanticizes days past, when patrons like Seneca lavishly dispensed gifts: "No one asks for the gifts sent to his humble friends by Seneca, the gifts good Piso and Cotta used to dispense. In those days, you know, the glory of giving (*donandi gloria*) was prized more highly than titles and symbols of office." Translation of Susanna Morton Braund, *Juvenal and Persius* (LCL; Cambridge, MA: Harvard University Press, 2004).
44. See n. 38 above on Seneca's use of hyperbole.
45. It is to the extraordinarily wealthy that Seneca's gift-giving advice is directed. Aubutius Liberalis, to whom *De Beneficiis* is dedicated, was himself a wealthy benefactor, perhaps of equestrian rank (Griffin, *Seneca,* 455–56).
46. Friesen, "Poverty in Pauline Studies," 353–54; Friesen, "Prospects for a Demography," 368, places Philemon at level 4 (moderate surplus of resources)

or 5 (stable near subsistence) on his poverty scale; Longenecker, *Remember the Poor*, 245, concurs.

47. Benefits mentioned in the letter include Philemon's hosting the assembly in his household (v. 2) and Paul in a guest room (v. 22). For Paul's view that "love" is manifested through gift-giving, see 1 Cor 8:8, where he refers to the collection for the Jerusalem assembly.
48. On households (such as Philemon's) as the "Basiselemente" and "Keimzellen" of early Christian mission, see Müller, *Der Brief an Philemon*, 48.
49. Julien Ogereau ("Jerusalem Collection") has recently focused attention on Paul's use of *koinōnia* and its cognates (cp. also his "Business Partnership Among the First Christians?"); Ogereau, *Paul's Koinonia*.
50. Proponents of an "egalitarian" view of early Christian communities include Ehrensperger, *Paul and the Dynamics of Power;* Welborn, "'That There May Be Equality'"; Briones, "Mutual Brokers of Grace"; Barclay, "Manna and the Circulation of Grace"; Ogereau, "Jerusalem Collection."
51. That Paul construes himself as standing in a hierarchical relation with respect to the communities that he founds is conceded in Briones ("Mutual Brokers of Grace," 555): "This is not to deny Paul's apostolic authority, especially when he is, in many ways, superior to the Corinthians. . . . But his mutual dependency on the Corinthians should challenge any view that considers his *authority over* and *mutuality with* his churches an either-or option. The two are undeniably inseparable." Mutuality should not be confused with egalitarianism, however. Both authority and hierarchy presuppose the agreement and cooperation of subordinates. For analyses of the social dynamic involved, see Bell, *Ritual Theory, Ritual Practice,* 197–223; Lincoln, *Discourse and the Construction of Society,* 131–59; Bourdieu, *Language and Symbolic Power,* 163–70.
52. Note that Paul makes the issue semipublic by addressing not just Philemon, but the ecclesial functionaries Apphia and Archippus, as well as the assembly that meets in Philemon's household (vv. 1–3).
53. Peter Stuhlmacher observes: "Dementsprechend deutet Paulus hier mit dem sonst bei ihm ungebräuchlichen, massiven *epitassein* die Möglichkeit einer definitiven Anordnung an und weist in V 19 darauf hin, daß Philemon seine christliche Existenz dem Apostel verdankt (also ihm gegenüber besondere Verpflichtungen hat)" (*Der Brief an Philemon,* 37). Chris Frilingos ("'For My Child'") offers a perceptive analysis of Paul's use of the language of authority in the letter.
54. Translation of Walsh, *Pliny the Younger;* Latin text in Radice, *Pliny: Letters and Panegyricus* (2 vols., LCL; Cambridge, MA: Harvard University Press, and London: Heinemann, 1969).

55. NRSV.
56. So BDAG, s.v. *xenia*.
57. For an analysis of the early Christian assemblies (albeit in Corinth, not Colossae) in terms of patronage practices, see Chow, *Patronage and Power*.
58. For a more detailed treatment of the "heavenly patronage" depicted in Apuleius, see Blanton, "*De caelo patrocinium*."
59. Text and translation in J. Arthur Hanson, *Apuleius: Metamorphoses* (2 vols., LCL; Cambridge, MA: Harvard University Press, 1989).
60. Compare Stuhlmacher: "Philemon ist verpflichtet, dem Apostel in der Mission zu dienen" (*Der Brief an Philemon*, 50).
61. Briones, "Mutual Brokers of Grace," 553. Barclay's formulation: "Paul backs off from making himself patron of the churches, anticipating instead a mutual patronage, where each will have something to contribute to the other" ("Manna and the Circulation of Grace," 424).
62. For the view that Paul's letters accord a "material exchange value" to "nonmaterial, discursive products, such as the promise of deliverance from an eschatological judgment imagined to be imminent," see chapter 2 herein. See also Stuhlmacher, *Der Brief an Philemon*, 50–51 and n. 126.
63. Saller, "Patronage and Friendship," 51–52, 60–61 (quoted). Saller cites Proculus's comments in Justinian's *Digest* 49.15.7.1.
64. Saller has pointed out that the terms *patronus* and *cliens* were often avoided, as it was viewed as unseemly to call attention to the asymmetry involved in such relationships, which were often euphemized as "friendship" (*amicitia*) rather than patronal relations (*Personal Patronage*, 8–11). Although the Greek equivalents of *patronus* (*euergetēs*, *sōtēr*, or the loanword *patrōn*) and of *cliens* (*pelatēs*; cp. Dionysius of Halicarnassus, *Ant. Rom.* 1.83.3; Plutarch, *Romulus* 13) do not appear in Paul's letter to Philemon, Osiek ("Politics of Patronage," 147) notes: "[A word of] caution should be raised against the assumption that if the usual language for patronage is not present, neither is the social construct to which it refers." It is Paul's language of debt and obligation (Phlm 19), as well as Paul's paternal language (v. 10), that establishes the patronal context. On the "debt" owed by a recipient to the giver of a gift, see Dixon, "Meaning of Gift and Debt," 451–64. On the patron as "father," see Neyrey, "God, Benefactor and Patron," 468, 471–72.
65. Since Paul's rhetoric and practice both mimic and invert aspects of Roman patronage, Steven Friesen's argument that Paul attempts to avoid patronage practices seems unwarranted ("Paul and Economics"). Paul neither wholly adopts nor unequivocally rejects Roman patronage practices; he modifies and adapts them to the local conditions of particular house-churches.

66. Schütz, *Paul and the Anatomy of Apostolic Authority,* passim (on Philemon, see 221–24); Polaski, *Paul and the Discourse of Power,* 23–51.

Chapter 4. Gift or Commodity?

1. Mauss, *The Gift.*
2. Carrier, "Gifts, Commodities, and Social Relations"; Carrier, "Gift in Theory and Practice"; Carrier, "Emerging Alienation in Production."
3. Herrmann, "Gift or Commodity."
4. Herrmann, "Gift or Commodity," 910.
5. Miller, "Gift, Sale, Payment, Raid."
6. I define "commodity" as any good that is exchanged (sold or bartered) under the conditions of market transaction and "gift" as any good that is exchanged under nonmercantile conditions. Arjun Appadurai's ("Introduction") use of the term "commodity" to apply to goods or services exchanged in both mercantile and gift-giving contexts unduly broadens the meaning of the term; however, Appadurai's point that commodities are not unique to capitalist economic systems is well taken.
7. Mauss, *The Gift,* esp. 1–14, 39–43.
8. Mauss, *The Gift,* 33–39.
9. Mauss, *The Gift,* 47–83.
10. Mauss, *The Gift,* 67.
11. Carrier acknowledges a debt to Gregory (*Gifts and Commodities*) in his use of Marxian categories to explicate Mauss; "Gifts, Commodities, and Social Relations," 122.
12. Carrier, "Gifts, Commodities, and Social Relations," 122.
13. Carrier, "Gifts, Commodities, and Social Relations," 132.
14. Hermann, "Gift or Commodity," 910–11.
15. Hermann, "Gift or Commodity," 918.
16. Hermann, "Gift or Commodity," 920.
17. Hermann, "Gift or Commodity," 919. The idea that the status of a particular good as "gift" or "commodity" may change over time, and on that basis can be said to have a "life history" or "cultural biography," is to be credited to Igor Kopytoff ("Cultural Biography of Things").
18. Miller, "Gift, Sale, Payment, Raid," 18–50.
19. Miller, "Gift, Sale, Payment, Raid," 42.
20. The model proposed here differs significantly from that of Ronald F. Hock, who bases his model on parallels with Cynic philosophers (*Social Context of Paul's Ministry,* 52–59). Hock proposes four modes of support: charging fees

for lectures, becoming the client of a wealthy politician or merchant, begging, and working to earn a living. There is, however, no evidence in the first century CE that Christian evangelists garnered economic support through charging fees for lectures or by begging. Gerd Theissen incorrectly identifies the practice of hospitality (see text above, mode no. 1) as a form of "begging" (*Social Setting of Pauline Christianity*, 31). Beggars were offered handouts in a public space, not granted room and board. A. E. Harvey notes the absence of any reference to the *pēra*, or beggar's pouch (as worn by Cynics) in the missionary's list of approved travel accouterments in Mark 6:8 and parallels ("'Workman Is Worthy,'" 218). There is clear evidence that some evangelists worked a trade to earn money, and there is some overlap between early Christian hospitality and the patron-client relationship. Thus Hock's typology provides at best two models of early Christian economic support for ecclesial functionaries; it overlooks several important modes of support, which appear in the text below. On finances in Pauline assemblies, see also Datiri, "Finances in the Pauline Churches"; Briones, *Paul's Financial Policy;* Ogereau, *Paul's Koinonia;* see chapter 2 n. 26 herein for criticisms of Ogereau's thesis.

21. Luke 10:5-7 reads: "Into whichever house you enter, first say, 'Peace to this house.' And if there is a 'son of peace' there, your peace will remain upon him. But if not, it will return to you. Remain in that house, eating and drinking what they provide, for the worker deserves his wage." Note that the symmetry of the gift exchange, in which the evangelist's blessing ("peace") upon the household is recompensed by food, drink, and temporary lodging, is broken by the last line, which constitutes a discursive attempt to shift from the gift exchange mode into the mode of business and commodity. The Matthean version of the saying does not attempt to shift the practice into commodity mode; it avoids the use of the term *misthos*, "wage." Instead, it reads "The worker deserves his nourishment" (*trophē;* Matt 10:10). In the Gospel of Matthew, the gift mode is emphasized (10:8): "You have received freely, give freely."

22. Josephus (*J.W.* 2.8.4, §125): "On the arrival of any of the (Essene) sect from elsewhere, all the resources of the community are put at their disposal, just as if they were their own; and they enter the houses of men whom they have never seen before as though they were their most intimate friends" (translation of H. St. J. Thackeray in LCL 203: *Josephus: The Jewish War* 2:370). For overviews, see John Koenig, "Hospitality," *ABD* 3:299-301; Fitzgerald, "Hospitality." For the Roman context, see Nicols, "*Hospitium* and Political Friendship"; Nicols, "Hospitality Among the Romans"; Nicols, "Practice of *Hospitium*."

23. Davies and Allison, *Gospel According to St. Matthew*, 2:626-27. The Greek form Cephas derives from the Aramaic *kephāʾ*.

24. John Nicols notes that the phrases *hospes atque cliens* ("guest-client") and *patroni atque hospites* ("patron-hosts" or "patron-guests") are attested ("*Hospitium* and Political Friendship," 101). Both Marshall (*Enmity in Corinth*, 143-47) and Chow (*Patronage and Power*) interpret the situation in Corinth in relation to patronage practices. On the indignities suffered by clients, see Lucian of Samosata, "On Salaried Posts in Great Houses" (A. M. Harmon, *Lucian* [LCL; London: Heinemann, and New York: Putnam, 1921], 3:412-81).
25. *OCD*, s.v. "Friendship, ritualized," 611-13 (612).
26. If the term *timē* in 1 Tim 5:17 refers to an honorarium or stipend, it would appear that by the early second century CE, some Christian functionaries had begun to receive pay in monetary form. However, there is no evidence for such a practice in the first century.
27. For a discussion of the relation of early Christian missionaries to their hosts and the modifications that the relation entails vis-à-vis patron-client relations, see chapter 7 herein.
28. Rom 16:1-2; Florence Gillman, "Phoebe," *ABD* 5:348-49.
29. Acts 13:1-3; Gal 2:1; Jon Daniels, "Barnabas," *ABD* 1:610-11.
30. As, for example, in Acts 15:1-5.
31. So BDAG, s.v. *propempō*.
32. The standard work on Paul's occupation as leatherworker remains Hock, *Social Context*. On Paul's association with Priscilla (or Priska) and Aquila, see Murphy-O'Connor, *Paul: A Critical Life*, 261.
33. So Hock, *Social Context*, 37-42.
34. A possible sixth mode may be mentioned. Independently wealthy individuals who commanded the necessary resources could travel and preach at their own expense. Although the book of Acts may portray Paul in this light (if one is to suppose that he rents at his own expense an Ephesian lecture hall in which to speak in Acts 19:9-10, as some commentators assume), it is unlikely that the picture is accurate, as it conflicts with the apostle's own statements as to his relative impoverishment (on Paul's economic location, see chapter 3 herein). Acts appears to have systematically distorted its picture of Paul to make him appear far wealthier than he actually was. In view of the likelihood that few, if any, members of early Christian communities commanded more than a moderate surplus of resources (Friesen, "Poverty in Pauline Studies" and "Prospects for a Demography"), it is unlikely that this mode was practiced in the first century CE.
35. *OCD*, s.v. "Friendship, ritualized," 612.
36. That the pronouncement of "peace" was more then a simple greeting is clearly indicated by Luke 10:6. On the Matthean parallel in Matt 10:13, Davies and

Allison write, "Peace is here spoken of as though it had an objective existence and as though it were subject to the disciples' commands" (*Gospel According to St. Matthew*, 2:176).
37. Lucian, "On Salaried Posts," §§4–6, 10–11, 13, 20–21, 24, 36, 38; Martial, *Epigrams* 3.7, 60; 4.26, 68; 10:27; 14.125. Early in the Roman imperial period, the standard payment was twenty-five asses (so Ernst Badian, *OCD*, s.v. *salutatio*).
38. On the charges to which Paul responds, see Senft, *La Première Épitre*, 117–20. Senft, however, does not clearly distinguish the literal use of *misthos*, "salary" or "wage," from the practice of providing room and board (i.e., hospitality; cp. his comments on vv. 14 and 18, pp. 121–22). In view of 1 Cor 9:4 ("Do we not have the right to eat and drink?") and the use of the term *opsōnion*, which refers to a soldier's provisions (Caragounis, "*OPSŌNION*"), the latter is more likely at issue in 1 Cor 9. Note that in 9:17, Paul uses the term *misthos* in the context of a counterfactual statement, and in v. 18, his *misthos*, "payment," is that he gives away the gospel free of charge. Neither verse provides evidence that he was offered a "salary" in Corinth (see also Caragounis, "*OPSŌNION*," 52–53).
39. Joseph A. Fitzmyer (*First Corinthians*, 353–54), Richard B. Hays (*First Corinthians*, 146–49), Helmut Merklein (*Der erste Brief*, 2:211, 217), Wolfgang Schrage (*Der erste Brief*, 2:278–83), and Christian Wolff (*Der erste Brief*, 184–85) note that the use of the term *exousia* as well as the reference to "food and drink" serve to link the contents of 1 Cor 9 with the discussion of the "rights" of members of the Corinthian assemblies to eat meat that had originated in sacrifices to Greco-Roman deities, discussed in 1 Cor 8 and 10 (esp. 8:9). For additional links between 1 Cor 9 and its immediate context, see Willis, "An Apostolic Apologia?" Willis overplays his hand when he denies that Paul responds to criticism in the chapter, as 9:3 clearly indicates.
40. On "expenses," see Caragounis, "*OPSŌNION*," 52.
41. Although NA[28] sets the phrase "the one who plows should plow" in italics, indicating that it is a quotation, that is unlikely, since no known text includes the statement. More likely, the verse glosses the meaning of Deut 25:4 by extending it to other agricultural roles (so Fitzmyer, *First Corinthians*, 364; Fee, *First Epistle*, 409, n. 68; otherwise Schrage, *Der erste Brief*, 302).
42. Paul Millett, *OCD*, s.v. "wages."
43. The distinction between human and divine authority is implied in 1 Cor 9:8: "I am not saying these things on human authority; does not the law itself say them?"
44. So Schrage (*Der erste Brief*, 303, n. 152), who points to similar agrarian metaphors in 1 Cor 3:6–8 and Mark 4:3–9.

45. On the exchangeability of "spiritual" and material things in Paul's discourse and practice, see chapter 2 herein.
46. Cp. Luke 10:7; Matt 10:10.
47. Harry Nasuti writes: "Instead of receiving a *misthos,* Paul claims to have been entrusted with a stewardship (*oikonomia*). When seen solely from the perspective of its involuntary origins, it is not entirely clear why such an *oikonomia* should rule out a *misthos*" ("Woes of the Prophets," 259). The reason is that *oikonomoi* (stewards or household administrators) were often slaves (see Stegemann and Stegemann, *Jesus Movement,* 45-46, commenting on Luke 16:1-9).
48. The term "gain" (*kerdainō*) bears strong economic connotations, even though, as BDAG (s.v. *kerdainō,* 1b), Fitzmyer (*First Corinthians,* 368-69), and others point out, it is often used to refer to the result of missionary activity in terms of "gaining" adherents within the context of a religious movement.
49. Similarly Gordon Fee: "Since [Paul] is under 'compulsion,' he cannot receive 'pay,' for 'pay' implies voluntary labor. His labor has been 'involuntary' in the sense of v. 16, that divine destiny has prescribed his task—he is a slave entrusted with a charge (v. 17)" (*First Epistle,* 415).
50. Broneer, "Isthmian Victory Crown"; Murphy-O'Connor, *St. Paul's Corinth,* 106. Both pine and celery were used in the Isthmian games at different periods.
51. Murphy-O'Connor, *St. Paul's Corinth,* 12-15.
52. Paul also compares himself favorably with a different group of evangelists in 2 Cor 11:21b-33.
53. On the rhetorical figure of aposiopesis, see Smyth, *Greek Grammar,* §3015.
54. See Blanton, "Boasting." Nasuti points out that Paul also adduces his renunciation of support from the Corinthians as grounds for boasting in 2 Cor 10-13 ("Woes of the Prophets," 255).
55. Seneca, *Ben.* 3.6.1-10.1; on contracts, see also Mauss, *The Gift,* 47-64.
56. On the social expectations underlying Seneca's views, see above in this chapter and chapter 2 herein; Mauss, *The Gift,* 3-4.
57. Compare the similar implication that an addressee owes Paul a "gift-debt" in Phlm 19; see chapter 3 herein.
58. See, for example, Carrier, "Gifts, Commodities, and Social Relations," 119-36; Miller, "Gift, Sale, Payment, Raid," 18-50.
59. Seneca, *Ben.* 1.3.4-5; 1.4.2.
60. The same instability is evident in the parallel Matthean and Lukan version of Jesus' missionary mandate (cp. n. 21 above).

Chapter 5. Classification and Social Relations

1. Godbout and Caillé, *World of the Gift,* 9.
2. The chapter's subtitle is derived from Sherry, McGrath, and Levy, "Dark Side of the Gift." See also Marcoux, who repeatedly uses the phrase "the dark side of the gift" in "Escaping the Gift Economy."
3. Davis, *Gift in Sixteenth-Century France,* 67–84. The title below, "Gifts Gone Wrong in Corinth," is indebted to a chapter similarly titled in Davis's book.
4. Marcoux, "Escaping the Gift Economy," 671–85.
5. Mauss, *The Gift,* 13.
6. *Ben.* 3.1.4.
7. *Ben.* 3.1.1. Translation of J. W. Basore, *Seneca: Moral Essays* (3 vols., LCL; Cambridge, MA: Harvard University Press, and London: Heinemann, 1935 [repr. 1964]).
8. Peter Sidney Darow, *OCD,* s.v. "Laelius, Gaius," 811.
9. Ernst Badian, *OCD,* s.v. "Cornelius Scipio Aemilianus Africanus (Numantinus), Publius," 397–98.
10. *Amic.* 10.35; translation of William A. Falconer, *Cicero: De senectute, De amicitia, De divinatione* (LCL; Cambridge, MA: Harvard University Press, 1992 [1923]), 147.
11. See chapter 4 herein.
12. So Hock, *Social Context,* 59–64; Marshall, *Enmity in Corinth,* 174–77, 247; Chow, *Patronage and Power,* 109–10; Welborn, *End to Enmity,* 398–400.
13. So also Collins, *Second Corinthians,* 216, 220; Thrall, *Critical and Exegetical Commentary,* 2:689–90, 703–4; Furnish, *II Corinthians,* 506–9; Martin, *2 Corinthians,* 348; Harris, *Second Epistle,* 766–67.
14. So Thrall, *Critical and Exegetical Commentary,* 842; Furnish, *II Corinthians,* 556; Martin, *2 Corinthians,* 438; Harris, *Second Epistle,* 869, 877–79.
15. Peter Marshall has made this point forcefully: "Paul's acceptance of the Philippian gifts does appear to have been understood by the Corinthians within the conventions of friendship and enmity. By his refusal [to accept gifts in Corinth] he has insulted and dishonoured them, treated them as inferiors and showed them that he did not love them. . . . There is ample evidence of a hostile relationship between Paul and his enemies—invective, comparison, conspiracy, charges—and it does appear to result from Paul's refusal, and his consequent behaviour" (*Enmity in Corinth,* 246–47). Welborn dissents: "Paul's decision to decline the offer of support from Gaius, whenever it came, must have occasioned consternation, as a departure from the paradigm of Greco-Roman friendship. But it need not have instigated enmity" (*End to*

Enmity, 400). In light of Cicero's statement in *Amic.* 10.35 (quoted above), it is evident that failure to accede to a friend's request constituted a breach of the "law of friendship," which would be expected to lead to recrimination. While a single breach need not destroy a friendship, "ceaseless recriminations" (*querella inveterata*) threaten to dissolve social intimacy and engender "everlasting enmities" (*odia . . . sempiterna*). It is the possibility that recrimination might degenerate into irreparable and "everlasting enmity" that Paul's assertion of his "love" (2 Cor 11:11) and his indication that he has done no "wrong" (12:13) attempt to forestall. He attempts to save the friendship by addressing the grounds on which the recrimination was based.

16. For overviews of the pertinent issues, see Betz, *2 Corinthians 8 and 9*, 3–36; Thrall, *Critical and Exegetical Commentary*, 1:1–49; Reimund Bieringer, "Teilungshypothesen zum 2. Korintherbrief: Ein Forschungsüberblick," in Bieringer and Lambrecht, *Studies on 2 Corinthians*, 67–105; Mitchell, "Corinthian Epistles"; Mitchell, "Paul's Letters to Corinth"; Schmeller, *Der zweite Brief an die Korinther*, 18–40.
17. Here I follow the dates suggested by Meeks and Fitzgerald, eds., *Writings of St. Paul*, 21–23, 44–46. For discussions of the chronology see, among others, Jewett, *Chronology of Paul's Life*; Lüdemann, *Paul*.
18. Various reconstructions of the background and ideology of these missionaries have been proposed; see, for example, Georgi, *Opponents of Paul*, 1–9; Sumney, *Identifying Paul's Opponents*; Reimund Bieringer, "Die Gegner des Paulus im 2. Korintherbrief," in Bieringer and Lambrecht, *Studies on 2 Corinthians*, 181–221; Thrall, *Critical and Exegetical Commentary*, 2:926–45; Blanton, *Constructing a New Covenant*, 109–21; Blanton, "Spirit and Covenant Renewal."
19. Cicero, *Reg. Deiot.* 11.30; *Verr.* 2.2.37. For additional evidence, see Marshall, *Enmity in Corinth*, 56–60.
20. So Furnish, *II Corinthians*, 498, 506; Barnett, *Second Epistle*, 521; Thrall, *Critical and Exegetical Commentary*, 2:693; Harris, *Second Epistle*, 752–53, 767.
21. Welborn, *End to Enmity*, 142. See also Welborn, "Paul's Caricature."
22. Welborn, *End to Enmity*, 139–50.
23. Welborn, *End to Enmity*, 140–50. Welborn's translation (139–40).
24. So Marshall: "It is clear enough that refusal of gifts and services or attempts to end a friendship could be and were construed as an act of hostility by the offended party. . . . By his refusal he has insulted and dishonoured them, treated them as inferiors and showed that he did not love them" (*Enmity in Corinth*, 246).

25. On Paul's assertions that he serves as "father" to the assemblies he founds, see White, "Paul and *Pater Familias*," esp. 470-71.
26. The asymmetry between benefits conferred by parents and their children was so great that Seneca addresses at length the question of whether children can ever surpass their parents' benefactions (*Ben.* 3.29.2-38.3).
27. Welborn relates this to the associations with patronage latent in an offer of hospitality: "Paul cleverly exploits the parent-child analogy to bring about a role-reversal in his relationship with the Corinthians; for in the analogy, Paul figures himself as the parental patron and the Corinthians his filial clients" (*End to Enmity*, 139).
28. Here Paul returns to a theme introduced in 1 Corinthians; see chapter 4 herein.
29. Marshall (*Enmity in Corinth*, 341-48) notes that Paul engages in the technique of non-naming, whereby one refers to one's enemies only obliquely; the technique amounts to a form of *damnatio memoriae*.
30. So Peterman, *Paul's Gift from Philippi*, 168-69; Hock, *Social Context*, 30 and n. 44.
31. Tacitus, *Annals* 2.38. Translation of John Jackson, *Tacitus: The Annals* (LCL; Cambridge, MA: Harvard University Press, and London: Heinemann, 1962 [1931]), slightly modified.
32. Translation of R. D. Hicks, *Diogenes Laertius: Lives of Eminent Philosophers* (LCL; London: Heinemann, and New York: Putnam, 1925), slightly modified.
33. BDAG defines the verb *hessoomai*, "to be put in lesser or worse circumstances or status." The term implies a diminution of status; thus the translation into idiomatic English, "to slight someone." BDAG suggests the translation, "in what respect, then, are you being made to feel less important than the other congregations" (s.v. *hessoomai*).
34. The Vulgate can translate both verbs with *gravare;* 2 Cor 12:13: *ego ipse non gravavi vos* (Greek *katanarkan*); 2 Cor 12:16: *ego vos non gravavi* (Greek *katabarein*).
35. Both glosses suggested by BDAG, s.v. *katanarkaō*.
36. Compare Welborn (*End to Enmity*, 134-35): "It cannot be that Paul employs *katanarkan* [in 2 Cor 11:9] simply for the sake of variation, since the term is repeated strategically in Paul's recapitulation of his defense in 12:13, and comes up again in 12:14. So we must assume that Paul has used this unusual word intentionally, and with consciousness of its original meaning." Welborn, however, prefers the meaning "to be slothful towards" (citing LSJ) in these instances.

37. Literally, "In what way have you been slighted (or, diminished) more than the other assemblies?" The use of *hyper* with the accusative indicates a comparison (cp. BDAG, s.v. *hyper*).
38. In favor of the letter's unity, see Fitzgerald, "Philippians, Epistle to the," esp. 320–22; in favor of the view that canonical Philippians consists of three originally independent letters, see Reumann, *Philippians*, 8–18.
39. On the economic context of Paul's language, see Ogereau, *Paul's Koinonia*; see, however, chapter 2 n. 26 herein for criticisms of the thesis.
40. Marshall, *Enmity in Corinth*, 34; Peterman, *Paul's Gift from Philippi*, 53–65. Cicero, *Amic.* 16.58, illuminates the social context: "It surely is calling friendship to a very close and petty accounting to require it to keep an exact balance of credits and debits [*ratio acceptorum et datorum*]. I think true friendship is richer and more abundant than that and does not narrowly scan the reckoning lest it pay out more than it has received; and there need be no fear that some bit of kindness will be lost, that it will overflow the measure and spill upon the ground, or that more than is due will be poured into friendship's bin." Translation of Falconer, *Cicero*, 169. See also Seneca, *Ben.* 1.2.3, and chapter 3 herein on Paul's keeping an imaginary account book listing credits and debits in his gift exchange relationships. Ogereau argues against the idea that reciprocal gift exchange is in view in Philippians (*Paul's Koinonia*, 28–42, 274–80), but Paul's comparison of the donations that Epaphroditus sent him with sacrifices, prototypical "gifts to God" (Phil 4:18), and his assurance that God would provide a countergift (v. 19) establish Paul's use of the gift exchange paradigm.
41. For a brief overview of the Roman carceral system, see Rapske, "Prison, Prisoner"; Rapske, *Book of Acts and Paul in Roman Custody*.
42. In Thessalonica as in Corinth, Paul labored as a leatherworker to support himself (1 Thess 2:9).
43. So Furnish, *II Corinthians*, 553, 556. Thrall objects that the use of the emphatic *autos egō* points to a contrast, not with "other churches," but with other missionaries, that is, those with whom Paul compares himself in 2 Cor 11:1–12:13 (*Critical and Exegetical Commentary*, 841–42). Thrall is only partially correct, since the contrast between Paul and his missionary rivals and that between his practices in Corinth and other communities are not mutually exclusive. The comparison between Paul and his rivals entailed judgments about their respective modes of support.
44. So Furnish, *II Corinthians*, 507. It is possible that other cities (Thessalonica and Beroea) were included; so Thrall, *Critical and Exegetical Commentary*, 685–86. Peterman, however, notes that "the evidence is too sparse to make a

decision" as to whether cities other than Philippi were in view (*Paul's Gift from Philippi,* 146, n. 134).
45. As calculated using "ORBIS: The Stanford Geospatial Network Model of the Roman World," http://orbis.stanford.edu/#using.
46. Contra Caragounis, who asserts that the *opsōnion* took the form of provisions: "in all probability, the gifts were in kind; they were provisions: foodstuff and perhaps clothes, though the possibility that some money also was included can not be ruled out" ("*OPSŌNION,*" 53).
47. Contra David Dungan, who asserts that Paul received from Philippi "financial support in sufficient amount so that it could be termed a salary" (cited in Martin, *2 Corinthians,* 346). It is not the amount, but the measured regularity with which it is given, that distinguishes salary from gift.
48. Welborn, *End to Enmity,* 380-481.
49. Plummer, *Second Epistle,* 364.
50. I am largely persuaded by Margaret Mitchell's recent arguments concerning the order in which the various letters now contained in 2 Corinthians were written ("Corinthian Epistles" and "Paul's Letters to Corinth"). Two caveats are in order. First, Thomas Schmeller, who argues that 2 Corinthians was written as a single letter, offers an important cautionary remark on the hypothetical and provisional nature of all reconstructions of the literary history of the letter or letters in 2 Corinthians: "*Jeder* der vorgetragenen Lösungsversuche bringt eigene Schwierigkeiten mit sich. Eine Abwägung ist nicht objektiv möglich" (*Der zweite Brief,* 37). The same holds true of the hypothesis of literary unity, however. The manuscript tradition provides "objective" evidence for the literary unity of 2 Corinthians only as the text was transmitted during the third-fourth centuries CE and later (i.e., from the time of our earliest manuscripts). If the various sections of 2 Corinthians ever existed in independent form, they had already been edited into a single document by that time. Failing objective evidence to establish the form in which 2 Corinthians, or its component parts, circulated in the mid-first century CE, the researcher must come to a decision on the basis of literary-critical issues, fully recognizing the provisional nature of his or her own position. Second, Larry Welborn (*End to Enmity,* xix-xxvii) has recently argued in favor of a "literary history" of the Corinthian correspondence similar to Mitchell's, although he places the apologetic letter of 2:14-7:4 (minus 6:14-7:1) after the "tearful letter" (2 Cor 10-13), rather than before it. For the purposes of the present argument, the placement of 2:14-7:4 in relation to 10-13 is not crucial. For a relative chronology of the events and letters of greatest significance to the present argument, see the Appendix.

51. On the patroness Phoebe, see Lampe, "Paul, Patrons, and Clients," 498–99.
52. NRSV (modified).
53. So Welborn, *End to Enmity,* 321–35; Dunn, *Romans,* 2:910–11; Murphy-O'Connor, *St. Paul's Corinth,* 182–83. It may have been in Gaius's house that the meetings for the Lord's supper, a communal meal commemorating the death of the early Christian community's "lord," Jesus, took place (1 Cor 11:17–34). On the Lord's supper and the problems of social stratification that it entailed in Corinth, see, among others, Theissen, *Social Setting of Pauline Christianity,* 145–74; Lampe, "Das korinthische Herrenmahl"; Murphy-O'Connor, *St. Paul's Corinth,* 178–85; Schmeller, *Hierarchie und Egalität,* 66–73; Welborn, *End to Enmity,* 358–65, 401–3.
54. So Welborn, *End to Enmity,* 243: "there is general agreement among scholars that Paul resided with Gaius on the occasion of his final visit to Corinth, and was, in this way, the recipient of Gaius' hospitality." Similarly, Dunn, *Romans,* 1:xliv; Jewett, *Chronology of Paul's Life,* "Graph of Dates and Time-spans" (n.p.); Fitzmyer, *Romans,* 85–88 (Corinth in the winter of 57–58 CE); Murphy-O'Connor, *Paul: A Critical Life,* 30–31, 331–32 (55–56 CE). A caveat is in order: Lüdemann (*Paul,* 178–79) views the three-month time span as a "round number" created by the redactor of Luke-Acts; he places Paul's third visit to Corinth in 51/52 CE (pp. 171–72).
55. John T. Fitzgerald notes that, although the terms *philia* and *philos* do not occur in Paul's letters, closely associated motifs appear frequently; friendship is thus an important category for Paul. See Fitzgerald, "Paul and Friendship." On shifts in Paul's thinking, see Fitzgerald, "Paul and Paradigm Shifts." Welborn holds a similar view (*End to Enmity,* 380–91): "Paul did not simply accommodate himself to the framework of Roman friendship, but shifted some of its conventional elements" (p. 391).
56. On the "dance of the Graces" as a metaphor for gift exchange, see chapter 2 herein.
57. Mitchell, "Paul's Letters to Corinth," 307–38.
58. Plutarch observes that parasites are "driven away and punished by everyone" (*Mor.* 778D–E; cited in Welborn, *End to Enmity,* 148).

Chapter 6. The Gift of Status

1. Mauss notes: "No less important in these transactions of the Indians [of the American Northwest] is the role played by the notion of honour. Nowhere is the individual prestige of a chief and that of his clan so closely linked to what

is spent and to the meticulous repayment with interest of gifts that have been accepted, so as to transform into persons having an obligation those that have placed you yourself under a similar obligation" (*The Gift*, 37). Note also the unilateral (and therefore accumulative) distribution of baskets and other valuables to the chief of the wife's clan during marriage exchanges in Polynesia described by Claude Lévi-Strauss in *Elementary Structures*, 63-65.

2. Mauss, *The Gift*, 5-7, 36-46.
3. C. A. Gregory explains the relationship between giving and status: "The accumulation of capital, whether in the form of pigs, blankets or money, is not the aim of a gift transactor. To the extent that gift transactors accumulate at all it is in the form of gift-credit. The big-man is the one with the most gift-credit for he has been able to maximise net-outgoings" ("Gifts to Men and Gifts to God," 638).
4. On the relations between economic and other forms of capital, see Bourdieu, "Forms of Capital"; Swartz, *Culture and Power*, 65-94; Robert Moore, "Capital," in Michael Grenfell, ed., *Pierre Bourdieu*, 101-17.
5. Mauss, *The Gift*, 37.
6. Gregory, "Gifts to Men and Gifts to God," 626-52.
7. See Saller, *Personal Patronage*, 128-29. The economic dependence and subordinate status of the client is illustrated by the poet Martial: "Yesterday, Caecilianus, when I came to bid you 'Good Morning,' I accidentally greeted you by name and forgot to call you 'My Lord.' How much did this liberty cost me? You knocked a dollar off my allowance" (*Ep.* 6.88). Translation of Shelton, *As the Romans Did*, 14.
8. *OLD*, s.v. status, 1-3.
9. *OLD*, s.v. status, 9-10.
10. John Scott, "Class and Stratification," in Geoff Payne, ed., *Social Divisions*, 25-64 (esp. 26-31). Compare Max Weber, "Class, Status, Party" and "Status Groups and Classes," reprinted in Grusky, ed., *Social Stratification*, 114-24, 124-28, respectively.
11. Scott, "Class and Stratification," 29.
12. Scott, "Class and Stratification," 29.
13. Scott, "Class and Stratification," 29.
14. Tepperman and Curtis, *Sociology*, 362.
15. Macionis, *Sociology*, 140.
16. Macionis, *Sociology*, 140-41.
17. Vanfossen, *Structure of Social Inequality*, 8-9.
18. Seneca the Younger, *Prov.* 2.5; *Ira* 2.21.1-6.

19. Pliny the Younger, *Ep.* 9.12.
20. See the discussion in Lincoln, *Ephesians,* 400–402, citing Dionysius of Halicarnassus, *Rom. Ant.* 2.26.1–4; Xenophon, *Mem.* 4.4.19–20; Cicero, *Offic.* 1.58; Epictetus, *Diss.* 2.17.31; 3.7.26.
21. Seymour M. Lipset ("Social Class") distinguished three "dimensions" of status: "(1) *objective* status, or aspects of stratification that structure environments differently enough to provoke differences in behavior; (2) *accorded* status, or the prestige accorded to individuals and groups by others; (3) *subjective* status, or the personal sense of location within the social hierarchy felt by various individuals" (p. 310).
22. *Claud.* 15.4; cited in Welborn, *Paul, the Fool of Christ,* 47.
23. See, for example, Seneca's ruminations on slaves who save the lives of their masters, thus achieving high accorded status (*Ben.* 3.18.1–29.1, esp. 23.5, 25), and Pliny the Younger's lament over Fannia, the second wife of Helvidius Priscus: "Yet how charming and genial she is, and how she inspires affection as much as respect, a quality granted to few! Will there be any woman after whom we can establish a model for our wives, and to whom we men can look for patterns of courage? Will there be any whom we can likewise gaze upon and listen to in admiration, like the heroines of history?" (*Ep.* 7.19). Translation of Walsh, *Pliny the Younger,* 176.
24. See most recently Friesen, "Junia Theodora of Corinth."
25. See Blanton, "Boasting": "since honor is based on communal judgment, it cannot be self-conferred: 'even the winners of the crown at the games are proclaimed victors by others, who thus remove the odium of self-praise' (Plutarch, *Mor.* 539C; cp. Quintilian, *Educ. Or.* 11.1.22). Attempts to confer honor on oneself risk arousing the envy (*phthonos*) of the hearers (Isocrates, *Antid.* 8, 13; Plutarch, *Mor.* 539D) and bringing dishonor (*adoxia; Mor.* 547E–F) to the speaker."
26. Translation of Walsh, *Pliny,* 251.
27. Compare Cicero, *Agr.* 2.2.3: *dignitas consularis,* "a being worthy of the office of consul"; cited in L&S, s.v. *dignitas,* I.
28. Walsh, *Pliny,* 364, note to 26.1. Sherwin-White concurs: "This is a rather obscurely worded recommendation of Rosianus for any posts in the emperor's service to which his present rank qualifies him" (*Letters of Pliny,* 596).
29. On the reciprocal exchange of gifts and services involved in patron-client relations, see chapter 2 herein (and the literature cited in notes 1–2 of that chapter).
30. Translation of Walsh, *Pliny,* 244.
31. So Sherwin-White, *Letters of Pliny,* 174.

32. The "right of three children" actually consists of two regulations: the *Lex Iulia de maritandis ordinibus* (18 BCE) and the *Lex Papia Poppaea* (9 CE); see Berger, *Encyclopedic Dictionary*, 553–54. It was sometimes granted as an honorary award even to those who did not have three children.
33. Translation of Walsh, *Pliny*, 243–44.
34. The term "friend" used here is a euphemism. On the avoidance of the term *cliens*, see Saller, *Personal Patronage*, 8–15, and Saller, "Patronage and Friendship." This is not to deny that genuine goodwill and positive regard may have existed between the two.
35. Although the book as a whole is highly illuminating, Zeba A. Crook's claim in *Reconceptualising Conversion*, 56–59, 64, that the "technical definition" of gift exchange necessarily entails equality between the parties to the exchange (i.e., that the recipient of a gift should be able to reciprocate on an equal basis) is problematic. He himself notes that the Greco-Roman literature speaks of "gifts" in exchanges both between patrons and clients and between humans and their gods (85–86, 98–99). Gift exchanges may occur within the context of either symmetric or asymmetric relations. "Gift" is a broad term that refers simply to "that which is given" in a wide variety of extramercantile contexts. See chapter 4 herein for the distinction between "gift" and "sale."
36. Translation of Griffin and Inwood, *Lucius Annaeus Seneca*, 53.
37. Sherwin-White, *Letters of Pliny*, 210.
38. Translation of Walsh, *Pliny*, 56–57 (slightly modified).
39. Sherwin-White, *Letters of Pliny*, 211.
40. So NRSV; lit. "are not a terror to the good deed, but to the bad."
41. There is not a wholly satisfying way to translate the term *leitourgos*. It refers to someone who performs a *leitourgia*—a sort of tax imposed upon wealthy individuals by cities in which the individuals were required to cover the expenses for some public work, such as outfitting ships for war. Although BDAG's gloss "servant" effectively captures the idea that the *leitourgos* provides a public service, it is misleading in that it may be taken to imply low status, a connotation not present with the Greek term. My translation "public service provider" attempts better to capture the connotations of the Greek. One caveat: contemporary "service providers" tend to charge fees, whereas liturgies were provided at the expense of the public benefactor.
42. On the structure of Rome's extractive economy, see Hanson and Oakman, *Palestine in the Time of Jesus*, 107–8. For the more recent view that Roman imperialism generated market conditions conducive to economic growth, even in the provinces, see Jongman, "Re-constructing the Roman Economy."
43. As, for example, in Mark 13:7; Matt 24:6, 14.

44. These beings he designates as the "elements of the world" whose power "enslaves" the majority of humanity (Gal 4:3). On the "elemental spirits," see Betz, *Galatians*, 204–5. In comparison with the superior rank and quality of the god of Israel, such beings cannot even lay claim to the designation "gods": in Paul's view, they are "those who by nature are not gods" (Gal 4:8).

45. The term occurs in Romans, 1 and 2 Corinthians, Galatians, Philippians, and 1 Thessalonians. In the letter to the Philippians, the term is used to designate Epaphroditus as an emissary of the assembly at Philippi (Phil 2:25); it is absent from the letter to Philemon.

46. See the discussions of the term in Betz, *Galatians*, 37–39, 74–75; Meeks, *First Urban Christians*, 131–33; Schütz, *Paul and the Anatomy of Apostolic Authority*, 22–34.

47. BDAG, s.v. *charis*, 4: refers to the "exceptional effect produced by generosity, *favor*," citing 1 Cor 15:10abc as examples.

48. NRSV translates "grace" each time the term *charis* appears in these verses. The theological appropriation and subsequent development of doctrines of "grace" by Augustine and Luther often obscures the logic of gift exchange in Paul's letters. I have attempted to restore the clarity of Paul's formulations by translating as "beneficence" and "favor" (in most cases following BDAG). It is, however, difficult to assign a specific nuance to the multivalent term in each case; it can refer alternately to a favorable disposition that might result in the giving of a gift, the gift itself, or thanksgiving in response to a gift. For a discussion, see Crook, *Reconceptualising Conversion*, 132–50; Harrison, *Paul's Language of Grace*, 273–79. Note, however, the criticisms of Harrison's work in Crook, *Reconceptualising Conversion*, 145–47, and Engberg-Pedersen, "Gift-Giving and Friendship," 17–18. John Barclay retains the translation "grace" but offers a history of the term's use in Christian theology in order to differentiate Paul's views from later developments; see his *Paul and the Gift*, 79–193.

49. So also Crook, *Reconceptualising Conversion*, 157–58.

50. BDAG, s.v. *charis*, 4.

51. So Fitzmyer, *Romans*, 237.

52. Compare BDAG, s.v. *charis*, 2: "a beneficent disposition toward someone, *favor, grace . . . goodwill*" (italics in original), citing Gal. 1:15 as an example.

53. Note, however, that the phrase "and, through his beneficence, called me" is missing from the c. 200 CE manuscript P[46].

54. On God as patron in the synoptic gospels, see Malina, "Patron and Client"; for patronage motifs in the New Testament and Greco-Roman religions, see

Neyrey, "God, Benefactor and Patron"; on patronage motifs in Paul, see Pickett, "Death of Christ"; Osiek, "Politics of Patronage." On God as Paul's patron, see Crook, *Reconceptualising Conversion,* 151-97, 243-50; Lampe, "Paul, Patrons, and Clients," esp. 505-7. David J. Downs ("Is God Paul's Patron?") rejects patronage as a model illuminating Paul's theology. He argues that Paul's language of God as "father" (rather than "patron") and the possibility for exploitation in patron-client relations indicate that patronage does not apply to Paul's constructions of divine-human relations. However, it is precisely in his role as imperial patron that Augustus was called *pater patriae* (cp. Favro, "Making Rome a World City," esp. 245-48), and, in the wake of Friedrich Nietzsche (e.g., *The Antichrist,* sections 42, 45), the possibility of religious exploitation on Paul's part cannot simply be dismissed without argument.

55. Crook, *Reconceptualising Conversion,* passim, esp. 151-97; Crook, "Divine Benefactions"; see also Jennings, "Patronage and Rebuke." For the exchange of services, or *officia,* in the Roman context, see Saller, *Personal Patronage,* 15-22. For a discussion of "heavenly patronage" in relation to the cultus of Isis, see Blanton, "*De caelo patrocinium,*" and Crook, *Reconceptualising Conversion,* 113, 122-23.

56. The point is acknowledged (or conceded) by most commentators; see, for example, Ehrensperger, *Paul and the Dynamics of Power,* 135-36, 150-51, 155, who, however, sees Paul's claims to power as temporally self-limiting; he does not seek to "establish a *permanent* structure of domination and control" (emphasis added; 136); Polaski, *Paul and the Discourse of Power,* 30-35; 104-11; 118-23; Castelli, *Imitating Paul,* 96, 100-102, 110-17; McNeel, *Paul as Infant and Nursing Mother,* 172; Økland, *Women in Their Place,* 176-77; Schmeller, *Hierarchie und Egalität,* 77. For a critique of the contrary position represented by Edwin Judge, see below, "'Anti-Status' Views of Paul."

57. Grant, *Paul in the Roman World,* 24.

58. According to Douglas Moo, "Paul would intend the 'gifts' to summarize those privileges of Israel that he enumerated in 9:4-5" (*Epistle to the Romans,* 732), where the "privileges" include the covenants and the patriarchs; for the covenant of circumcision, see Gen 17:9-14, where the connection between the patriarch Abraham and circumcision is also established.

59. Note that, in addition to the "gift" of status with respect to apostles, teachers, and the other positions to be surveyed, Paul construes marital status as a "gift" in 1 Cor 7:7. The context makes it clear that the sorts of "gifts" to which Paul refers are not the "spiritual gifts" of prophecy, glossolalia, and so on discussed in 1 Cor 12-14, but the gift of marital status.

60. This phrase is often translated as "concerning spiritual gifts," as in NRSV. The term "gifts," however, is not present in the Greek but is supplied on the basis of the context.
61. Greek *kybernēseis;* cp. *kybernētēs:* a ship's "steersman" or "pilot" (see MM and *EDNT* under the respective headings).
62. As noted by Garland, *1 Corinthians,* 598.
63. Fitzmyer, *First Corinthians,* 482. Fitzmyer's subsequent qualification that the ordinals "could be simply an indication of historical time when such functions emerged in the church" lacks support.
64. Longenecker, *Remember the Poor,* 282.
65. On the theme of *mimesis,* or imitation, and its implications for the hierarchical ordering of social relations within the assemblies, see Castelli, *Imitating Paul,* passim.
66. See the recent detailed work of McNeel on this passage: *Paul as Infant and Nursing Mother,* passim.
67. On the content of Paul's "gospel," see Sanders, *Paul,* 25–29.
68. Note that in Rom 1:5 and 15:18, obedience to Christ entails obedience to Paul's proclamation and directives.
69. Hospitality could be anticipated for most or all members of the early assemblies (e.g., Rom 16:1–2), but it is only apostles for whom room and board was considered a "right"; for others, it was a gift or favor. On hospitality in Greece, Rome, and early Judaism, see Fitzgerald, "Hospitality."
70. The citation continues: "The Father sent it as a helper of good men, and again to Zeus it goes, having been cast with the thunderbolt of God."
71. Verses 34–35 are placed after 14:40 in manuscripts D, F, G, and some Vulgate texts; they occur after v. 33b in Codex Sinaiticus, A, B, and other texts. For a detailed discussion, see Schrage, *Der erste Brief,* 4:457, 479–87. For an argument in favor of Pauline authorship, see Wire, "1 Corinthians," esp. 186–87.
72. On the "language of the gods," see Bader, *La langue des dieux;* Bader, "Language of the Gods in Homer"; Bernabé, "Las *Ephesia Grammata,*" 5–28; Brashear, "Greek Magical Papyri"; Clay, "Planktai and Moly"; Charles de Lamberterie, "Grec homérique *MŌLY*"; Graf, "Prayer in Magical and Religious Ritual."
73. See Hans-Josef Klauck, "Mit Engelszungen? Von Charisma der verständlichen Rede in 1 Kor 14," and "Von Kassandra bis zur Gnosis: Im Umfeld der frühchristlichen Glossolalie," repr. in Klauck, *Religion und Gesellschaft,* 145–67 and 119–44, respectively; Martin, "Tongues of Angels."
74. Lincoln, "Theses on Method." See esp. thesis 11.

NOTES TO PAGES 96-99

75. Judge, *Social Distinctives*, 105.
76. Judge, *Social Distinctives*, 105.
77. Judge, *Social Distinctives*, 108.
78. Judge, *Social Distinctives*, 108.
79. Martin, *Slavery as Salvation*. Martin states: "In the Greco-Roman world certain highly visible slaves, some of whom were downright famous, controlled substantial amounts of money. Greek and Roman authors were constantly carping about uppity slaves who were rich rather than honest, upstanding free men such as themselves. . . . Higher-placed imperial slaves are an obvious example of slaves with money. They were the most famous wealthy slaves in the first century" (pp. 7-8). See also Harrison, *Paul's Language of Grace*, 234-35.
80. Schmeller (*Hierarchie und Egalität*, 57) notes: "Das Prestige eines Patrons färbt gleichsam auf die Klienten ab."
81. Translation of J. W. Cohoon, *Dio Chrysostom* (LCL; London: William Heinemann, New York: G. P. Putnam's Sons, 1937), 1:129-31.
82. Veyne, *Bread and Circuses*, esp. 10-18, 246-60.
83. See Engberg-Pedersen's cogent critique of the dichotomy, "Gift-Giving and Friendship"; Briones, *Paul's Financial Policy*, 48-53.
84. Translation of Cohoon, *Dio Chrysostom*, 1:123.
85. So, for example, Taylor, *Paul, Apostle to the Nations*, 288: "In his intervention for Onesimus [in his letter to Philemon], Paul outlines some of the basics of life in the Christ-believing community, which is a family of siblings."
86. Cited in Schussler-Fiorenza, *In Memory of Her*, 255.
87. Schussler-Fiorenza, *In Memory of Her*, 205-50: "Paul's interpretation and adaptation of the baptismal declaration Gal 3:28 in his letters to the community of Corinth unequivocally affirm the equality and charismatic giftedness of women and men in the Christian community" (p. 235).
88. Attempts to escape the subordination of female to male in this passage by understanding *kephalē* as "source" rather than "head" are beside the point: whether based on a metaphor of derivation or elevation, a hierarchical relation is entailed; see rightly Økland, *Women in Their Place*, 174-83. Økland writes: "But in spite of recent attempts I find it impossible to strip Paul's use of the word *kephalē* from the hierarchical connotations the term has in other ancient contexts, or to eliminate value-judgements and power implications from the expression 'man is the head/source of woman.' 'Source' is not a neutral concept in Greco-Roman discourse! Rather, the source is more authentic, or in Elizabeth Castelli's words, the origin, the original or first-born, had priority and superior status vis-a-vis the imitation" (pp. 175-76).

89. Although in some instances Paul does use female imagery when referring to the god of Israel, the god is nevertheless classified as "male." On female imagery in Paul's depictions of the god of Israel, see most recently McNeel, *Paul as Infant and Nursing Mother;* note also my review in *RBL* (http://www.bookreviews.org/pdf/9921_10985.pdf). It is doubtful that Paul personifies the feminine-gendered "wisdom" as, for example, in Wisdom of Solomon 9:1–10:21.

90. Lincoln, *Discourse and the Construction of Society,* 142–59, esp. 145–48; Mitchell, *Paul and the Rhetoric of Reconciliation,* 157–64; Martin, *Corinthian Body,* 38–68.

91. See most recently Ogereau, "Jerusalem Collection," who notes: "It is therefore unlikely that by appealing to the principle of *isotēs* and Exod 16.18 Paul wished to impose an exact equalisation of resources across all the churches, an impractical, if not impossible objective to attain. Rather, his edited citation suggests that the goal was to achieve a relative, proportional equality by restoring a certain balance between need and surplus" (pp. 365–66). See also Welborn, "'That There May Be Equality.'"

92. Translation of W. D. Ross, cited in Pojman and Westmoreland, eds., *Equality,* 20.

93. For a concise overview of Aristotle's statements on equality, see Welborn, "'That There May Be Equality,'" 76, 81–82, citing Hirzel, *Themis, Dike und Verwandtes,* 277–81.

94. On this passage, see Welborn, "'That There May Be Equality,'" 86–88; Gaventa, "Economy of Grace"; Barclay, "Manna and the Circulation of Grace"; Jennings, "Patronage and Rebuke," esp. 126.

Chapter 7. Spiritual Gifts and Status Inversion

1. Meeks, *First Urban Christians,* 22–23, 54–55.
2. Meeks, *First Urban Christians,* 55.
3. Meeks, *First Urban Christians,* 54 (emphasis in original).
4. Meeks, *First Urban Christians,* 54–55, 174, 191.
5. Meeks, *First Urban Christians,* 54.
6. Meeks, *First Urban Christians,* 54. See also Seymour M. Lipset, "Social Class," in Sills, ed., *International Encyclopedia of the Social Sciences,* 296–316 (310).
7. Meeks, *First Urban Christians,* 54.
8. There is a tension between Meeks's theoretical formulations, which lack elements of time, change, and contestation, and his more nuanced analyses of

NOTES TO PAGES 106–111   183

Paul's letters, in which those factors do play a role (cp. Meeks, *First Urban Christians*, 117–25, where the notion of status, however, plays only a minor role in the analysis). Meeks does, however, note that "the weight of each dimension depends on who is doing the weighing" (p. 54). This statement opens the door to issues of contest and negotiation, but the insight is not further developed.

9. "Preface," in Ehrenreich, Crumley, and Levy, eds., *Heterarchy*, v. Crumley notes that the idea was developed as early as 1945 by Warren McColloch in an analysis of neural networks; see Crumley, "Heterarchy," 3.
10. Crumley, "Heterarchy," 1–5 (2).
11. Crumley, "Heterarchy," 3.
12. Mark Mosko, cited in Dmitri M. Bondarenko, "Homoarchic Alternative," 20. See also Bondarenko and Grinin, "Alternative Pathways"; Bondarenko, "Approaching 'Complexity.'"
13. Crumley, "Dialectical Critique," 163 (emphasis in original).
14. Crumley, "Dialectical Critique," 163.
15. Rautman, "Hierarchy and Heterarchy," 329.
16. Rautman, "Hierarchy and Heterarchy," 328, citing Brumfiel, "Heterarchy."
17. Meeks, *First Urban Christians*, 54.
18. Meeks, *First Urban Christians*, 54.
19. Translation of Kennedy, *Progymnasmata*, 50.
20. See chapter 3, n. 43 herein.
21. Branham and Kinney, eds., *Petronius*.
22. Judge, *Social Distinctives*, 43, 86–87, 164–74; Lampe, "Paul, Patrons, and Clients"; Lampe, "Das korinthische Herrenmahl"; Theissen, *Social Setting of Pauline Christianity*, 69–174; Marshall, *Enmity in Corinth*; Chow, *Patronage and Power*; Osiek, "Politics of Patronage"; Osiek and MacDonald, *A Woman's Place*, 194–219; Kirner, "Apostolat und Patronage (I)."
23. For a classic treatment of the rhetoric of inversion, see Lincoln, *Discourse and the Construction of Society*, 142–59.
24. So Taylor, *Paul, Apostle to the Nations*, 278–79.
25. See Friesen, "Poverty in Pauline Studies," 350; Friesen, "Prospects for a Demography of the Pauline Mission," esp. 368; Longenecker, *Remember the Poor*, 298–332.
26. Palmer, *Mood and Modality*, 80.
27. On *paraleipsis*, see Smyth, *Greek Grammar*, §3036.
28. So Dunn, *The Epistles*, 340: "It is universally inferred that the obligation referred to is Philemon's conversion under Paul's ministry (cp. Rom 15:27)." See also Moo, *Letters to Colossians and Philemon*, 430: "What Paul means by say-

ing that Philemon owes him his very 'self' (*seauton*) is that Philemon is in debt to Paul for his eternal life."

29. Crook, *Reconceptualising Conversion*, 73–74: "To the client seeking something from a patron too far removed by status, the broker is a benefactor or patron because he or she has provided a benefaction by acting as broker."

30. On the social implications of claims to apostolic status, see chapter 6 herein.

31. On the term, see Judge, *Social Distinctives*, 171–72; Meeks, *First Urban Christians*, 60; Dunn, *Romans*, 2:888–89. For a recent (and in my view unsuccessful) argument that Phoebe did not function as a patroness to the assembly, see MacGillivray, "Romans 16:2." The distinction between patronage and benefaction is not as clearly drawn as MacGillivray suggests, and the distinction between vertical ("dependency") and horizontal ("friendly") relations cannot simply be correlated with the two terms. Thomas Schmeller has provided weightier arguments against understanding Phoebe as a patroness: (1) her role as *prostatis* was "sehr offen; sie ist nicht *prostatis* ihrer Heimatgemeinde, sondern 'vieler' "; (2) the phrase *kai gar autē* connects Phoebe's role as *prostatis* with the preceding request that the Roman assembly "assist" ("beistehen") her, using the verb *parastēte;* (3) it is unlikely that Paul was related to Phoebe as her client. See Schmeller, *Hierarchie und Egalität*, 58–59. However, Junia Theodora is an example of a woman who served as patroness to "many," and not just a home community, and forms of material "assistance" (including lodging, as is apparently requested for Phoebe) were endemic to the "services" (*officia*) provided by patrons (see, for example, Lucian's "On Salaried Posts in Great Houses"). On Junia, see most recently Friesen, "Junia Theodora of Corinth." On the basis of an inversion of the usual patronal logic (the argument of this chapter), I agree that it is unlikely that either Paul or Phoebe considered Paul to be her client. This does not, however, indicate that "patroness" is an improper gloss of Phoebe's role (see the comments of Lampe quoted in the text following this note). One must concede that the role was, as Schmeller indicates, "sehr offen," due not least to the inversions and modifications that took place within the heterarchic situation of the early Christian assemblies.

32. So Meeks, *First Urban Christians*, 16.
33. Lampe, "Paul, Patrons, and Clients," 499.
34. Marshall, *Enmity at Corinth;* Peterman, *Paul's Gift*.
35. Peterman (*Paul's Gift*, 159) states: "Paul has not become socially obligated, and thereby in a sense inferior, by accepting their gifts. Rather, because he has accepted their gifts, they have been elevated to the place of partners in the gospel. Though Paul is in receipt of their gift and can mention his own ben-

efit from it (4.18a), in 4.17b he rather makes it appear that they are actually the ones benefitted. Their gift does bring them a return. It is an investment that reaps spiritual dividends. But ultimately the responsibility to reward them rests not with Paul, but with God (4.19)." Peterman, however, rests content merely to have explicated Paul's theological construction; he does not subject it to critical analysis or relate it to Paul's position of interest.

36. However, as Reumann (*Philippians*, 7, 17) notes, "it is unclear" whether Paul had already been imprisoned when he wrote Phil 4:10–20; it is possible that the gift entailed financial aid, rather than supplies for his stay in prison. Bormann (*Philippi*, 208) opines that Paul's reference to "distress" in v. 14 probably indicates imprisonment.

37. According to Brian Rapske, prison rations often failed to meet the requirements to sustain life; see Rapske, *Book of Acts and Paul in Roman Custody*, 209–16.

38. See Phil 4:10, where he notes that the Philippian assembly "lacked opportunity" to provide at an earlier date, perhaps politely euphemizing what he experienced as their neglect.

39. Hock, *Social Context of Paul's Ministry*, 36.

40. His audience consisted of "auditors" because his letters were read aloud in assembly meetings (1 Thess 5:27; 1 Cor 3:2).

41. On the negative assessments of Paul's oratorical ability, see Winter, *Philo and Paul*, 203–39; Litfin, *St. Paul's Theology of Proclamation*, 154–73; Peterson, *Eloquence and the Proclamation of the Gospel*, 60–66; Mihaila, *Paul-Apollos Relationship*, 82–94, 152–64; Finney, *Honour and Conflict*, 84; Welborn, *End to Enmity*, 101–22.

42. On the evaluation of "bodily presence" in ancient oratory, see Dulk and Langford, "Polycarp and Polemo," esp. 224–35; Winter, *Philo and Paul*, 113–16, 221–23.

43. The term *kolaphizō* denotes a closed-fisted attack and so is generally translated "to beat" or "cuff" (cp. BDAG). I have translated the term "slapped around" to convey the sense of physical abuse in more idiomatic English.

44. The term *perikatharma* indicates "that which is removed as the result of a thorough cleansing," that is, "refuse" or "off-scouring" (BDAG, s.v.). Again, I have translated to reflect the modern idiom: "dirty dishwater." The synonymous term *peripsēma* (BDAG: "that which is removed by the process of cleansing") I translate as "soap scum" in keeping with the dishwashing motif. The idiomatic rendition restores the sense of ignominy that is lost in most English translations.

45. Nguyen, "Identification of Paul's Spectacle of Death Metaphor," 497.

46. According to Michel Foucault (*Discipline and Punish*) punishment ceased to be construed as a "spectacle" that served to preserve the moral order and began to be understood as a means of "correcting the soul" in Europe in the late 1700s and early 1800s.
47. Nguyen, "God's Execution," 40.
48. The characterization of the evangelists with whom Paul compares himself in the passage need not detain us here; on the issue, see Blanton, "Spirit and Covenant Renewal"; Sumney, *Identifying Paul's Opponents;* Sumney, *"Servants of Satan";* Georgi, *Opponents of Paul*, 1–9; Reimund Bieringer, "Die Gegner des Paulus im 2. Korintherbrief," in Bieringer and Lambrecht, *Studies on 2 Corinthians*, 181–221; Thrall, *Critical and Exegetical Commentary*, 2:926–45; Harris, *Second Epistle to the Corinthians*, 67–87.
49. For a detailed examination of Paul's lists of hardships within the context of Greco-Roman *peristasis* catalogs, see Fitzgerald, *Cracks in an Earthen Vessel.*
50. On Paul's "boasting" or "bragging," see Edwin A. Judge, "Paul's Boasting in Relation to Contemporary Practice," *Australian Biblical Review* 16 (1968), 37–50 (repr. in Judge, *Social Distinctives*, 57–72); Betz, *Der Apostel Paulus*, 75–77; Hans Dieter Betz, "*De Laude ipsius* (*Moralia* 539A–547F)," in Betz, *Plutarch's Ethical Writings*, 367–93; Forbes, "Comparison, Self-Praise and Irony"; Danker, "Paul's Debt"; Mitchell, "Patristic Perspective"; David Aune, "Boasting," in Aune, *Westminster Dictionary*, 81–84; Watson, "Paul and Boasting"; Blanton, "Boasting."
51. On "weakness" as indicating a lack of sociopolitical efficacy, note Philo, *On Dreams:* "Are not private citizens continually becoming officials, and officials private citizens, rich men becoming poor men and poor men men of ample means, nobodies being celebrated, obscure people becoming distinguished, weak men [*astheneis*] strong [*ischyroi*], insignificant men powerful [*dynatoi*], foolish men wise men of understanding [*synetoi*], witless men sound reasoners?" (*Somn.* 155), cited in Theissen, *Social Setting*, 72.
52. David Graf, "Aretas," *ABD* 1:374–76.
53. Edwin Judge, "The Conflict of Educational Aims in the New Testament," *Journal of Christian Education* 9 (1966): 3–45; repr. in Judge, *First Christians*, 693–708 (708), writes: "But if it is realized that everyone in antiquity would have known that the finest military award for valour was the *corona muralis*, for the man who was first up the wall in the face of the enemy, Paul's point is devastatingly plain: he was first down."
54. *Pro Rabino* 5.16, cited in Welborn, "*Mōros genesthō*," 421.

NOTES TO PAGES 120-124

55. The older tripartite educational scheme, which places training in the art of declamation at the final stage, has been called into question by more recent studies, which note diversity in the ways in which the curriculum was ordered. For the older scheme, see Marrou, *History of Education;* for criticisms, see Dutch, *Educated Elite,* 58–91.
56. Timothy A. Brookins has recently argued that Paul's references to "wisdom" imply philosophical traditions rather than oratory, as Duane Litfin and others have maintained; see Brookins, *Corinthian Wisdom,* 8–61.
57. See Martin, *Corinthian Body,* 40–44; Theissen, *Social Setting,* 70–73.
58. Welborn, "On the Discord in Corinth," 101, citing Herodotus 5.66.
59. Gerd Theissen (*Social Setting,* 70–72) has demonstrated the social significance of the phrases *ta onta* ("the things that are"; i.e., "somebodies") and *ta mē onta* ("the things that are not"; i.e., "nobodies") in 1 Cor 1:28.
60. See also Martin, *Corinthian Body,* 47–63.
61. Mysteries were associated with Isis and Serapis, Demeter and Kore; sanctuaries were associated with each of those deities in Corinth. Nancy Bookidis notes that "the popularity of Sarapis and Isis at Corinth is manifested in four sanctuaries to the deities at the base of Acrocorinth, in a fifth to Sarapis in the South Stoa . . . on a column from the theater, dedicated to both deities by C. Iulius Syros in the first century, and possibly in two more heads identified as Sarapis." See Bookidis, "The Sanctuaries of Corinth," in Williams and Bookidis, eds., *Corinth,* 247–59 (257). There was also a sanctuary of Demeter and Kore in the city that was in use during the Roman period. It is impossible to determine from these archaeological data, however, whether mystery initiations took place in connection with those deities in the first century. Apuleius's fictive depictions of Lucius's initiations into the mysteries of Isis in his novel *The Metamorphoses* (or *The Golden Ass*) date from the second century CE. Nevertheless, well-known mystery initiations took place at Eleusis from the sixth century BCE; those associated with Dionysus-Bacchus are attested only slightly later; see Burkert, *Ancient Mystery Cults,* 2.
62. On the initiation ceremonies, see Burkert, *Ancient Mystery Cults,* 89–114; Meyer, *Ancient Mysteries,* 1–14; Klauck, *Religious Context,* 81–89; Bowden, *Mystery Cults of the Ancient World,* 6–25.
63. On the theme of panoptic vision in Paul's letters, see Becklin, "'The One Who Searches the Hearts,'" and Glowacki, "All Things to All People"; both depend on Foucault, *Discipline and Punish,* 195–228.
64. The inversion between the politically powerful and powerless is characteristic of Jewish apocalyptic (e.g., Dan 7), wisdom (e.g., Prov 3:34), and narrative

(e.g., Deut 28:13) traditions. Paul nuances the basic scenario by relating it to the negative evaluations that he had received in Corinth.
65. Bruce Lincoln notes: "The shift from aesthetic or ethical to religious discourse effects a qualitative transformation of enormous importance. Human propositions, precepts, and preferences are (mis)represented as distinctly more than human, with the result that they are insulated against criticism by mere mortals." Citation in Lincoln, *Holy Terrors,* 55; see also Lincoln, *Gods and Demons,* 5.
66. Schmeller, *Hierarchie und Egalität,* 57: "Das Prestige eines Patrons färbt gleichsam auf die Klienten ab." On the prestige that may accrue to slaves on the basis of association with more prestigious masters, see Martin, *Slavery as Salvation,* 47–48; Hellerman, *Reconstructing Honor,* 106–8.
67. Compare Betz, *Der Apostel Paulus,* 44–57, who draws a parallel with assessments of philosophers on the basis of their *schēma,* or external appearance and dress.
68. These chapters may well stem from two originally independent letters; what is relevant to the argument at hand, however, is that both were written after 1 Corinthians. On the partition theories of 2 Corinthians, see Thrall, *Critical and Exegetical Commentary,* 1:1–49; Betz, *2 Corinthians 8 and 9,* 3–36; Furnish, *II Corinthians,* 29–48; Reimund Bieringer, "Teilungshypothesen zum 2. Korintherbrief. Ein Forschungsüberblick," in Bieringer and Lambrecht, *Studies on 2 Corinthians,* 67–105; Blanton, *Constructing a New Covenant,* 107–9; Mitchell, "Corinthian Epistles"; Schmeller, *Der zweite Brief,* 1–38.
69. On the "inner human being," see Markschies, "Innerer Mensch"; Burkert, "Towards Plato and Paul"; Betz, "Concept of the 'Inner Human Being.'"
70. Bruce Winter (*Philo and Paul,* 158–59, 162–63) notes that the terminology of 1 Cor 2:4 reflects that of Greco-Roman oratory.
71. On the order in which the various sections of canonical 2 Corinthians were written, see most recently Mitchell, "Corinthian Epistles"; Mitchell, "Paul's Letters to Corinth"; and Welborn, *End to Enmity,* xix–xxvii.
72. Lampe, "Paul, Patrons, and Clients," 498.
73. Bourdieu, *Language and Symbolic Power,* 168: "Dominant class fractions, whose power rests on economic capital, aim to impose the legitimacy of their domination either through their own symbolic production, or through the intermediary of conservative ideologues. . . . The dominated fraction (clerics or 'intellectuals' and 'artists,' depending on the period) always tend to set the specific capital, to which it owes its position, at the top of the hierarchy of the principles of hierarchization."

Chapter 8. Summary and Conclusions

1. To borrow the apt phrase of Godbout and Caillé, *World of the Gift,* 9.
2. I borrow the phrase from Gregory, "Gifts to Men and Gifts to God," 630, 638. Gregory credits Andrew Strathern with coining the phrase.
3. As, for example, Mauss, *The Gift,* 14–18; Godelier, *Enigma of the Gift,* 170–200.

Bibliography

Appadurai, Arjun. "Introduction: Commodities and the Politics of Value." In Appadurai, ed., *The Social Life of Things*, 6–16.

Appadurai, Arjun, ed. *The Social Life of Things: Commodities in Cultural Perspective*. Cambridge: Cambridge University Press, 1986.

Arnal, William E. "Definition." In Braun and McCutcheon, eds., *Guide to the Study of Religion*, 21–34.

Arzt-Grabner, Peter. *Philemon*. Papyrologische Kommentare zum Neuen Testament 1; Göttingen: Vandenhoeck & Ruprecht, 2003.

Aune, David. *The Westminster Dictionary of the New Testament and Early Christian Literature and Rhetoric*. Louisville, KY: Westminster John Knox, 2003.

Bader, Françoise. "The Language of the Gods in Homer." In Christidis, Arapopoulou, and Chriti, eds., *A History of Ancient Greek*, 1376–99.

———. *La langue des dieux, ou l'hermétisme des poètes indo-européens*. Pisa: Giardini, 1989.

Barclay, John M. G. "Grace Within and Beyond Reason: Philo and Paul in Dialogue." In Paul Middleton, Angus Paddison, and Karen Wennell, eds., *Paul, Grace and Freedom: Essays in Honor of John K. Riches*, 9–21. London: T&T Clark, 2009.

———. "Manna and the Circulation of Grace: A Study of 2 Corinthians 8:1–15." In Wagner, Rowe, and Grieb, eds., *The Word Leaps the Gap*, 409–26.

———. "Money and Meetings: Group Formation Among Diaspora Jews and Early Christians." In Gutfeld and Koch, eds., *Vereine, Synagogen und Gemeinden im kaiserzeitlichen Kleinasien*, 113–27.

———. *Paul and the Gift*. Grand Rapids, MI: Eerdmans, 2015.

———. "Paul, Philemon, and the Dilemma of Christian Slave-ownership." *NTS* 37 (1991): 161–86.

Barnett, Paul. *The Second Epistle to the Corinthians*. NICNT; Grand Rapids, MI: Eerdmans, 1997.

Barth, Markus, and Helmut Blanke. *The Letter to Philemon: A New Translation with Notes and Commentary*. Eerdmans Critical Commentary; Grand Rapids, MI: Eerdmans, 2000.

Becklin, Hans E. "'The One Who Searches the Hearts': Paul's Panoptic Theology in Romans 8:26–27." Unpublished paper, Lutheran School of Theology at Chicago, 2014.

Bell, Catherine. *Ritual Theory, Ritual Practice.* New York: Oxford University Press, 1992.
Benveniste, Émile. "Gift and Exchange in the Indo-European Vocabulary." In Schrift, ed., *The Logic of the Gift,* 33–42.
Berger, Adolf. *Encyclopedic Dictionary of Roman Law.* Transactions of the American Philological Association, New Series 43.2 (1953); repr. Union, NJ: Lawbook Exchange, 2002.
Bernabé, Alberto. "Las *Ephesia Grammata:* Génesis de una Fórmula Mágica." *MHNH: Revista Internacional de Investigación sobre Magia y Astrología Antiguas* 3 (2003): 5–28.
Betz, Hans Dieter. *Der Apostel Paulus und die sokratische Tradition: Eine exegetische Untersuchung zu seiner "Apologie" 2 Korinther 10–13.* Beiträge zur historischen Theologie 45; Tübingen: Mohr Siebeck, 1972.
———. "The Concept of the 'Inner Human Being' (*ho esō anthrōpos*) in the Anthropology of Paul." *NTS* 46 (2000): 315–41.
———. *Galatians: A Commentary on Paul's Letter to the Churches in Galatia.* Hermeneia; Philadelphia: Fortress, 1979.
———. *Plutarch's Ethical Writings and Early Christian Literature.* Studia ad Corpus Hellenisticum Novi Testamenti 4; Leiden: Brill, 1978.
———. *2 Corinthians 8 and 9: A Commentary on Two Administrative Letters of the Apostle Paul.* Hermeneia; Philadelphia: Fortress, 1985.
Bieringer, Reimund, and Jan Lambrecht. *Studies on 2 Corinthians.* BETL 112; Leuven: Leuven University Press, 1994.
Blanton, Thomas R. "The Benefactor's Account-book: The Rhetoric of Gift Reciprocation in Seneca and Paul." *NTS* 59.3 (2013): 396–414.
———. "Boasting." In Hans-Josef Klauck, Bernard McGinn, et al., eds., *Encyclopedia of the Bible and Its Reception,* Vol. 4: *Birsha–Chariot of Fire,* 245–47. Berlin: Walter de Gruyter, 2011.
———. *Constructing a New Covenant: Discursive Strategies in the Damascus Document and Paul's Second Corinthians.* WUNT 2/233; Tübingen: Mohr Siebeck, 2007.
———. "*De caelo patrocinium:* The Economy of Divine Patronage in Apuleius' Metamorphoses." In Blanton, Calhoun, and Rothschild, eds., *The History of Religions School Today,* 283–96.
———. "Gift, Film." In Dale C. Allison, Jr., Volker Leppin, et al., eds., *Encyclopedia of the Bible and Its Reception,* Vol. 10: *Genocide–Hakkoz,* 254–55. Berlin: Walter de Gruyter, 2015.

———. "Gift, NT." In Dale C. Allison, Jr., Volker Leppin, et al., eds., *Encyclopedia of the Bible and Its Reception*, Vol. 10: *Genocide–Hakkoz*, 240–42. Berlin: Walter de Gruyter, 2015.

———. "Spirit and Covenant Renewal: A Theologoumenon of Paul's Opponents in 2 Corinthians." *JBL* 129.1 (2010): 153–75.

Blanton, Thomas R., Robert Matthew Calhoun, and Clare K. Rothschild, eds. *The History of Religions School Today: Essays on the New Testament and Related Ancient Mediterranean Texts*. WUNT 1/340; Tübingen: Mohr Siebeck, 2014.

Blau, Peter. *Exchange and Power in Social Life*. New Brunswick, NJ: Transaction, 2008 (1964).

Boissevain, Jeremy. *Friends of Friends: Networks, Manipulators, and Coalitions*. Pavilion Series in Social Anthropology; Oxford: Basil Blackwell, 1974.

Bondarenko, Dmitri M. "Approaching 'Complexity' in Anthropology and Complexity Studies: The Principles of Sociopolitical Organization and the Prospects for Bridging the Interdisciplinary Gap." *Emergence: Complexity & Organization* 9.3 (2007): 55–67.

———. "A Homoarchic Alternative to the Homoarchic State: Benin Kingdom of the 13th–19th Centuries." *Social Evolution and History* 4.2 (2005): 18–88.

Bondarenko, Dmitri M., and Leonid E. Grinin. "Alternative Pathways of Social Evolution." *Social Evolution and History* 1.1 (2002): 54–79.

Bormann, Lukas. *Philippi: Stadt und Christengemeinde zur Zeit des Paulus*. NovTSup 78; Leiden: Brill, 1995.

Bourdieu, Pierre. "The Forms of Capital." In J. G. Richardson, ed., *Handbook of Theory and Research for the Sociology of Education*, 183–98. New York: Greenwood, 1986. Translation of "Ökonomisches Kapital, kulturelles Kapital, soziales Kapital," in Reinhard Kreckel, ed., *Soziale Ungleichheiten*. Soziale Welt 2; Göttingen: Schwartz, 1983.

———. "Genèse et structure du champ religieux." *Revue française de sociologie* 12.3 (1971): 295–334.

———. *Language and Symbolic Power*. Cambridge, MA: Harvard University Press, 1991. Translation by Gino Raymond and Matthew Adamson of *Ce que parler veut dire. L'économie des échanges linguistiques*. Paris: Fayard, 1982.

———. *The Logic of Practice*. Stanford, CA: Stanford University Press, 1980. Translation by Richard Nice of *Le sens pratique*. Paris: Minuit, 1980.

———. "Marginalia—Some Notes on the Gift." In Schrift, ed., *The Logic of the Gift*, 231–41.

———. *Outline of a Theory of Practice*. Cambridge: Cambridge University Press, 1977. Translation by Richard Nice of *Esquisse d'une théorie de la pratique, précédé de trois études d'ethnologie kabyle*. Geneva: Droz, 1972.

———. *Practical Reason: On the Theory of Action*. Stanford, CA: Stanford University Press, 1998. Translation of *Raisons pratiques. Sur la théorie de l'action*. Paris: Seuil, 1994.

Bowden, Hugh. *Mystery Cults of the Ancient World*. Princeton, NJ: Princeton University Press, 2010.

Branham, R. Bracht, and Daniel Kinney, eds. *Petronius: Satyrica*. Berkeley: University of California Press, 1997.

Brashear, William M. "The Greek Magical Papyri: An Introduction and Survey; Annotated Bibliography (1928–1994)." *ANRW* 2.18.5: 3380–684.

Braun, Willi, and Russell McCutcheon, eds. *Guide to the Study of Religion*. London: Cassell, 2000.

Briones, David. "Mutual Brokers of Grace: A Study in Corinthians 1:3–11." *NTS* 56 (2010): 536–56.

———. *Paul's Financial Policy: A Socio-Theological Approach*. LNTS 494; London: Bloomsbury T&T Clark, 2013.

Broneer, Oscar. "The Isthmian Victory Crown." *American Journal of Archaeology* 66.3 (1962): 259–63.

Brookins, Timothy A. *Corinthian Wisdom, Stoic Philosophy, and the Ancient Economy*. SNTSMS 159; New York: Cambridge University Press, 2014.

Brumfiel, Elizabeth M. "Heterarchy and the Analysis of Complex Societies: Comments." In Ehrenreich, Crumley, and Levy, eds., *Heterarchy and the Analysis of Complex Societies*, 125–31.

Burkert, Walter. *Ancient Mystery Cults*. Cambridge, MA: Harvard University Press, 1987.

———. *Creation of the Sacred: Tracks of Biology in Early Religions*. Cambridge, MA: Harvard University Press, 1996.

———. "Towards Plato and Paul: The 'Inner' Human Being." In Yarbro Collins, ed., *Ancient and Modern Perspectives on the Bible and Culture*, 59–82.

Callahan, Allen Dwight. *Embassy of Onesimus: The Letter of Paul to Philemon*. New Testament in Context; Valley Forge, PA: Trinity Press International, 1997.

Caragounis, Chrys C. "*OPSŌNION:* A Reconsideration of Its Meaning." *NovT* 16.1 (1974): 35–57.

Carrier, James. "Emerging Alienation in Production: A Maussian History." *Man* 27.3 (1992): 539–58.

———. "The Gift in Theory and Practice in Melanesia: A Note on the Centrality of Gift Exchange." *Ethnology* 31.2 (1992): 185–93.
———. "Gifts, Commodities, and Social Relations: A Maussian View of Exchange." *Sociological Forum* 6.1 (1991): 119–36.
Castelli, Elizabeth A. *Imitating Paul: A Discourse of Power.* Louisville, KY: Westminster/John Knox, 1991.
Chow, John K. *Patronage and Power: A Study of Social Networks in Corinth.* JSNTSup 75; Sheffield: Sheffield Academic Press, 1992.
Christidis, Anastassios-Fivos, Maria Arapopoulou, and Maria Chriti, eds. *A History of Ancient Greek: From the Beginnings to Late Antiquity.* Cambridge: Cambridge University Press, 2007.
Clay, Jenny. "The Planktai and Moly: Divine Naming and Knowing in Homer." *Hermes* 100 (1972): 127–31.
Collins, Raymond F. *Second Corinthians.* Paideia Commentaries on the New Testament; Grand Rapids, MI: Baker Academic, 2013.
Crook, Zeba A. "The Divine Benefactions of Paul the Client." *JGRChJ* 2 (2001–2005): 9–26.
———. "Grace as Benefaction in Galatians 2:9, 1 Corinthians 3:10, and Romans 12:3; 15:15." In Dietmar Neufeld, ed., *The Social Sciences and Biblical Translation*, 25–38. SBL Symposium Series; Atlanta: Society of Biblical Literature, 2008.
———. "Reciprocity: Covenantal Exchange as a Test Case." In Philip F. Esler, ed., *Ancient Israel: The Old Testament in Its Social Context*, 78–91. Minneapolis: Fortress, 2005.
———. *Reconceptualising Conversion: Patronage, Loyalty, and Conversion in the Religions of the Ancient Mediterranean.* BZNW 130; Berlin: Walter de Gruyter, 2004.
———. "Reflections on Culture and Social-Scientific Models." *JBL* 124 (2005): 515–20.
Crumley, Carole L. "A Dialectical Critique of Hierarchy." In Patterson and Gailey, eds., *Power Relations and State Formation*, 155–69.
———. "Heterarchy and the Analysis of Complex Societies." In Ehrenreich, Crumley, and Levy, eds., *Heterarchy and the Analysis of Complex Societies*, 1–5.
Danker, Frederick W. *Benefactor: Epigraphic Study of a Graeco-Roman and New Testament Semantic Field.* St. Louis, MO: Clayton, 1982.
———. "Paul's Debt to the *De Corona* of Demosthenes: A Study of Rhetorical Techniques in Second Corinthians." In Watson, ed., *Persuasive Artistry*, 262–80.

Datiri, Dachollom C. "Finances in the Pauline Churches: A Socio-Exegetical Study of the Funding of Paul's Mission and the Financial Administration of His Congregations." PhD diss., University of Sheffield, 1996.

Davies, W. D., and Dale Allison. *The Gospel According to St. Matthew*. 3 vols., ICC; Edinburgh: T&T Clark, 1988–97.

Davis, Natalie Zemon. *The Gift in Sixteenth-Century France*. Madison: University of Wisconsin Press, 2000.

Derrida, Jacques. *Given Time: 1. Counterfeit Money*. Chicago: University of Chicago Press, 1992.

———. "The Time of the King." In Schrift, ed., *The Logic of the Gift*, 121–47.

De Ste. Croix, G. E. M. "Greek and Roman Accounting." In Littleton and Yamey, eds., *Studies in the History of Accounting*, 14–74.

De Vivo, Arturo, and Elio Lo Cascio, eds. *Seneca uomo politico e l'età di Claudio e di Nerone: Atti del Convegno internazionale (Capri 25–27 marzo 1999)*. Bari: Edipuglia, 2003.

Dixon, Suzanne. "The Meaning of Gift and Debt in the Roman Elite." *Echos du Monde Classique/Classical Views* 12 (1993): 451–64.

Downs, David J. "Is God Paul's Patron? The Economy of Patronage in Pauline Theology." In Longenecker and Liebengood, eds., *Engaging Economics*, 129–56. Grand Rapids, MI: Eerdmans, 2009.

———. *The Offering of the Gentiles: Paul's Collection for Jerusalem in Its Chronological, Cultural, and Cultic Contexts*. WUNT 2/248; Tübingen: Mohr Siebeck, 2008.

Dulk, Matthijs den, and Andrew M. Langford. "Polycarp and Polemo: Christianity at the Center of the Second Sophistic." In Blanton, Calhoun, and Rothschild, eds., *The History of Religions School Today*, 211–40.

Dunn, James D. G. *The Epistles to the Colossians and to Philemon*. NIGTC; Carlisle: Paternoster, and Grand Rapids, MI: Eerdmans, 1996.

———. *Romans*. 2 vols., WBC 38A–B; Dallas: Word Books, 1988.

Dutch, Robert S. *The Educated Elite in 1 Corinthians: Education and Community Conflict in Graeco-Roman Context*. JSNTSup 271; London: T&T Clark, 2005.

Edart, Jean-Baptiste. *L'Épître aux Philippiens: rhétorique et composition stylistique*. Études Bibliques 45; Paris: Gabalda, 2002.

Ehrenreich, Robert M., Carole L. Crumley, and Janet E. Levy, eds. *Heterarchy and the Analysis of Complex Societies*. Archaeological Papers of the American Anthropological Association 6; Arlington, VA: American Anthropological Association, 1995.

Ehrensperger, Kathy. *Paul and the Dynamics of Power: Communication and Interaction in the Early Christ-Movement.* LNTS 325; London: T&T Clark, 2007.

Eisenstadt, S. N., and Luis Roniger. *Patrons, Clients, and Friends: Interpersonal Relations and the Structure of Trust in Society.* Cambridge: Cambridge University Press, 1984.

Elliott, J. K. *The Apocryphal New Testament: A Collection of Apocryphal Christian Literature in an English Translation.* Oxford: Oxford University Press, 2005 (1993).

Elliott, Scott S. "'Thanks but No Thanks': Tact, Persuasion, and the Negotiation of Power in Paul's Letter to Philemon." *NTS* 57 (2010): 51–74.

Engberg-Pedersen, Troels. "Gift-Giving and Friendship: Seneca and Paul in Romans 1–8 and the Logic of God's *Charis* and Its Human Response." *Harvard Theological Review* 101.1 (2008): 15–44.

———. "Gift-Giving and God's *Charis:* Bourdieu, Seneca and Paul in Romans 1–8." In Schnelle, ed., *The Letter to the Romans,* 95–111.

Engberg-Pedersen, Troels, ed. *Paul Beyond the Judaism/Hellenism Divide.* Louisville, KY: Westminster John Knox, 2001.

Evans, Craig A., and Stanley E. Porter, eds. *Dictionary of New Testament Background.* Downers Grove, IL: InterVarsity, 2000.

Faraone, Christopher, and Dirk Obbink, eds. *Magika Hiera: Ancient Greek Magic and Religion.* New York: Oxford University Press, 1991.

Favro, Diane. "Making Rome a World City." In Galinsky, ed., *The Cambridge Companion to the Age of Augustus,* 234–63.

Fee, Gordon D. *The First Epistle to the Corinthians.* NICNT 7; Grand Rapids, MI: Eerdmans, 1987.

———. *Paul's Letter to the Philippians.* NICNT 11; Grand Rapids, MI: Eerdmans, 1995.

Finley, Moses. *The Ancient Economy.* Sather Classical Lectures 43; Berkeley: University of California Press, 1999 (1973).

Finney, Mark T. *Honour and Conflict in the Ancient World: 1 Corinthians in Its Greco-Roman Social Setting.* LNTS 460; London: T&T Clark, 2012.

Fitzgerald, John T. *Cracks in an Earthen Vessel: An Examination of the Catalogs of Hardships in the Corinthian Correspondence.* SBLDS 99; Atlanta: Scholars Press, 1999.

———. "Hospitality." In Evans and Porter, eds., *Dictionary of New Testament Background,* 522–25.

———. "Paul and Friendship." In Sampley, ed., *Paul in the Greco-Roman World,* 319–43.

———. "Paul and Paradigm Shifts: Reconciliation and Its Linkage Group." In Engberg-Pedersen, ed., *Paul Beyond the Judaism/Hellenism Divide*, 241–62.

———. "Philippians, Epistle to the." *ABD* 5:318–26.

Fitzgerald, John T., ed. *Greco-Roman Perspectives on Friendship*. SBL Resources for Biblical Study 34; Atlanta, GA: Scholars Press, 1997.

———, ed. *Passions and Moral Progress in Greco-Roman Thought*. New York: Routledge, 2008.

Fitzmyer, Joseph A. *First Corinthians: A New Translation with Introduction and Commentary*. AYB 32; New Haven, CT: Yale University Press, 2008.

———. *Romans*. AYB 33; New York: Doubleday, 1992.

Forbes, Christopher. "Comparison, Self-Praise and Irony: Paul's Boasting and the Conventions of Hellenistic Rhetoric." *NTS* 32 (1986): 1–30.

Foucault, Michel. *Discipline and Punish: The Birth of the Prison*. 2nd ed., New York: Vintage, 1995 (1977).

Friesen, Stephen J. "Junia Theodora of Corinth: Gendered Inequalities in the Early Empire." In Friesen, James, and Schowalter, eds., *Corinth in Contrast*, 203–26.

———. "Paul and Economics: The Jerusalem Collection as an Alternative to Patronage." In Given, ed., *Paul Unbound*, 27–54.

———. "Poverty in Pauline Studies: Beyond the So-Called New Consensus." *JSNT* 26.3 (2004): 323–61.

———. "Prospects for a Demography of the Pauline Mission: Corinth Among the Churches." In Schowalter and Friesen, eds., *Urban Religion in Roman Corinth*, 351–70.

Friesen, Stephen J., Sarah A. James, and Daniel N. Schowalter, eds. *Corinth in Contrast: Studies in Inequality*. NovTSup 155; Leiden: Brill, 2014.

Frilingos, Chris. "'For My Child, Onesimus': Paul and Domestic Power in Philemon." *JBL* 119.1 (2000): 91–104.

Furnish, Victor Paul. *II Corinthians*. AYB 32A; New York, 1984.

Galinsky, Karl, ed. *The Cambridge Companion to the Age of Augustus*. Cambridge: Cambridge University Press, 2005.

Garland, David E. *1 Corinthians*. Baker Exegetical Commentary on the New Testament; Grand Rapids, MI: Baker Academic, 2003.

Garnsey, Peter, and Richard Saller. *The Roman Empire: Economy, Society, and Culture*. Berkeley: University of California Press, 1987.

Gaventa, Beverly Roberts. "The Economy of Grace: Reflections on 2 Corinthians 8 and 9." In Johnston, Jones, and Wilson, eds., *Grace upon Grace*, 51–62.

Gellner, Ernest, and John Waterbury, eds. *Patrons and Clients in Mediterranean Societies.* London: Duckworth, 1977.

Georgi, Dieter. *The Opponents of Paul in Second Corinthians.* Philadelphia: Fortress, 1986. Translation of *Die Gegner des Paulus im 2. Korintherbrief: Studien zur religiösen Propaganda in der Spätantike.* Wissenschaftliche Monographien zum Alten und Neuen Testament 11; Neukirchen-Vluyn: Neukirchener Verlag, 1964.

———. *Remembering the Poor: The History of Paul's Collection for Jerusalem.* Nashville, TN: Abingdon, 1992.

Gill, Christopher, Norman Postlethwaite, and Richard Seaford, eds. *Reciprocity in Ancient Greece.* Oxford: Oxford University Press, 1998.

Given, Mark D., ed. *Paul Unbound: Other Perspectives on the Apostle.* Peabody, MA: Hendrickson, 2010.

Glowacki, David R. "All Things to All People: Unraveling the Structure of the Apostolic Panopticon." *Journal for Cultural and Religious Theory* 11.1 (2010): 78–91.

Godbout, Jacques, and Alain Caillé. *The World of the Gift.* Montreal: McGill-Queen's University Press, 2000. Translation by Donald Winkler of *L'Esprit du don.* Paris: La Découverte, and Montréal: Boréal, 2000.

Godelier, Maurice. *The Enigma of the Gift.* Chicago: University of Chicago Press, 1999. Translation by Nora Scott of *L'Énigme du don.* Paris: Fayard, 1996.

Gouldner, Alvin. "The Norm of Reciprocity: A Preliminary Statement." *American Sociological Review* 25.2 (1960): 161–78; repr. in Schmidt, Scott, Landé, and Guasti, eds., *Friends, Followers, and Factions,* 28–43.

Graf, Fritz. "Prayer in Magical and Religious Ritual." In Faraone and Obbink, eds., *Magika Hiera,* 188–213.

Grant, Robert M. *Paul in the Roman World: The Conflict at Corinth.* Louisville, KY: Westminster John Knox, 2001.

Gregory, C. A. *Gifts and Commodities.* London: Academic Press, 1982.

———. "Gifts to Men and Gifts to God: Gift Exchange and Capital Accumulation in Contemporary Papua." *Man* 15.4 (1980): 626–52.

Grenfell, Michael, ed. *Pierre Bourdieu: Key Concepts.* Durham: Acumen, 2008.

Griffin, Miriam. "*De Beneficiis* and Roman Society." *JRS* 93 (2003): 92–113.

———. *Seneca: A Philosopher in Politics.* Oxford: Clarendon, 1992 (1976).

———. "Seneca as a Sociologist: De Beneficiis." In De Vivo and Lo Cascio, eds., *Seneca uomo politico e l'età di Claudio e di Nerone,* 89–122.

Griffin, Miriam, and Brad Inwood. *Lucius Annaeus Seneca: On Benefits.* Chicago: University of Chicago Press, 2011.

Griffiths, J. Gwyn. *The Isis-Book: Metamorphoses, Book XI*. Etudes préliminaires aux religions orientales dans l'Empire romain 39; Leiden: Brill, 1975.

Grusky, David B., ed. *Social Stratification: Class, Race, and Gender in Sociological Perspective*. 3rd ed., Boulder: Westview, 2008.

Gutfeld, Andreas, and Dietrich-Alex Koch, eds. *Vereine, Synagogen und Gemeinden im kaiserzeitlichen Kleinasien*. Studien und Texte zu Antike und Christentum 25; Tübingen: Mohr Siebeck, 2006.

Hanson, K. C., and Douglas E. Oakman. *Palestine in the Time of Jesus: Social Structures and Social Conflicts*. 2nd ed., Minneapolis: Fortress, 2008.

Harris, Murray J. *The Second Epistle to the Corinthians*. NIGTC; Grand Rapids, MI: Eerdmans, and Milton Keynes: Paternoster, 2005.

Harrison, James R. "The Brothers as the 'Glory of Christ' (2 Cor 8: 23): Paul's *Doxa* Terminology in Its Ancient Benefaction Context." *NovT* 52.2 (2010): 156–88.

———. *Paul's Language of Grace in Its Greco-Roman Context*. WUNT 2/172; Tübingen: Mohr Siebeck, 2003.

Hartog, Paul. "'Not Even Among the Pagans' (1 Cor 5:1): Paul and Seneca on Incest," in John Fotopoulos, ed., *The New Testament and Early Christian Literature in Greco-Roman Context: Studies in Honor of David E. Aune*, 51–64. NovTSup 122; Leiden: Brill, 2006.

Harvey, A. E. "'The Workman Is Worthy of His Hire': Fortunes of a Proverb in the Early Church." *NovT* 24.3 (1982): 209–21.

Hays, Richard B. *First Corinthians*. Interpretation; Louisville, KY: John Knox, 1997.

Heim, Maria. *Theories of the Gift in South Asia: Hindu, Buddhist, and Jain Reflections on Dana*. New York: Routledge, 2004.

Hellerman, Joseph H. *Reconstructing Honor in Roman Philippi: Carmen Christi as Cursus Pudorum*. SNTSMS 132; Cambridge: Cambridge University Press, 2005.

Herrmann, Gretchen. "Gift or Commodity: What Changes Hands in the U.S. Garage Sale?" *American Ethnologist* 24.4 (1997): 910–30.

Hewitt, J. "The Terminology of 'Gratitude' in Greek." *Classical Philology* 22 (1927): 142–61.

Hirzel, Rudolf. *Themis, Dike und Verwandtes: Ein Beitrag zur Geschichte der Rechtsidee bei den Griechen*. Leipzig: S. Hirzel, 1907.

Hock, Ronald F. *The Social Context of Paul's Ministry: Tentmaking and Apostleship*. Minneapolis: Fortress, 2007 (1980).

Horn, Christoph. "Der Zeitbegriff der antiken Moralphilosophie und das Zeitverständnis des Neuen Testaments," in Friedrich Wilhelm Horn and

Ruben Zimmermann, eds., *Jenseits von Indikativ und Imperativ*, 117-34. WUNT 1/238; Tübingen: Mohr Siebeck, 2009.

Inwood, Brad. "Politics and Paradox in Seneca's De Beneficiis," in Laks and Schofield, eds., *Justice and Generosity*, 241-65.

James, Wendy, and J. N. Allen, eds. *Marcel Mauss: A Centenary Tribute*. New York: Berghahn, 1998.

Jennings, Mark A. "Patronage and Rebuke in Paul's Persuasion in 2 Corinthians 8-9." *JGRChJ* 6 (2009): 107-27.

Jewett, Robert. *A Chronology of Paul's Life*. Philadelphia: Fortress, 1979.

Johnson, Luke Timothy. *Among the Gentiles: Greco-Roman Religion and Christianity*. New Haven, CT: Yale University Press, 2009.

Johnston, Robert K., L. Gregory Jones, and Jonathan R. Wilson, eds. *Grace upon Grace: Essays in Honor of Thomas A. Langford*. Nashville, TN: Abingdon, 1999.

Jongman, Willem. "Re-constructing the Roman Economy." In Neal and Williamson, eds., *The Cambridge History of Capitalism*, 1:75-100.

Joubert, Stephan. "'Homo reciprocus': Seneka, Paulus en weldoenerskap." Hervormde teologiese studies 55.4 (1999): 1022-38. (Afrikaans with English abstract.)

———. *Paul as Benefactor: Reciprocity, Strategy, and Theological Reflection in Paul's Collection*. WUNT 2/124; Tübingen: Mohr Siebeck, 2000.

Judge, Edwin A. *The First Christians in the Roman World: Augustan and New Testament Essays*. Edited by James R. Harrison. WUNT 1/229; Tübingen: Mohr Siebeck, 2008.

———. *Social Distinctives of the Christians in the First Century: Pivotal Essays by E. A. Judge*. Edited by David M. Scholer. Peabody, MA: Hendrickson, 2008.Kennedy, George A. *Progymnasmata: Greek Textbooks of Prose Composition and Rhetoric*. SBL Writings from the Greco-Roman World 10; Leiden: Brill, 2003.

Kirner, Guido O. "Apostolat und Patronage (I): Methodischer Teil und Forschungsdiskussion." *ZAC* 6 (2002): 3-37.

———. "Apostolat und Patronage (II): Darstellungsteil: Weisheit, Rhetorik und Ruhm im Konflikt um die apostolische Praxis des Paulus in der frühchristlichen Gemeinde Korinth (1Kor 1-4 u. 9; 2Kor 10-13)." *ZAC* 7 (2003): 27-72.

Klauck, Hans-Josef. *2. Korintherbrief.* Neue Echter Bibel. Neues Testament 8; Würzburg: Echter Verlag, 1994 (1986).

———. *Religion und Gesellschaft im frühen Christentum: Neutestamentliche Studien*. WUNT 1/152; Tübingen: Mohr Siebeck, 2003.

———. *The Religious Context of Early Christianity: A Guide to Graeco-Roman Religions*. Minneapolis: Fortress, 2003.
Kopytoff, Igor. "The Cultural Biography of Things: Commoditization as Process." In Appadurai, ed., *The Social Life of Things*, 64–91. Cambridge: Cambridge University Press, 1986.
Laidlaw, James. "A Free Gift Makes No Friends." *Journal of the Royal Anthropological Institute* 6.4 (2000): 617–34.
Laks, André, and Malcolm Schofield, eds. *Justice and Generosity: Studies in Hellenistic Social and Political Philosophy*. Cambridge: Cambridge University Press, 1995.
Lamberterie, Charles de. "Grec homérique MŌLY: Étymologie et poétique." *Lalies* 6 (1984): 129–38.
Lampe, Peter. "Keine 'Sklavenflucht' des Onesimus." *ZNW* 76 (1985): 135–37.
———. "Das korinthische Herrenmahl im Schnittpunkt hellenistisch-römischer Mahlpraxis und paulinischer Theologia Crucis (1Kor 11,17–34)." *ZNW* 82 (1991): 183–213.
———. "Paul, Patrons, and Clients." In Sampley, ed., *Paul in the Greco-Roman World*, 488–523.
Lévi-Strauss, Claude. *The Elementary Structures of Kinship*. Boston: Beacon, 1969.
Lincoln, Andrew T. *Ephesians*. WBC 42; Dallas: Word Books, 1990.
Lincoln, Bruce. *Discourse and the Construction of Society: Comparative Studies of Myth, Ritual, and Classification*. New York: Oxford University Press, 1989.
———. *Gods and Demons, Priests and Scholars: Critical Explorations in the History of Religions*. Chicago: University of Chicago Press, 2012.
———. *Holy Terrors: Thinking About Religion After September 11*. 2nd ed., Chicago: University of Chicago Press, 2006 (2003).
———. "Theses on Method." *Method and Theory in the Study of Religions* 8 (1996): 225–27. Online at http://religion.ua.edu/thesesonmethod.html.
Lipset, Seymour M. "Social Class." In Sills, ed., *International Encyclopedia of the Social Sciences*, 296–316.
Litfin, Duane. *St. Paul's Theology of Proclamation: 1 Corinthians 1–4 and Greco-Roman Rhetoric*. SNTSMS 79; Cambridge: Cambridge University Press, 1994.
Littleton, A. C., and B. S. Yamey, eds. *Studies in the History of Accounting*. Homewood, IL: Richard D. Irwin, and London: Sweet and Maxwell, 1956.
Lohse, Eduard. *Colossians and Philemon*. Hermeneia; Philadelphia: Fortress, 1971.

Longenecker, Bruce W. *Remember the Poor: Paul, Poverty, and the Greco-Roman World*. Grand Rapids, MI: Eerdmans, 2010.

Longenecker, Bruce W., and Kelly D. Liebengood, eds. *Engaging Economics: New Testament Scenarios and Early Christian Reception*. Grand Rapids, MI: Eerdmans, 2009.

Lüdemann, Gerd. *Paul, Apostle to the Gentiles: Studies in Chronology*. Philadelphia: Fortress, 1984.

MacGillivray, Erlend D. "Romans 16:2, *prostatis/prostatēs*, and the Application of Reciprocal Relationships to New Testament Texts." *NovT* 53 (2011): 183-99.

Macionis, John J. *Sociology*. 8th ed., Upper Saddle River, NJ: Prentice Hall, 2001.

Malherbe, Abraham. "Hellenistic Moralists and the New Testament." *ANRW* 2.26.1:267-333.

Malina, Bruce. "Patron and Client: The Analogy Behind Synoptic Theology." *Forum* 4 (1988): 2-32.

Marcoux, Jean-Sébastien. "Escaping the Gift Economy." *Journal of Consumer Research* 36.4 (2009): 671-85.

Markschies, Christoph. "Innerer Mensch." *Reallexikon für Antike und Christentum* 18 (1997): 266-312.

Marrou, Henri Irénée. *A History of Education in Antiquity*. Madison: University of Wisconsin Press, 1982 (1956).

Marshall, Peter. *Enmity in Corinth: Social Conventions in Paul's Relations with the Corinthians*. WUNT 2/23; Tübingen: Mohr Siebeck, 1987.

Martin, Dale B. *The Corinthian Body*. New Haven, CT: Yale University Press, 1995.

———. *Slavery as Salvation: The Metaphor of Slavery in Pauline Christianity*. New Haven, CT: Yale University Press, 1990.

———. "Tongues of Angels and Other Status Indicators." *Journal of the American Academy of Religion* 59.3 (1991): 547-89.

Martin, Luther H. *Hellenistic Religions: An Introduction*. New York: Oxford University Press, 1987.

Martin, Ralph P. *2 Corinthians*. WBC 40; Nashville, TN: Thomas Nelson, 1986.

Mauss, Marcel. *The Gift: The Form and Reason for Exchange in Archaic Societies*. New York: W. W. Norton, 1990. Translation by W. D. Halls of *Essai sur le don, forme et raison de l'échange dans le sociétés archaïques*. Paris: Presses Universitaires de France, 1950 (1925).

———. "An Intellectual Self-Portrait." In James and Allen., eds., *Marcel Mauss*, 29-42.

McNeel, Jennifer Houston. *Paul as Infant and Nursing Mother: Metaphor, Rhetoric, and Identity in 1 Thessalonians 2:5-8.* Early Christianity and Its Literature 12; Atlanta: SBL Press, 2014.

Meeks, Wayne A. *The First Urban Christians: The Social World of the Apostle Paul.* 2nd ed., New Haven, CT: Yale University Press, 2003 (1983).

Meeks, Wayne A., and John T. Fitzgerald, eds. *The Writings of St. Paul: Annotated Texts, Reception, and Criticism.* Norton Critical Edition; New York: Norton, 2007.

Merklein, Helmut. *Der erste Brief an die Korinther.* 3 vols., Ökumenischer taschenbuch-Kommentar 7/1-3; Gütersloh: Gütersloher Verlagshaus Gerd Mohn, and Würzburg: Echter, 1992-2005.

Meyer, Marvin W. *The Ancient Mysteries, A Sourcebook: Sacred Texts of the Mystery Religions of the Ancient Mediterranean World.* Philadelphia: University of Pennsylvania Press, 1987.

Mihaila, Corin. *The Paul-Apollos Relationship and Paul's Stance Toward Greco-Roman Rhetoric: An Exegetical and Socio-historical Study of 1 Corinthians 1-4.* LNTS 402; London: T&T Clark, 2009.

Miller, William. "Gift, Sale, Payment, Raid: Case Studies in the Negotiation and Classification of Exchange in Medieval Iceland." *Speculum* 61.1 (1986): 18-50.

Mitchell, Margaret M. "Corinthian Epistles." In Hans Dieter Betz, Don S. Browning, Bernd Janowski, and Eberhard Jüngel, eds., *Religion Past and Present: Encyclopedia of Theology and Religion,* 3:489-92. Leiden: Brill, 2007.

———. "A Patristic Perspective on Pauline *periautologia.*" *NTS* 46 (2001): 354-71.

———. *Paul and the Rhetoric of Reconciliation: An Exegetical Investigation of the Language and Composition of 1 Corinthians.* Louisville, KY: Westminster/John Knox, 1991.

———. "Paul's Letters to Corinth: The Interpretive Intertwining of Historical and Literary Reconstruction." In Schowalter and Friesen, eds., *Urban Religion in Roman Corinth,* 307-38.

Moo, Douglas. *The Epistle to the Romans.* NICNT; Grand Rapids, MI: Eerdmans, 1996.

———. *The Letters to Colossians and Philemon.* PNTC; Grand Rapids, MI: Eerdmans, 2008.

Müller, Peter. *Der Brief an Philemon.* Kritisch-exegetischer Kommentar über das Neue Testament 9/3; Göttingen: Vandenhoeck & Ruprecht, 2012.

Murphy-O'Connor, Jerome. *Paul: A Critical Life.* New York: Oxford University Press, 1996.

———. *Paul: His Story.* Oxford: Oxford University Press, 2004.

———. *St. Paul's Corinth: Texts and Archaeology*. 3rd ed., Collegeville, MN: Liturgical Press, 2002 (1983).

Nasuti, Harry. "The Woes of the Prophets and the Rights of the Apostle: The Internal Dynamics of 1 Corinthians 9." *Catholic Biblical Quarterly* 50 (1988): 246-64.

Neal, Larry, and Jeffrey G. Williamson, eds. *The Cambridge History of Capitalism*. Cambridge: Cambridge University Press, 2014.

Neyrey, Jerome H. "God, Benefactor and Patron: The Major Cultural Model for Interpreting the Deity in Greco-Roman Antiquity." *JSNT* 27.4 (2005): 465-92.

Nguyen, V. Henry T. "God's Execution of His Condemned Apostles: Paul's Imagery of the Roman Arena in 1 Cor 4,9." *ZNW* 99 (2008): 33-48.

———. "The Identification of Paul's Spectacle of Death Metaphor in 1 Corinthians 4.9." *NTS* 53 (2007): 489-501.

Nickle, Keith F. *The Collection: A Study in Paul's Strategy*. Studies in Biblical Theology 48; Naperville, IL: Allenson, 1966.

Nicols, John. "Hospitality Among the Romans." In Michael Peachin, ed., *The Oxford Handbook of Social Relations in the Roman World*, 422-37. Oxford: Oxford University Press, 2011.

———. "*Hospitium* and Political Friendship in the Late Republic." In Michael Peachin, ed., *Aspects of Friendship in the Graeco-Roman World*, 99-108. Journal of Roman Archaeology Supplementary series 43; Portsmouth, RI: Journal of Roman Archaeology, 2001.

———. "The Practice of *Hospitium* on the Roman Frontier." In Olivier Hekster and Ted Kaizer, eds., *Frontiers in the Roman World: Proceedings of the Ninth Workshop of the International Network Impact of Empire (Durham, 16-19 April 2009)*, 321-33. Leiden: Brill, 2011.

Nietzsche, Friedrich. "The Antichrist." In Walter Kaufmann, ed., *The Portable Nietzsche*, 565-656. Viking Portable Library; New York: Penguin, 1976.

Nongbri, Brent. *Before Religion: A History of a Modern Concept*. New Haven, CT: Yale University Press, 2013.

O'Brien, Peter T. *The Epistle to the Philippians: A Commentary on the Greek Text*. NIGTC; Grand Rapids, MI: Eerdmans, 1991.

Ogereau, Julien. "The Jerusalem Collection as *koinōnia:* Paul's Global Politics of Socio-Economic Equality and Solidarity." *NTS* 58 (2012): 360-78.

———. *Paul's Koinonia with the Philippians*. WUNT 2/377; Tübingen: Mohr Siebeck, 2014.

Økland, Jorunn. *Women in Their Place: Paul and the Corinthian Discourse of Gender and Sanctuary Space*. London: T&T Clark, 2004.

Osiek, Carolyn. *Philippians, Philemon.* Abingdon New Testament Commentaries; Nashville, TN: Abingdon, 2000.

———. "The Politics of Patronage and the Politics of Kinship: The Meeting of the Ways." *Biblical Theology Bulletin* 39 (2009): 143–52.

Osiek, Carolyn, and Margaret Y. MacDonald. *A Woman's Place: House Churches in Earliest Christianity.* Minneapolis: Fortress, 2006.

Osteen, Mark, ed. *The Question of the Gift: Essays Across Disciplines.* London: Routledge, 2002.

Palmer, F. R. *Mood and Modality.* 2nd ed., Cambridge Textbooks in Linguistics; Cambridge: Cambridge University Press, 2001.

Patterson, Thomas C., and Christine W. Gailey, eds. *Power Relations and State Formation.* Washington, DC: American Anthropological Association, 1987.

Payne, Geoff, ed. *Social Divisions.* 2nd ed., New York: Palgrave Macmillan, 2006.

Peterman, Gerald W. *Paul's Gift from Philippi: Conventions of Gift-Exchange and Christian Giving.* SNTSMS 92; Cambridge: Cambridge University Press, 1997.

———. "'Thankless Thanks': The Epistolary Social Convention in Philippians 4:10–20." *Tyndale Bulletin* 42.2 (1991): 261–70.

Peterson, Brian K. *Eloquence and the Proclamation of the Gospel in Corinth.* SBLDS 163; Atlanta: Scholars Press, 1998.

Petitat, André. "Le don: espace imaginaire normatif et secret des acteurs." *Anthropologie et Sociétés* 19.1–2 (1995): 17–44.

Pickett, Raymond W. *The Cross in Corinth: The Social Significance of the Death of Jesus.* JSNTSup 143; Sheffield: Sheffield Academic Press, 1997.

———. "The Death of Christ as Divine Patronage in Romans 5:1–11." In *SBL Seminar Papers 1993,* 726–39. Society of Biblical Literature Seminar Papers. 32; Atlanta: Scholars Press, 1993.

Plummer, Alfred. *The Second Epistle of St. Paul to the Corinthians.* ICC; Edinburgh: T&T Clark, 1960 (1915).

Pojman, Louis P., and Robert Westmoreland, eds. *Equality: Selected Readings.* New York: Oxford University Press, 1997.

Polaski, Sandra Hack. *Paul and the Discourse of Power.* Sheffield: Sheffield Academic Press, 1999.

Rapske, Brian. *The Book of Acts and Paul in Roman Custody,* Vol. 3 of *The Book of Acts in Its First Century Setting,* ed. Bruce W. Winter. Grand Rapids, MI: Eerdmans, and Carlisle: Paternoster, 1994.

———. "Prison, Prisoner." In Evans and Porter, eds., *Dictionary of New Testament Background,* 827–30.

———. "The Prisoner Paul in the Eyes of Onesimus." *NTS* 37 (1991): 187–203.

Rautman, Alison E. "Hierarchy and Heterarchy in the American Southwest: A Comment on McGuire and Saitta." *American Antiquity* 63.2 (1998): 325–33.

Reumann, John. *Philippians: A New Translation with Commentary.* AYB 33B; New Haven, CT: Yale University Press, 2008.

Rives, James B. "The Priesthood of Apuleius." *American Journal of Philology* 115.2 (1994): 273–90.

Roetzel, Calvin J. *The Letters of Paul: Conversations in Context.* 4th ed., Louisville, KY: Westminster John Knox, 1998.

———. *Paul: The Man and the Myth.* Minneapolis: Fortress, 1999.

Sahlins, Marshall. *Stone Age Economics.* New York: Aldine, 1972.

Said, Edward W. *Culture and Imperialism.* New York: Vintage, 1993.

Saller, Richard. "Patronage and Friendship in Early Imperial Rome: Drawing the Distinction." In Wallace-Hadrill, ed., *Patronage in Ancient Society,* 49–62.

———. *Personal Patronage Under the Early Empire.* Cambridge: Cambridge University Press, 1982.

———. "Promotion and Patronage in Equestrian Careers." *JRS* 70 (1980): 44–63.

Sampley, J. Paul, ed. *Paul in the Greco-Roman World: A Handbook.* Harrisburg, PA: Trinity Press International, 2003.

Sanders, E. P. *Paul: A Very Short Introduction.* Oxford: Oxford University Press, 2001.

Satlow, Michael L., ed. *The Gift in Antiquity.* Chichester: Wiley-Blackwell, 2013.

Scheidel, Walter. "Finances, Figures, and Fiction." *Classical Quarterly* 46 (1996): 222–38.

Scheidel, Walter, and Stephen Friesen. "The Size of the Economy and the Distribution of Income in the Roman Empire." *JRS* 99 (2009): 61–91.

Schino, Gabriele, and Filippo Aureli. "Grooming Reciprocation Among Female Primates: A Meta-Analysis." *Biological Letters* 4 (2008): 9–11.

———. "The Relative Roles of Kinship and Reciprocity in Explaining Primate Altruism." *Ecology Letters* 13 (2010): 45–50.

Schmeller, Thomas. *Hierarchie und Egalität: Eine sozialgeschichtliche Untersuchung paulinischer Gemeinden und griechisch-römischer Vereine.* Stuttgarter Biblestudien 162; Stuttgart: Verlag Katholisches Biblewerk, 1995.

———. *Der zweite Brief an die Korinther,* Teilbd. 1: 2 Kor 1,1–7,4. EKK 8.1; Neukirchen-Vluyn: Neukirchener Theologie, 2010.

Schmidt, Steffen W., James C. Scott, Carl Landé, and Laura Guasti, eds. *Friends, Followers, and Factions: A Reader in Political Clientelism.* Berkeley: University of California Press, 1977.

Schneemelcher, Wilhelm, Edgar Hennecke, and R. McL. Wilson, eds. *New Testament Apocrypha*. 2 vols., Louisville, KY: Westminster/John Knox, 1992.

Schnelle, Udo, ed. *The Letter to the Romans*. BETL 226; Leuven: Peeters, 2009.

Schowalter, Daniel, and Stephen Friesen, eds. *Urban Religion in Roman Corinth: Interdisciplinary Approaches*. Harvard Theological Studies 53; Cambridge, MA: Harvard University Press, 2005.

Schrage, Wolfgang. *Der erste Brief an die Korinther*. 4 vols., EKK VII/1–4; Düsseldorf: Benziger, and Neukirchen-Vluyn: Neukirchener, 1991–2001.

Schrift, Alan D., ed. *The Logic of the Gift: Toward an Ethic of Generosity*. New York: Routledge, 1997.

Schussler-Fiorenza, Elizabeth. *In Memory of Her: A Feminist Reconstruction of Christian Origins*. New York: Crossroad, 1983.

Schussler-Fiorenza, Elizabeth, ed. *A Feminist Commentary*, Vol. 2 of *Searching the Scriptures*. New York: Crossroad, 1994.

Schütz, John Howard. *Paul and the Anatomy of Apostolic Authority*. SNTSMS 26; Oxford: Cambridge University Press, 1976.

Schwartz, Seth. *Were the Jews a Mediterranean Society? Reciprocity and Solidarity in Ancient Judaism*. Princeton, NJ: Princeton University Press, 2010.

Senft, Christophe. *La première épitre de Saint Paul aux Corinthiens*. 2nd ed., Commentaire du Nouveau Testament, 2nd series 7; Geneva: Labor et Fides, 1990 (1979).

Sevenster, J. N. *Paul and Seneca*. NovTSup 4; Leiden: Brill, 1961.

Shelton, Jo-Ann. *As the Romans Did: A Sourcebook in Roman Social History*. New York: Oxford University Press, 1988.

Sherry, John, Mary Ann McGrath, and Sidney Levy. "The Dark Side of the Gift." *Journal of Business Research* 28 (1993): 225–44.

Sherwin-White, A. N. *The Letters of Pliny: A Historical and Social Commentary*. Oxford: Clarendon, 1985.

Sills, David L., ed. *International Encyclopedia of the Social Sciences*. New York: Macmillan, New York: Free Press, 1968.

Smith, Jonathan Z. *Drudgery Divine: On the Comparison of Early Christianities and the Religions of Late Antiquity*. Chicago: University of Chicago Press, 1990.

———. "The 'End' of Comparison: Redescription and Rectification." In Kimberly C. Patton and Benjamin C. Ray, eds., *A Magic Still Dwells: Comparative Religion in the Postmodern Age*, 237–42. Berkeley: University of California Press, 2000.

———. *Imagining Religion: From Babylon to Jonestown*. Chicago: University of Chicago Press, 1982.

———. *Relating Religion: Essays in the Study of Religion*. Chicago: University of Chicago Press, 2004.

Smyth, Herbert Weir. *Greek Grammar*. Cambridge, MA: Harvard University Press, 1984 (1920).

Stegemann, Ekkehard, and Wolfgang Stegemann. *The Jesus Movement: A Social History of Its First Century*. Minneapolis: Fortress, 1999.

Stuhlmacher, Peter. *Der Brief an Philemon*. 4th ed., EKK 18; Düsseldorf: Benziger, and Neukirchen-Vluyn: Neukirchener, 2004.

Sumney, Jerry L. *Identifying Paul's Opponents: The Question of Method in 2 Corinthians*. JSNTSup 40; Sheffield: Sheffield Academic Press, 1990.

———. *"Servants of Satan," "False Brothers" and Other Opponents of Paul*. Journal of the Study of the Old Testament: Supplement Series 188; Sheffield: Sheffield Academic Press, 1999.

Swartz, David. *Culture and Power: The Sociology of Pierre Bourdieu*. Chicago: University of Chicago Press, 1997.

Taylor, Mark C., ed. *Critical Terms for Religious Studies*. Chicago: University of Chicago Press, 1998.

Taylor, Walter F. *Paul, Apostle to the Nations: An Introduction*. Minneapolis: Fortress, 2012.

Tepperman, Lorne, and James Curtis. *Sociology: A Canadian Perspective*. Don Mills, Ontario: Oxford University Press, 2004.

Theissen, Gerd. *The Social Setting of Pauline Christianity: Essays on Corinth*. Philadelphia: Fortress, 1982.

Thrall, Margaret E. *A Critical and Exegetical Commentary on the Second Epistle to the Corinthians*. 2 vols., ICC; Edinburgh: T&T Clark, 1994, 2000.

Thurston, Bonnie B., and Judith M. Ryan. *Philippians and Philemon*. Sacra Pagina 10; Collegeville, MN: Liturgical Press, 2005.

Vanfossen, Beth E. *The Structure of Social Inequality*. Boston: Little, Brown, 1979.

Veyne, Paul. *Bread and Circuses: Historical Sociology and Political Pluralism*. London: Penguin, 1990. Translation by B. Pierce of *Le Pain et le cirque: sociologie historique d'un pluralisme politique*. Paris: Éditions du Seuil, 1976.

———. *Seneca: The Life of a Stoic*. New York: Routledge, 2003.

Vining, Peggy. "Comparing Seneca's Ethics in *Epistulae Morales* to Those of Paul in Romans." *Restoration Quarterly* 47.2 (2005): 83–104.

Waal, Frans B. M. de. "The Chimpanzee's Service Economy: Food for Grooming." *Evolution and Human Behavior* 18.6 (1997): 375–86.

Wagner, J. Ross, C. Kavin Rowe, and A. Katherine Grieb, eds. *The Word Leaps the Gap: Essays on Scripture and Theology in Honor of Richard B. Hays.* Grand Rapids, MI: Eerdmans, 2008.

Wallace, Daniel B. *Greek Grammar Beyond the Basics: An Exegetical Syntax of the New Testament.* Grand Rapids, MI: Zondervan, 1996.

Wallace-Hadrill, Andrew, ed. *Patronage in Ancient Society.* London: Routledge, 1989.

Walsh, P. G. *Pliny the Younger: Complete Letters.* Oxford World's Classics; Oxford: Cambridge University Press, 2006.

Watson, Duane F. "Paul and Boasting." In Sampley, ed., *Paul in the Greco-Roman World,* 77–100.

Watson, Duane F., ed. *Persuasive Artistry: Studies in New Testament Rhetoric in Honor of George A. Kennedy.* JSNTSup 50; Sheffield: Sheffield Academic Press, 1991.

Welborn, L. L. *An End to Enmity: Paul and the "Wrongdoer" of Second Corinthians.* BZNW 185; Berlin: De Gruyter, 2011.

———. "*Mōros genesthō:* Paul's Appropriation of the Role of the Fool in 1 Corinthians 1–4." *Biblical Interpretation* 10.4 (2002): 420–35.

———. "On the Discord in Corinth: 1 Corinthians 1–4 and Ancient Politics." *JBL* 106.1 (1987): 85–111.

———. "Paul's Caricature of His Chief Rival as a Pompous Parasite in 2 Corinthians 11.20." *JSNT* 3.1 (2009): 39–56.

———. *Paul, the Fool of Christ: A Study of 1 Corinthians 1–4 in the Comic-Philosophic Tradition.* JSNTSup 293; London: T&T Clark, 2005.

———. "'That There May Be Equality': The Contexts and Consequences of a Pauline Ideal." *NTS* 59.1 (2013): 73–90.

White, L. Michael. "Paul and *Pater Familias.*" In Sampley, ed., *Paul in the Greco-Roman World,* 457–87.

Williams, Charles K., and Nancy Bookidis, eds. *Corinth, The Centenary: 1896–1996.* Athens: American School of Classical Studies at Athens, 2007.

Willis, Wendell. "An Apostolic Apologia? The Form and Function of 1 Corinthians 9." *JSNT* 24 (1985): 33–48.

Winter, Bruce W. *Philo and Paul Among the Sophists: Alexandrian and Corinthian Responses to a Julio-Claudian Movement.* 2nd ed., Grand Rapids, MI: Eerdmans, 2002.

Winter, Sara C. "Methodological Observations on a New Interpretation of Paul's Letter to Philemon." *Union Seminary Quarterly Review* 39 (1984): 203–12.

———. "Paul's Letter to Philemon." *NTS* 33 (1987): 1–15.

Wire, Antoinette. "1 Corinthians." In Schussler-Fiorenza, ed., *Searching the Scriptures,* vol. 2, 153–95.
Witt, R. E. *Isis in the Ancient World.* Baltimore: Johns Hopkins University Press, 1971.
Wolff, Christian. *Der erste Brief des Paulus an die Korinther.* Theologischer Handkommentar zum Neuen Testament 7; Leipzig: Evangelische Verlagsanstalt, 1996.
Yarbro Collins, Adela, ed. *Ancient and Modern Perspectives on the Bible and Culture: Essays in Honor of Hans Dieter Betz.* Atlanta: Scholars Press, 1998.

Index of Subjects

Apocalypticism, 7–8, 19, 25–26, 31, 39, 54, 56, 87–88, 111, 120, 122, 126, 128–29, 151n15, 158n21, 187n64
Apostle (film), 3–4
Aretas IV (Nabataean monarch), 119
Athletic competition, 52–53, 56

Barnabas (evangelist), 47, 49
Boasting, 53–54, 71, 176n25, 186n50

Cephas/Peter (evangelist), 46, 49, 53, 56, 58, 69, 97
Charis (grace/gift/beneficence), 11, 19, 21, 54, 88–89, 129–30, 178nn47,48
Classification, 13, 44–60, 62–63, 74–75, 135–36
Claudius (emperor), 32, 80
Collection for Jerusalem, 19–21

Disinterest, 9, 11, 156n11
Do ut des, 11, 137, 140

Economic support, early Christian, 46–50, 135, 164n20, 166n34. *See also* Hospitality; Travel funding
Economy of symbolic goods, 12, 15–26, 134–35, 137–38, 141, 150n10, 151n15
Egalitarianism, 36, 95–101
Epaphroditus, 22, 30, 114, 172n40, 178n45
"Equality," proportional, 99–100

Fraud, financial, 69–70

Gaius (member of Christian assembly in Corinth), 69–71, 75, 131, 169n15, 174nn53,54

Garage sale, 41, 43–44
Gift/reciprocity: constraint and freedom, 9, 11; "free gift," 3–5, 134; gift and commodity, 13, 41–45, 54–60, 135, 164n6; gift and market exchange, 1–5, 7, 10, 15, 34, 152nn25,26; gift and social relations, 3, 10, 13, 55, 59, 61–75, 134; gift, "dark side" of, 61–62; gift, definition, 8–11, 149n38; gift-debt, 17, 24–25, 30–32, 34, 38, 58, 85, 102, 111; gifts, "spiritual," 90–95, 116, 119–30, 133, 139; God as gift-giver, 4, 11, 22–23, 54, 88–90, 115, 135, 137, 139; reciprocity, human, 1–3, 5–7, 9, 15–18, 34; reciprocity, human/divine, 4, 16, 19–26, 137–41; reciprocity, primate, 7–8
Glory (divine luminescence), 23, 128, 136. *See also* Honor/prestige
Glossolalia, 90, 94–95, 180nn72,73
Graces, dance of the, 16–17, 21, 54, 72, 75, 156n8, 174n56
Gratitude, 10–11, 17, 28, 34, 138, 158n20

Harpocras (physician), 82
Harvest (gifting metaphor), 17, 20–21
Heterarchy, 14, 105–13, 131–33, 136–37
Hierarchy, sociopolitical, 36–38, 90–103, 131–33, 161n40
Honor/prestige, 12, 14, 18, 29–30, 35, 54, 59, 83, 98, 116, 119–21, 132–33, 136
Hospitality, 46–48, 55, 62–65, 71–72, 93, 101, 109, 135, 180n69

Icelandic saga, 41, 44–45
Interdisciplinary study, 5–8, 139–41
Internal/external dichotomy, 126–31

213

Isis (goddess), 38, 179n55, 187n61
Iulia Agrippina (mother of Nero), 32

James (brother of Jesus), 53, 56, 58, 69, 97
Jesus of Nazareth: crucifixion and resurrection, 3–4, 19, 31, 128–29, 137; divine being, 87–88, 136; gift-giver, 4, 11, 137
John (evangelist), 97

Kinship, fictive, 36, 98

Lucius (character in Apuleius's *Metamorphoses*), 38

Magic, 38
Marx, Karl, 42
Maturus, Arrianus (equestrian), 84–86
Maximus, Vibius (prefect), 84–86
Methods in the study of religion, 5–6
Moses (lawgiver), 49–50
Mysteries and mystery initiations, 122, 125–26, 187nn61,62

Nero (emperor), 32, 86, 159n29
Nerva (emperor), 82–83

Oikonomia, 2, 50, 147n6
Onesimus (slave), 23–25, 30–32, 110
Oratory, 116, 120–21, 124, 126, 129

Patronage, 34, 36–39, 46–47, 73, 77, 80–85, 89, 108–15, 131–32, 161n41, 163n65, 184n31
Paul of Tarsus: apostle, 49, 88–93, 111–12; craftsman, 33, 47, 62, 116, 160n32; economic location, 33, 109, 117–18; evangelist, 5; lacking prestige, 116–19, 127, 130–31, 160n32; mediator of gifts from God, 11, 38–39, 45–46, 111–12, 114–15, 135, 140
Philemon (member of early Christian assembly in Colossae), 23–25, 30–32, 36–40, 109–12
Philippi, gifts to Paul from, 22–23, 67–68, 114–15
Phoebe (member of early Christian assembly in Cenchreae), 47, 70, 112–13
Pliny the Younger, 6, 13, 81–85
Potlatch, 76–77
Priest, 50–51
Priscilla and Aquila (craftspeople), 47, 166n32
Prophet, 51–52, 89, 93–94

Religion (analytic category), 8, 11–12, 148n30, 149n41
Romanus, Voconius (equestrian), 82–84

Scipio, Publius (Roman general), 62, 169n9
Seneca the Younger, 3, 6, 12, 16–17, 27–35, 40; use of hyperbole, 35, 160n38
Status, 13, 37, 39–40, 76–78; positional and accorded status, 13, 78–80, 136–37; status, gift of, 80–89, 102–3; status inconsistency, 14, 104–5, 131–33, 137; status inversion, 14, 36, 39, 109–33

Teacher, 95
Tiberius (emperor), 32, 66
Titus (evangelist), 70, 72
Trajan (emperor), 13, 81–84, 89, 93
Travel funding (for evangelists), 47, 55–56

Wage, 46, 48, 50, 54, 68, 167nn37,38

Index of Modern Authors

Appadurai, A., 164n6
Aune, D., 186n50

Bader, F., 180n72
Badian, E., 167n37, 169n9
Barclay, J., 18, 38, 149n39, 150n12, 152n20, 159nn22,25, 162n50, 163n61, 178n48, 182n94
Barnett, P., 170n20
Barth, M. and H. Blanke, 154n31, 155n34
Becklin, H., 187n63
Bell, C., 162n51
Benveniste, E., 149n39
Berger, A., 177n32
Berger, K., 151n13
Bernabé, A., 180n72
Betz, D., 149n42, 152nn19,22, 170n16, 178nn44,46, 186n50, 188nn67-69
Bieringer, R., 152n19, 170nn16,18, 186n48, 188n68
Blanton, T., 147n15, 154n27, 163n58, 168n54, 170n18, 176n25, 179n55, 182n89, 186nn48,50, 188n68
Blau, P., 161n40
Boissevain, J., 149n3
Bondarenko, D., 183n12
Bookidis, N., 187n61
Bormann, L., 185n36
Bourdieu, P., 1-2, 12, 15-17, 25, 27, 147nn5-6, 149n5, 150n9, 156n2, 157n11, 162n51, 175n4, 188n73
Bowden, H., 187n62
Brashear, W., 180n72
Briones, D., 18, 38, 150n12, 158n19, 162nn50-51, 163n61, 165n20, 181n83
Broneer, O., 168n50
Brookins, T., 187n56

Brumfiel, E., 106-7, 183n16
Burkert, W., 149n39, 187n61, 188n69

Callahan, A., 155n34, 159n25
Caragounis, C., 167nn38,40, 173n46
Carrier, J., 13, 41-44, 164nn2,11-13, 168n58
Castelli, E., 179n56, 180n65
Chow, J., 108, 160n37, 163n57, 166n24, 169n12
Clay, J., 180n72
Collins, R., 169n13
Conzelmann, H., 151n13
Crook, Z., 18, 89, 150n12, 177n35, 178nn48-49, 179nn54-55, 184n29
Crumley, C., 14, 104-7, 136, 183nn9-11, 13-14

Daniels, J., 166n29
Danker, F., 150nn10-11, 186n50
Darow, P., 169n8
Datiri, D., 165n20
Davies, W. and D. Allison, 165n23, 166n36
Davis, N., 61, 169n3
Derrida, J., 1-3, 8-9, 147nn1-4,8
De Ste. Croix, G., 156n10
Dixon, S., 156n3, 163n64
Douglas, M., 148nn20,22
Downs, D., 150n12, 151n16, 153n27, 179n54
Dulk, M. den, and A. Langford, 185n42
Dunn, J., 154n31, 155nn34-35, 157nn13,16, 158nn18,22, 159n27, 174nn53-54, 183n28, 184n31
Durkheim, É., 6
Dutch, R., 187n55

215

Edart, J.-B., 153n25
Ehrensperger, K., 162n50, 179n56
Eisenstadt, S. and L. Roniger, 149n2, 150n6
Elliott, J., 156n1
Elliott, S., 155n33
Engberg-Pedersen, T., 18, 150n12, 151n13, 156n1, 178n48, 181n83

Falconer, W., 153n25
Favro, D., 179n54
Fee, G., 154nn28–29, 167n41, 168n49
Finley, M., 147n6
Finney, M., 185n41
Fitzgerald, J., 151n14, 156n1, 165n22, 172n38, 174n55, 180n69, 186n49
Fitzmyer, J., 167nn39,41, 168n48, 174n54, 178n51, 180n63
Forbes, C., 186n50
Foucault, M., 186n46, 187n63
Friesen, S., 33, 151n16, 160nn35–37, 161n46, 163n65, 166n34, 176n24, 183n25, 184n31
Frilingos, C., 162n53
Furnish, V., 169n13, 170n20, 172nn43–44, 188n68

Garland, D., 180n62
Garnesy, P. and R. Saller, 149n2
Gaventa, B., 152n20, 182n94
Gellner, E. and J. Waterbury, 149n2, 156n4
Georgi, D., 151n16, 170n18, 186n48
Gill, C., N. Postlethwaite, and R. Seaford, 149n2, 156n4
Gillman, F., 166n28
Glowacki, D., 187n63
Godbout, J. and A. Caillé, 3, 75, 147n10, 148n23, 169n1, 189n1
Godelier, M., 189n3
Gouldner, A., 6–7, 148n21, 150n6, 156n4
Graf, D., 186n52

Graf, F., 180n72
Grant, R., 90, 96, 179n57
Gregory, C., 77, 164n11, 175nn3,6, 189n2
Griffin, M., 28, 150n6, 151n14, 156nn3,7, 159nn28–30, 160n38, 161n45
Griffin, M. and B. Inwood, 156nn3,6,8–9

Hanson, K. and D. Oakman, 177n42
Harris, M., 169n13, 170n20, 186n48
Harrison, J., 151n12, 153n27, 178n48, 181n79
Hartog, P., 156n1
Harvey, A., 165n20
Hays, R., 167n39
Hellerman, J., 188n66
Herrmann, G., 13, 41, 43–45, 58, 164nn3–4,14–17
Hirzel, R., 182n93
Hock, R., 116, 160n32, 164n20, 166nn32–33, 169n12, 171n30, 185n39
Horn, C., 156n1

Inwood, B., 156n11, 160n38

Jennings, M., 158n19, 179n55, 182n94
Jewett, R., 170n17, 174n54
Jongman, W., 177n42
Joubert, S., 18, 150n12, 151n16, 156n1
Judge, E., 96–100, 108, 119, 149n40, 179n56, 181nn75–78, 183n22, 184n31, 186nn50,53

Kirner, G., 183n22
Klauck, H.-J., 180n73, 187n62
Koenig, J., 165n22
Kopytoff, I., 164n17

Lamberterie, C. de, 180n72
Lampe, P., 108, 112–13, 131, 150n12, 154n31, 157nn12–13, 158n19, 174nn51,53, 179n54, 183n22, 184n33, 188n72

Lévi-Strauss, C., 175n1
Lincoln, A., 176n20
Lincoln, B., 96, 99, 162n51, 180n74, 182n90, 183n23, 188n65
Lipset, S., 176n21, 182n6
Litfin, D., 185n41
Lohse, E., 159n26
Longenecker, B., 92, 151n16, 152n21, 160n35, 162n46, 180n64, 183n25
Lüdemann, G., 170n17, 174n54

MacGillivray, E., 184n31
Macionis, J., 78–79, 175nn15–16
Malherbe, A., 155n1
Malina, B., 158n19, 178n54
Marcoux, J.-S., 61, 169nn2,4
Markschies, C., 188n69
Marrou, H., 187n55
Marshall, P., 108, 113–14, 160n37, 166n24, 169nn12,15, 170nn19,24, 171n29, 172n40, 183n22, 184n34
Martin, D., 97, 99, 180n73, 181n79, 182n90, 187nn57,60, 188n66
Martin, L., 151n15
Martin, R., 169n13, 173n47
Mauss, M., 6, 8–9, 12, 41–42, 61, 76–77, 140, 148nn20,31,33–35, 149nn36–37,42, 150n6, 164nn1,7–10, 168nn55–56, 169n5, 174n1, 175nn2,5, 189n3
McNeel, J., 179n56, 180n66, 182n89
Meeks, W., 14, 104–8, 132, 137, 178n46, 182nn1–8, 183nn17–18, 184nn31–32
Meeks, W. and J. Fitzgerald, 152n18, 154nn30,32, 170n17
Merklein, H., 167n39
Meyer, M., 187n62
Mihaila, C., 185n41
Miller, W., 13, 41, 44–45, 58, 164nn5,18–19, 168n58
Millett, P., 167n42
Mitchell, A., 151n14

Mitchell, M., 72, 99, 170n16, 173n50, 174n57, 182n90, 186n50, 188nn68,71
Momigliano, A. and T. Cornell, 161n41
Moo, D., 155n35, 158n18, 179n58, 183n28
Moore, R., 175n4
Mosko, M., 106
Müller, P., 157n15, 158n22, 159n23, 162n48
Murphy-O'Connor, J., 160n33, 166n32, 168nn50–51, 174nn53–54

Nasuti, H., 168nn47,54
Neyrey, J., 158n19, 163n64, 179n54
Nguyen, H., 117–18, 185n45, 186n47
Nickle, K., 151n16
Nicols, J., 165n22, 166n24
Nietzsche, F., 179n54
Nongbri, B., 148n30, 149n4

O'Brien, P., 154n28
Ogereau, J., 153n26, 157n16, 162nn49–50, 165n20, 172nn39–40, 182n91
Økland, J., 179n56, 181n88
Osiek, C., 152n25, 154n31, 157nn13,16, 158n22, 163n64, 179n54, 183n22

Palmer, F., 110, 183n26
Peterman, G., 18, 113–14, 150n12, 171n30, 172nn40,44, 184nn34–35
Peterson, B., 185n41
Petitat, A., 2–3, 147nn7,9,12, 149n38
Pickett, R., 179n54
Plummer, A., 69, 173n49
Polaski, S., 164n66, 179n56

Rapske, B., 152n24, 157n13, 172n41, 185n37
Rautman, A., 106–7, 183nn15–16
Reumann, J., 172n38, 185n36
Riesenfeld, H., 155n36
Roetzel, C., 152nn18,23, 154nn30,32, 157n13
Römer, C., 156n1

Said, E., 148n32
Saller, R., 34, 39, 149n2, 150nn10–11, 151n14, 156nn4–5, 158n19, 160n39, 161n42, 163nn63–64, 175n7, 177n34, 179n55
Sanders, E., 180n67
Scheidel, W., 33, 159n30
Scheidel, W. and S. Friesen, 159n31
Schino, G. and F. Aureli, 7, 148nn25–28
Schmeller, T., 126, 170n16, 173n50, 174n53, 179n56, 181n80, 184n31, 188nn66,68
Schmidt, S., J. Scott, C. Landé, and L. Guasti, 150n11
Schneemelcher, W., E. Hennecke, and R. Wilson, 156n1
Schrage, W., 167nn39,41,44, 180n71
Schussler-Fiorenza, E., 98, 181nn86–87
Schütz, J., 164n66, 178n46
Schwartz, S., 151n12
Scott, J., 78–79, 175nn10–13
Senft, C., 167n38
Sevenster, J., 155n1
Sherry, J., M. McGrath, and S. Levy, 169n2
Sherwin-White, A., 85, 176nn28,31, 177nn37,39
Smith, J. Z., 5–6, 8, 147nn16–17, 148nn18–19,29, 149n41, 149n4
Smyth, H., 158n17, 168n53, 183n27
Stegemann, E. and W. Stegemann, 168n47
Stuhlmacher, P., 162n53, 163nn60,62
Sumney, J., 170n18, 186n48
Swartz, D., 175n4

Taylor, W., 181n85, 183n24
Tepperman, L. and J. Curtis, 78–79, 175n14
Theissen, G., 108, 165n20, 174n53, 183n22, 186n51, 187nn57,59
Thrall, M., 152n19, 169n13, 170nn16,18,20, 172nn43–44, 186n48, 188n68
Thurston, B. and J. Ryan, 154n31, 155n34, 157n13

Vanfossen, B., 79, 175n17
Veyne, P., 15, 98, 149n1, 150n11, 156nn3–4, 159n28, 181n82
Vining, P., 155n1

Waal, F. de, 7, 148n24
Wallace, D., 155n36
Wallace-Hadrill, A., 149n2, 156n4, 158n19
Walsh, P., 81, 176n28
Ware, J., 156n1
Watson, D., 186n50
Weber, M., 175n10
Welborn, L., 64, 69, 162n50, 169nn12,15, 170nn21–23, 171nn27,36, 173nn48,50, 174nn53–55,58, 176n22, 182nn91,93,94, 185n41, 186n54, 187n58, 188n71
White, M., 171n25
Willis, W., 167n39
Winter, B., 185nn41–42, 188n70
Winter, S., 154nn31,33, 157n12, 159n26
Wire, A., 180n71
Wolf, E., 150n11
Wolff, C., 167n39

Index of Biblical and Early Jewish Sources

Hebrew Bible

Genesis
17:9–14	179n58

Exodus
16:18	100, 182n91

Leviticus
2:1–2	115

Deuteronomy
25:4	49, 167n41
28:13	187n64

Proverbs
3:34	187n64
22:8a (LXX)	20

Isaiah
49:1	89

Jeremiah
1:5	89
20:7–9	51

Daniel
7	187n64

New Testament

Matthew
10:5–13	46
10:8	165n21
10:10	165n21, 168n46
10:13	166n36
16:26	39
24:6–14	177n43

Mark
4:3–9	167n44
6:8	165n20
8:37	39, 111
13:7	177n43

Luke
10:1–9	46
10:1–12	48
10:5–7	165n21
10:6	166n36
10:7	168n46
16:1–9	168n47

Acts
13:1–3	166n29
15:1–5	166n30
18:1–4	47
18:3	62
19:9–10	166n34
20:2–3	71

Romans
1:1	92, 97
1:5	88, 92, 112, 180n68
1:9	92
1:16	128
1:18	25, 31
1:20	126
2:5	21, 25, 31
2:5–7	151n15
2:7	126
2:10	126
2:16	126
2:20–23	95
3:23	126

Romans (continued)

3:24–26	19
4:20	126
5:2	19, 23, 126
5:5	123
5:8	158n21
5:15	19
5:17	19
5:19	158n21
8:15	123
8:27	93
8:32	99
9:4–5	179n58
9:22	158n21
9:22–24	111
9:23	126
9:27–29	151n15
10:6–7	88
10:8–9	31
10:14–17	31
11:28–29	90
11:36	126
12:6	94
12:6–7	95
12:19	151n15
13:1–7	86
14:19	36
15:2	36
15:12	88
15:15–16	89
15:18	92, 180n68
15:19	128
15:24	33, 47
15:25–26	20
15:26–27	19, 26
15:27	20, 50, 153n26, 155n35, 158n18, 183n28
16	70
16:1–2	112, 166n28, 180n69
16:2c	112
16:23	71, 131

1 Corinthians

1–4	124
1:4–9	54
1:17	92
1:20–25	119
1:21	123
1:26–29	121
1:28	124, 187n59
2:3	120
2:4	128, 188n70
2:6–9	121
2:6–13	38
2:7	126
2:7–8	128
2:8	88, 126
2:9–12	93
2:10	123
2:10–13	122
2:14–16	123, 124
3:1–2	92
3:2	54, 185n40
3:6–8	167n44
3:8	54
3:10	54, 88, 112
3:10–15	92
3:14	54
3:18	130
4:1	54, 97, 123
4:1–5	125
4:3–4	124
4:5	93, 126
4:9	117
4:10	121
4:10–12	116
4:10–13	128
4:10b–13	117, 127
4:11	33
4:11–12	109

4:12	33	12:1–14:40	90
4:14	99	12:4–11	94
4:14–15	73	12:8	91, 94
4:14–16	92	12:9–10	91
4:21	37, 92	12:10	94
5:3–5	93	12:27–31a	91
5:4	128	12:28	88, 90
6:11	115	13:1	94
6:19	123	14:1	94
7:7	90, 178n59	14:3	93
7:21–24	159n25	14:4	93
8:8	162n47	14:5	94
9	54, 113	14:6–25	95
9:1–18	71, 153n26	14:13	94
9:2	90	14:25	93
9:3–6	46	14:29–33	93
9:3–12	93	14:33	180n71
9:4–5	53	14:34–35	94, 180n71
9:4–12	49	14:40	180n71
9:8	167n43	15:4	88
9:11	50	15:9–10	88, 112
9:12b–15	93	15:10	53, 54, 178n47
9:13–19	50–51	15:24–25	87
9:15	53, 72	15:24–27	129
9:16	51	15:24–28	126
9:16–17	168n49	15:25–57	23
9:18	55, 56	15:28	99
9:19	51, 97	15:35–55	31
9:23	51	15:35–57	19, 128, 129
9:24	126	15:49–55	111
9:24–29	52	15:51	123
9:25	52	15:58	54
9:26–27	53	16:1–4	20, 69
10:3–24	36	16:6	47, 55
11:2	93	16:6–7	55
11:3	99	16:11	47
11:4–5	93		
11:17	93	2 Corinthians	
11:17–34	174n53	1:1–2:13	70, 131
12	90, 101	1:16	47
12–14	179n59	1:22	123

2 Corinthians (continued)
1:24	101
2:4	63, 70
2:5-7	70
2:9	72
2:14-7:4	173n50
2:17	65
3:17-18	128
3:18	129
4:5	97
4:7-10	127
4:7-18	127
4:16-18	127
4:17	23, 126
5:5	123
5:10	126, 129
5:12	127
5:21-6:1	19
6:4	126
6:14-7:1	173n50
6:18	99
7:5-16	70, 131
7:6-8	70
7:7	70
7:12	69, 70
7:15	70, 72, 92
8	167n39
8-9	20, 45, 153n26
8:9	21, 167n39
8:15	100
8:16-24	69
8:19-21	20
9	70, 167nn38,39
9:1-5	70
9:3	167n39
9:4	167n38
9:6-15	20-21
9:7	20
9:14	167n38
9:17-18	167n38
9:18	65
10	167n39
10-13	63, 64, 65, 66, 68, 69, 70, 73, 168n54, 173n50
10:4-5	93
10:6	92, 93
10:8	92
10:8-9	101
10:10	63, 116
10:12	63
11:1-12:13	172n43
11:4	123
11:6	63
11:7	65, 116
11:7-11	71
11:8-9	22, 67, 68
11:9	64, 68
11:9-10	71
11:10	72
11:11	62, 170n15
11:12	64, 71, 72
11:13-15	63
11:20	64
11:20-21	72
11:21-33	168n52
11:23-33	118
11:27	33, 109
11:32-33	119
12:1-4	151n15
12:9-10	127, 129
12:13-16	66
12:13	62, 68, 170n15, 171n34
12:13-14	171n36
12:14	64, 65, 68
12:14-15	73
12:16	68, 171n34
12:16-18	69
13:2	92
13:2-4	93
13:4	128
13:11-13	70

INDEX OF BIBLICAL AND EARLY JEWISH SOURCES 223

Galatians
- 1:1 — 88
- 1:4 — 115
- 1:10 — 97
- 1:15 — 178n52
- 1:15–16a — 89
- 1:18–19 — 69
- 2:6–9 — 97
- 2:9 — 89
- 2:15 — 158n21
- 2:17 — 158n21
- 2:19–21 — 19
- 3:2 — 123
- 3:5 — 123
- 4:3–8 — 178n44
- 4:6 — 99, 123
- 4:25–26 — 151n15
- 6:10 — 152n21

Philippians
- 1:1 — 97
- 1:5 — 67
- 1:9–10 — 151n15
- 1:22 — 153n26
- 1:28 — 158n21
- 2:6–8 — 21
- 2:9–11 — 129
- 2:10–11 — 87
- 2:25 — 178n45
- 3:12–14 — 53
- 3:14 — 126, 151n15
- 3:17 — 92
- 3:19 — 158n21
- 3:20 — 151n15
- 3:28 — 181n87
- 4 — 23
- 4:1 — 53
- 4:5 — 67
- 4:10 — 185n38
- 4:10–20 — 185n36
- 4:14 — 185n36
- 4:14–19 — 114
- 4:15–16 — 47
- 4:15–18 — 22
- 4:15–20 — 46
- 4:16 — 22
- 4:16–17 — 68
- 4:17 — 22, 153n26
- 4:17–18 — 47, 152n25
- 4:17–19 — 184n35
- 4:18 — 67, 153n26
- 4:18–19 — 172n40
- 4:19 — 115, 153n26
- 4:20 — 115

Colossians
- 4:7 — 154n32

1 Thessalonians
- 1:10 — 21, 25, 31, 38
- 2:4 — 92
- 2:7–8 — 92
- 2:9 — 33, 47, 62, 109, 172n42
- 2:11–12 — 99
- 2:19–20 — 53
- 4:13–18 — 19, 23, 31, 151n15
- 4:15–17 — 111
- 4:16–17 — 151n15
- 5:1–10 — 25, 31
- 5:3 — 111, 158n21
- 5:27 — 185n40

Philemon
- 1 — 36
- 1–3 — 162n52
- 2 — 37, 162n47
- 3 — 36
- 5 — 36
- 6 — 36
- 7 — 36, 37
- 8 — 37, 155n33
- 8–9 — 93
- 8–14 — 24

Philemon (continued)

10	23, 31, 154n33, 157n14
11	38
12	155n35, 157n13
13	25, 30, 38, 40, 155n35, 159n25
13–14	32, 155n33
14	37
15–16	31
16	109
17	36, 38, 157nn15,16
17–18	110
17–19	30, 31, 157n16
17–20	24
18	25
18–19	110, 157n15, 158n22
19	25, 31, 36, 38, 155n33, 162n53, 163n64, 168n57
20	36, 110, 155n35, 157n15
21	24, 32, 37, 92, 110, 155n33, 157n15
22	33, 37, 71, 92, 109, 110, 155n33, 162n47

Early Jewish Texts

Ben Sira

41:19 (42:11 LXX)	152n25
42:7	152n25

Dead Sea scrolls

1QpHab VII.5–14	122
1QS IV.6–7	122
1QS XI.3–9a	122

Josephus, *Jewish War*

2.8.4, §125	46, 165n22

Philo, *On Dreams*

155	186n51

Wisdom of Solomon

5:9–14	158n21
5:15	158n21
9:1–10:21	182n89

Index of Greek and Roman Sources

Aelius Theon

Exercises
109–110   108

Apuleius of Madauros

Met.
11.6–18   38, 151n12

Aristotle

Pol.
1.1259b   98
Nic. Eth.
5.3.7   99
5.3.14–15   99

Cicero

Agr.
2.2.3   176n27
Amic.
10.35   169n10, 170n15
16.58   172n40
Lael.
58   153n25
Offic.
1.58   176n20
Pro Rabino
5.16   186n54
Reg. Deiot.
11.30   170n19
Republic
6.17   151n15
Verr.
2.2.37   170n19

Dio Chrysostom

Or.
1.45–46   97
3.39   98
3.55–57   97–98

Diogenes Laertius

Lives of Eminent Philosophers
5.4.65   66

Dionysius of Halicarnassus

Rom. Ant.
2.26.1–4   176n20

Epictetus

Diss.
2.17.31   176n20
3.7.26   176n20

Herodotus

Hist.
5.66   187n58

Homer

Il.
6.224–25   46

Isocrates

Antid.
8–13   176n25

Juvenal

Satires
5.107–111   108, 161n43

Lucian of Samosata

Alex.
40   93
Icaromenippus   151n15
"On Salaried Posts"   166n24, 167n37

Martial

Ep.
    167n37
6.88   175n7
12.36   108, 161n43

Pliny the Younger

Ep.
2.13   82
3.2.1–6   85
7.19   176n23
9.12   176n19
9.21   37
10.4.1–6   82
10.5.1   82
10.5.1–2   82
10.6.2   82
10.7   82
10.26.2–3   81
12.36   108

Plutarch

Mor.
539C–D   176n25
540A   53
541F   53
547E–F   176n25
778D–E   174n58

Pseudo-Aristotle

Oeconomica,   147n6

Ptolemy

Tetrabiblos   151n15

Quintilian

Educ. Or.
11.1.22   176n25

Seneca the Younger

Ben.
1.1.2   17
1.1.3   29
1.1.9   17
1.1.13–1.2.2   28
1.2.3   17, 29, 160n38, 172n40
1.2.4   17, 34
1.2.5   29
1.3.1   29
1.3.4–5   168n59
1.3.4–1.4.1   156n8
1.3.8–1.4.1   28
1.4.2   147n11, 168n59
1.4.2–4   17
1.4.4   28
1.10.4   17
1.10.5   28
1.15.1   30
2.4.3   158n20
2.6.2   17, 160n38
2.7.1   29
2.9.1–2.10.3   160n38
2.10.4   17
2.11.4   17
2.11.4–5   28
2.11.6   29
2.13.1–3   29

2.17.3	28	4.14.4	35
2.17.3–5	28	4.22.3	35
2.17.5	29	4.22.4	35
2.22.1	28	5.1.4	30
2.24.1	28	7.8.2	28
2.24.4	28	7.23.2	160n38
2.25.3	17, 28, 156n8	*Ira*	
2.29.1	84	2.21.1–6	175n18
2.29.4–5	84	*Prov.*	
2.29.5	84	2.5	175n18
2.30.1–2	151n12	*De Vita Beata*	
2.30.2	28	24.2	161n42
2.31.2	17		
2.32.1–4	28		

Suetonius

Claud.	
15.4	176n22

2.33.3	29		
2.35.1	17, 28, 160n38		
2.35.5	28, 160n38		

Tacitus

3.1.1	17, 169n7		
3.1.4	169n6	*Ann.*	
3.6.1–2	17	2.38	171n31
3.6.1–10.1	168n55	13.42	32, 159n30
3.12.2	29	13.42.4	159n29
3.14.2	28, 29	14.53.5–6	159n29
3.13.2	29		

Xenophon

3.13.3–4	29		
3.18.1–29.1	176n23	*Mem.*	
3.22.1	28	4.4.19–20	176n20
3.29.2–38.3	171n26	*Oeconomicus*	147n6
4.13.3	160n38